MEN W
DIFI

Daniel Evans Jr.—Discarding his college deferment, he volunteered for the Army and to go to Vietnam. After a ten-week crash course in military medicine, he shipped out on what he imagined to be a great adventure. But amid the chaos and carnage of battle, he would learn a true lesson in war . . . and in courage.

Captain Byron Holley—Chief Surgeon, 4th Battalion, 39th Infantry, he took Dan Evans under his wing. He told the eager young medic: "Don't get yourself killed trying to prove something." It was advice Evans often and willfully ignored . . . at his peril.

PRAISE FOR
CHARLES W. SASSER

"**Few writers know men of war as well as Chuck Sasser.**"
—Jim Morris, author of *War Story*

"**Sasser draws his characters so vividly, depicts the emotions—good and evil—so strongly, that the reader lives the terrors and frustrations . . . with him.**"
—*Mostly Murder*

MEN WHO MADE A

Sergeant John Svatek—Handsome, blond and tan, he would have looked more at home on a surfboard in Malibu than on patrol in the Mekong Delta. But again and again, he proved his mettle under fire, including the time he dropped his weapon and faced down a crazed GI aiming a loaded M16 at his heart.

Joe "Slim" Holleman—A homeboy with an attitude, in the barracks he gave lectures on black power and the coming revolution against white America. But once in the field of battle, he knew who his true brothers were—the fellow men in his platoon, no matter the color of their skin.

PRAISE FOR
CHARLES W. SASSER'S
ONE SHOT—ONE KILL

"Shocking and brutal. . . . The reality of sniping is achieved superbly by personal accounts. . . . Each account is remarkable, detailing vivid memories of combat action."

—*Marine Corps Gazette*

James "Billy" Scott—Evans's fellow medic, he was a deeply religious conscientious objector who refused to carry a rifle. Initially paralyzed by fear, Scott soon became a paragon of pure courage. Unarmed and undeterred, covered in the blood of those he treated, he found the strength to offer profound spiritual comfort to the wounded and dying.

Colonel David Hackworth—The most highly decorated soldier in the U.S. Army, he was a man of extraordinary charisma and leadership. Taking command when morale in the 4th Battalion had dropped to its lowest ebb, he gave the troops purpose—turning the 4th into the feared and fearsome "Hardcore Battalion," and turning its men into true warriors.

PRAISE FOR
CHARLES W. SASSER'S
HOMICIDE!

"**Authentic. . . . Gives us a personal look at the triumphs and frustrations of those we pay to face those horrors every working day.**"

—*Publishers Weekly*

"**Brings to life the ugly realities, black humor, and battle-scarred idealism of a veteran cop's world.**"

—*Action Digest*

Books by Charles W. Sasser

Doc: Platoon Medic
  (and Daniel E. Evans Jr.)
First SEAL
  (with Roy Boehm)
Smokejumpers
Last American Heroes
  (with Michael W. Sasser)
Shoot to Kill
Always a Warrior
Homicide!
The 100th Kill
One Shot—One Kill
  (with Craig Roberts)
The Walking Dead
  (with Craig Roberts)

Published by POCKET BOOKS

DOC:PLATOON
✚
MEDIC

Daniel E. Evans Jr.
and
Charles W. Sasser

POCKET BOOKS
New York   London   Toronto   Sydney   Tokyo   Singapore

An *Original* Publication of POCKET BOOKS

POCKET BOOKS, a division of Simon & Schuster Inc.
1230 Avenue of the Americas, New York, NY 10020

Copyright © 1998 by Dan Evans and Charles W. Sasser

ISBN: 0-671-56058-1

First Pocket Books printing January 1998

10 9 8 7 6 5 4 3 2 1

POCKET and colophon are registered trademarks of Simon & Schuster Inc.

Unless otherwise indicated, all photos are courtesy of author's collection.

Printed in the U.S.A.

To David Ernest Gardner, Richard Joseph Forte, Francis Craig Sollers, Robert Henry Sinclair Jr., James Thomas Pence, Nigel Frederick Poese, Earl Marshall Hayes, Joe Earl Holleman, Dennis R. Richards, William James Torpie, Frank J. G. Ellis Jr., William W. Schoth II, Walter Lee Nutt III, Donald Everett Dalton, and Sharon A. Lane.

And to all the combat medics who served in Vietnam.

ACKNOWLEDGMENTS

This book was created from the input of over sixty men and three families who lost their sons to the Vietnam War. Special thanks go to my mother, who saved all my letters from the war; to Jim Robertson, who spent many hours editing the early manuscript; and to my wife, Sandy, and my two children, Ryan and Kelly, who suffered with me through the writing of this book.

Others who should be singled out are Don Wallace, who helped locate other platoon members and who has a terrific memory for events in Vietnam; Dr. Byron Holley, who gave moral support beyond this book; Ron Sulcer, who assisted with the research into medical training; Dana Peck, a World War II P.O.W. from the 9th Infantry Division, who helped provide the unit history; and Craig Roberts, who did research on combat medics. A special thank-you goes to Colonel David Hackworth for his encouragement and support.

Special thanks also to Brent Barton of Scrivelsby for his help in locating old war friends. Vietnam veterans who have lost contact with friends might want to get in touch with him:

Scrivelsby
Box 219052
Portland, Oregon 97225
503-297-5402

My sincere thanks also to the following men for their support:

Gene Abrahamson   Arles Brown   John F. Carbone
Timothy Bauer   David J. Bryan   William Casey
Thomas Bever   Fred Buehler   Robert Celphane

ACKNOWLEDGMENTS

Dan Conney
Joe Connor
James H. Craig
James R. Craig
Teddy Creech
Timothy Dingley
Tommy Diveley
Larry Dixon
Freddie Downs
Glenn Ellis
James Fabrizio
Larry Faulkenberg
Larry Fentress
Eusebio Fernandez
Dale Fite
Albert Fletcher

Elijah Frazier
Calvin Freeman
Arnold Dale Gass
Robert Goldberg
Bill Gregory
Colonel Frank Hart
L. J. Henderson
Michael Hill
Ed Hogue
Rick Hudson
William Joye
Roger Keppel
Robert Knapp
Alvaro Melchor
Marty Miles
Dan Moreno

Ron Miller
Larry Neumann
Eugene O'Dell
Jim Richardson
James "Billy" Scott
Jim Silva
Tom Smith
Mario Sotello
Ross Sterling
Willis Stevens
Kenneth Sugimura
Matthew Sumas
John Svatek
James Sweeney
James Whitmore

—Daniel E. Evans Jr.

AUTHORS' NOTE

Actual names are used throughout this book except in those rare instances in which correspondents could not recall names or in which public identification would serve no useful purpose. In various instances, dialogue and scenes have by necessity been re-created. Where this occurs, we have tried to match personalities with the situation and the action while maintaining factual content. The recounting of some events may not correspond precisely with the memories of all involved. Much time has passed since the events in this book occurred. Time has a tendency to erode memory in some areas and selectively enhance it in others. Where such errors occur, the authors must accept full responsibility and ask to be forgiven.

The authors must apologize to anyone who has been omitted, neglected, or slighted in the preparation of this book. While some interpretational mistakes are bound to have occurred, we are certain that the content of this book is true to the spirit and the reality of the medics and soldiers who served in the Vietnam War. To that end, we are confident that we have not neglected anyone.

FOREWORD

This book tells the story of a combat medic's tour in Vietnam. It also shows in unique detail what medics do in battle, and concurrently you witness some of the most remarkable reporting of infantry fights I have ever read.

You are there with a grunt rifle company in the rice paddies and along the canals, hearing the sickening sing of bullets zinging over and the dull thud when steel-coated slugs strike flesh and bone. You hear the call of "Medic!" and witness the heroism of young combat medics selflessly putting their stricken infantry comrades ahead of themselves. The combat scenes are so real that you can see, smell, hear, taste, and feel the horror of close combat.

This is mainly the story of one medic, one rifle platoon, and one rifle company that fought in Vietnam circa 1968–69. I knew most of the key players well, as I had the privilege of being their battalion commander. They were not an elite parachute unit, a daring Special Forces outfit, or a crack Ranger unit, but mainly muddy-boot draftees sucked into a bad war who stood tall and fought as well as or better than centurions. None were Harvard, Princeton, or Yale graduates whose connections permitted them to sit out the war in an ivory tower. No, these boy-men were like this fine book's writer, Dan Evans, unconnected teenagers from mainly small-town USA who did the dirty killing and dying work not unlike their dads or older brothers did at Anzio or Pork Chop Hill.

There is no job in the insanity of close combat that requires more bravery, steadfastness, and coolness under fire than that of combat medic. Medics go into the very center of the hell storm of battle—where the grunt has fallen and where the enemy waits to strike again—and perform major and minor miracles. Almost always an enemy prime target, they do their thing with seemingly total disregard for themselves: find the wounded, stop the bleeding, patch the wound, administer morphine and good cheer, and then drag and pack shattered bodies of the men they love as brothers back to the safety of a paddy wall or a fold in the ground that provides a little protection from direct-fire weapons.

The men you meet on these pages are the salt of the earth, who, much to my discomfort way back then, defiantly scrawled on their steel pots FTA—Fuck The Army. Yet, without a doubt, they were the finest group of fighters I was privileged to skipper in twenty-six years in the soldiering business.

"Doc" Evans spent almost ten years putting this work together. First he painstakingly chased down the majority of Company "B," 4th Battalion, 39th Infantry (The Hardcore), who served with him. He interviewed most of these line doggies and has told their tale in riveting and gripping detail.

No such combat memoir has grabbed me as *Doc: Platoon Medic*. It ranks with the WW I classic *All Quiet on the Western Front* and the WW II masterpiece *Those Devils in Baggy Pants*.

The reader will come away from this remarkable book with a firm understanding of how the war was fought on the ground in Vietnam and also appreciate the camaraderie, brotherhood and love that warriors have for each other after they have been forged together on the crucible of the killing field. And you'll see how the medic becomes the grunts' best friend, rabbi, priest, preacher, last hope, lucky rabbit's foot and sacred guardian angel.

No man in the profession of arms deserved more honor and respect than the soldier who wears the coveted Combat Medic badge. They are true studs who are honored, cherished and loved by the fighting men they care for. Theirs is a noble, but damn dangerous profession, and this fine book tells how and why.

Dan Evans is a quiet and self-effacing man who hardly looks or acts the part of a great American hero. He didn't have to be in the trenches but volunteered time and again to leave a position of relative comfort and safety in a rear echelon hospital to wade through the mud, sleep on wet

FOREWORD

ground, be attacked by every creepy crawly known to humankind and to live the desperate life of being hunted by another human being whose intent was to inflict maximum bodily harm.

He did all this and did it well. Now by telling the story of the brave medical shepherds of Infantry Grunts he provides a lasting tribute to those who have from time immemorial selflessly tended their flock—the COMBAT MEDIC.

David Hackworth
Colonel, U.S. Infantry, Retired

INTRODUCTION

Ironically, the first American serviceman killed in the Vietnam War, on December 22, 1961, was a man sent to *save* lives. He was Specialist 4/C James T. Davis, an army combat medic. Just as ironically, he died not in the process of tending the wounded on the battlefield but instead while wielding an M16 himself, fighting back against a Vietcong ambush. He set the tone for combat medics who followed him into Vietnam. They were truly *combat* medics, rifle in one hand, aid bag in the other; firing at the enemy with the one hand, saving the lives of fallen comrades with the other. Over 1,300 army medics gave their lives during the war.

Combat medics in Vietnam suffered heat and rain and fear and loneliness alongside the line troops with whose lives and well-being they were entrusted. Throughout the bloody history of that Asian war, some 58,000 American GIs died and another 303,704 were wounded as a result of enemy action. The toll could have been much higher; 82 percent of those who fell in combat survived. Their survival was attributed to speedy helicopter evacuation from the battlefield— and to the Docs, the combat medics, who at the lowest field level with the platoons were there on site to treat the wounded even while bullets still flew and grenades exploded.

Heroism, it has been said, was prerequisite for a combat medic. He went to work when things went bad. He had to swallow his own terror and risk his life to render what aid and comfort he could to those mangled and torn by the horrid mechanisms of war. He had to instill in shattered men a will to survive. And when there was no hope, he whispered words of courage into their ears and held their hands to help them cross into that final no-man's-land.

Troops expected *their* Doc to possess the skill of a surgeon, the diagnostic insight of an internist, the patience of a saint, and the heart of a lion. Few medics ever disappointed *their* troops. Few soldiers wounded in combat ever forgot the name or the face of the Doc who patched them up under fire.

While there is no glory to war, there are men in war who have managed to bring a certain glory to humanity. Often these men are combat medics. This is the story of one of them, Daniel E. Evans Jr., U.S. Army, 9th Infantry Division. He arrived in Vietnam nauseated by the mere sight of blood; before his tour ended, he found himself bathed in it as he fought fate, nature, and the enemy for the lives of *his* young GIs.

Daniel E. Evans Jr.
Charles W. Sasser

DOC:PLATOON
+ MEDIC

1

Twilight Zone. It was so macabre. I couldn't wake up to escape the nightmare. Uncle Sam, through the courtesy of the U.S. Army, was sending me, Private Dan Evans Jr., to Vietnam, where I would be a combat medic. Sucking chest wounds, traumatic amputations, shock, bellies blown open. Blood.

I'd pass out. I knew I'd faint. The first wounded soldiers who started screaming, "Medic! Medic!" would expose me for a fraud. I couldn't be a medic, even though I'd been through the ten-week Band-Aid course at Fort Sam Houston. The sight of blood nauseated me. It made me breathe hard. It made my head spin. I could almost hear my commander now as he ripped the buttons off my uniform: "Private Evans, the Department of Army has made a huge mistake. You're simply not the caliber the army requires of its gallant fighting men in the Republic of Vietnam. We're returning you immediately to Ohio in disgrace."

If I was such an obvious fraud, why was I being kept under guard at Fort Ord? Ord was the departure point for soldiers bound overseas for the meat grinder in Asia. The departure point was like a large aircraft hangar partitioned into areas for sleeping, watching TV, playing Ping-Pong, snacking or simply waiting. Young troops in khakis crowded into the building to wait their assigned flights on world-famous Flying Tigers Airlines, which I'd never heard of.

The first thing I noticed after assignment to the holding building was guards with holstered .45s at all the doors. Loudspeakers blaring out departure flight numbers twenty-four hours a day kept everyone in a constant state of excitement and agitation.

"There's only one way out of this building," said Private

1

Christine, one of six soldiers sharing a sleeping cubicle with me. He pointed a finger at the roof. "You have to go through Vietnam to get back to Ohio or Wyoming or Oklahoma."

"There's no assurance I'll ever see the U.S. again," one kid cried. "I may die over there and never come back."

"Oh, you always come back," said a guard, smartasslike. "It may be in a body bag, but they always bring you back."

Some men came and went in as little as a day. Engine trouble delayed my flight for three days. I had one uniform that I had worn for a week. Those of us in the holding pen were never left without supervision for even a minute. It was as if the army was afraid we'd bolt from duty to God and country if someone didn't watch us every hour, day and night. Guards stood at the doors while we slept. They escorted us to chow and back. Roll call came over the loudspeakers four or five times a day. No one escaped. It was just as Private Christine said: there was only one way back home—and that was through Vietnam.

The guards weren't called guards, but that was what they were.

"What if I wanted to step outside for some fresh air?" I asked a corporal, taking off my glasses to wipe the lenses. The guard looked up at me suspiciously. He was short and stocky and had to tilt his head to meet my eyes. I was about six feet tall and lanky with the new meat's short haircut.

"What are you, a wiseass?" he growled.

"I'm a medic. At least I'm *supposed* to be a medic. How about some fresh air?"

He smirked. "Yeah? Where? In Omaha?"

Not a bad idea.

"No one is allowed to leave for any reason," said the corporal.

"Why?"

"They may call your flight."

"I could catch the next flight."

"You have to go on your assigned flight. That's the rule."

I had tried to psych myself up for this. After I graduated from the combat medic course at Fort Sam Houston, Texas, the army had given me sixteen days' leave and a sealed envelope containing orders for Vietnam. I had listened to "The Ballad of the Green Berets" sung by Barry Sadler and watched John Wayne in *The Sands of Iwo Jima* and *The Green Berets*. I got goose bumps. As long as I was at home, I felt indestructible, invincible. I felt immortal.

"Nothing is going to happen to me in Vietnam," I assured my wife, Dianne. "I have a guardian angel to look over me."

I celebrated my twenty-first birthday while on leave. I was practically an old man, compared to the average troop's age of nineteen.

My sense of immortality deserted me like a cheap whore the moment I stepped into the holding building and saw the guards and their frightened captives and heard the loudspeakers. I realized through the sudden dryness in my throat and the way my pulse pounded—*pounded,* in my temples—that this was it. This was *real.* Dan Evans was going to war just like his old man did during World War II. Big scared eyes stared back at me from the mirror when I shaved.

Evans, I told myself, there are guys who haven't been wounded yet who will depend on you to save their lives. You won't be able to do it, Evans, because you're a fake, a phony, an impostor, a fraud. . . .

Jesus. I didn't know if I could do this or not.

Kids from Kentucky and Arkansas and Mississippi, black kids and white kids all mixed together, rose up like zombies from whatever they were doing when they heard their flight numbers announced. They looked dry-mouthed and wide-eyed. They shook hands solemnly with those not yet summoned. Some of them tried on a macho air, but it seldom lasted long. They disappeared out the doors past the stern guards with the manner of Jews going to the trains in Hitler's Berlin.

My flight number was announced during one of my favorite TV shows, *Mission Impossible.* The show was a two-parter, the conclusion to be broadcast the following week. I felt as if I could have drunk about a gallon of water as I rose to leave with Private Christine.

"I don't mind staying another week to watch the second half," I tried to joke.

3

No one laughed.

The Flying Tigers Airline had been created to haul freight to Asia after World War II by the remnant pilots of a highly decorated fighter plane squadron of the same name. American soldiers were just so much freight bound for Vietnam.

2

In the attic of my parents' house in Mineral Ridge, Ohio, was a small box containing my father's mementos from World War II. When I was a little kid, I used to sneak up into the attic on quiet afternoons and approach the box with near-reverent curiosity. In it were coins from different European countries, a pair of souvenir wooden shoes from Holland, and Dad's patches and combat ribbons.

Dad seldom spoke of the war. It was as if his wartime experiences were too personal to share with someone who had not been there and who therefore could not possibly understand. About all I knew was that the U.S. Navy had inducted him in 1942, one week after he graduated from high school. A draftee in those days served for the duration of the war plus six months. Dad fought aboard a ship in the Atlantic and the Mediterranean without coming home even once in four years.

Somehow, my father's reluctance to talk about his war made it all the more intriguing and glamorous in the eyes of a young boy. The strong, silent warrior tempered and molded by battle has long commanded an honorable place in American folklore. I envied Dad his rite of passage into adulthood. I yearned for and dreamed of my own.

President Lyndon Johnson had started the American buildup of combat forces in Vietnam in 1965 when I graduated from high school. I was eighteen years old and had two things on my mind that were much more important than any little war on the other side of the world—playing college football and marrying Dianne, my high school sweetheart. I had received a full athletic scholarship to Northern Michigan University.

As it turned out, however, I was too small to play college-caliber football. Although I was about six feet tall, additional weight refused to fill out my lean, even gangly, frame. The coach stripped me of my football scholarship after the first semester. It wasn't until after I married Dianne and ended up working part-time while I attended Youngstown University as a premed student that the Vietnam War began intruding into my thoughts. It was on the news all the time. I watched, mesmerized, while Dianne cast worried glances at me from the corners of her pretty eyes.

"Don't even think of it," she said. "You stay in school and keep your student deferment. I don't want to be a widow before I'm twenty years old. This war is all wrong. It's insanity."

In January 1968 the North Vietnamese had the U.S. Marine base at Khe Sanh under siege. It was on TV every night. Young gyrenes slamming big shells into the breeches of howitzers. Marines with gaunt faces and hollow eyes and muddy boots slogging back in from patrols, carrying their wounded in ponchos.

I watched as Vietcong attacked the American embassy in Saigon during the Tet offensive and dueled it out in bitter fighting in Hue. Brigadier General Nguyen Loan of the Army of the Republic of Vietnam shot a VC in the head with his pistol and fifty million Americans watched it, aghast, on TV that night. Peter Arnett of the Associated Press uttered his famous quote about the fighting at Ben Tre: "It became necessary to destroy the town to save it."

My own father had served when our country called. A vague guilt haunted me that here I was, hiding like a coward behind my 2-S deferment, when I was *needed*. The guiltier I felt about it, the more determined Dianne became to dissuade me from doing anything stupid. After all, she pointed out, look at all the people at home protesting an unjust war. Draft resisters were fleeing to Canada. Young guys were burning their draft cards.

5

Fine. That was *them*. This was *me*. I stood up and placed my hand over my heart when "The Star-Spangled Banner" was played at basketball games. John Wayne was my hero. I tried to explain to Dianne that I couldn't be like most of the other college students majoring in draft dodging. This was my country, right or wrong, and Uncle Sam needed me. I felt this overwhelming urge to go to war, as my father had, and *prove* myself. I felt Dianne's resentment growing daily. I think she knew that eventually I would succumb to the long call of the bugle and the roll of the drums.

I finally volunteered for the draft and reported for induction on April 4, 1968.

"Dan? You don't *have* to go. Please?" Dianne pleaded.

She didn't understand. I *did* have to go.

My two years of college plus my high test scores qualified me for officer candidate school if I cared to extend for an additional year. Draftees served only two years. I declined. Poor eyesight prevented my becoming a fighter pilot, which was the only reason I would ever have wanted to be an officer.

"What else would you want to do in the army, then?" the sergeant interviewer asked, filling out a form.

Since I had been a premed student, I said, "I guess I want to be a medic."

Medics, the way I understood it, were noncombatants. I'd never have to kill anyone.

"How are you ever going to be a doctor if you faint when you see blood?" asked Dan Hurst, another inductee who volunteered to be a medic. I had confided in him about my affliction.

"I figure the army will help me get over it," I said.

"You don't want to be a medic," the army interviewer cautioned me. "Almost all medics are going to Vietnam. What's your next choice?"

He didn't understand. I *wanted* to go to Vietnam, but I said, "I don't care."

"You scored best on clerical work. I'll put you down to go to clerk school."

"I don't know how to type."

"No problem. The army will teach you. Now, where would you like to be stationed in the United States?"

That was easy. "Hawaii."

"Where would you like to be stationed overseas?"

"Vietnam."

He looked up in surprise. "Are you sure you want to go to Vietnam?"

"Yes."

"It's your funeral."

He erased something on the form. The interview ended.

My class was the first to go through basic combat training (BCT) with the new rapid-fire M16 rifle. Dianne and my parents came to Fort Knox for the graduation ceremony. I stood in ranks afterward for orders. Names were called in alphabetical order.

"Evans, Daniel. Fort Sam Houston. Medic."

We young troopers were all such innocents back then that we thought the common army initialism "FTA" stood for "fun, travel, and adventure."

3

The ten-week Basic Army Medical School at Fort Sam Houston was a much-accelerated, bare-minimum, no-frills medical education: stop the bleedin' and keep 'em breathin'. Emphasis was on the four lifesaving steps: clear the airway; stop the bleeding; treat the wound; prevent shock. The would-be medics heard all the stories. People died out there. "Out there" meaning Vietnam.

Could I do my job? Could I really save lives? It was a lot to ask of a green twenty-one-year-old with ten weeks of medical training. And I was older than most of the others.

"The day will come when you will be called upon," the instructors preached. "Here, now, is when and where you must prepare yourself. The troops will depend upon you. Their lives will be in your hands."

7

Oh, Lord, no!

Officer candidate school suddenly sounded good. Where did I sign up for a twenty-year hitch just to get out of the medical corps? How in hell could I ever treat a casualty in Vietnam? The casualty would have to treat *me* when I fainted.

Still, I couldn't force myself to quit. The army psyops' brainwashing was having its desired effect. We medics were the most *important* troops on the battlefield. We were *essential* to high morale and the fighting spirit. Soldiers *depended* on us, looked up to us. Medics were some of the most *highly decorated* soldiers in any war.

The army knew how to get to me. Play them bugles, boy. Pound them drums. March me off to that war with a voice-over of John Wayne telling the world how much we were *needed* over there, how much we were *depended* upon: "Your left, your right—now step it on out."

I sucked it up. That was one of the army expressions I learned, along with FTA and its various meanings: Suck it up, boy. Learn to take it. You're needed.

I swallowed my gorge and learned how to treat every variety of wound that might be sustained on the modern battlefield. We pretended, and we used mulages—realistic plastic wounds—to provoke our imaginations as we trained and practiced treatments.

Abdominal wounds, we learned, sometimes resulted in the intestines slithering out of their cavities like wet fat snakes to be dragged and stepped on. A medic never attempted to stuff the guts back in where they came from; they were filthy, contaminated. Scoop them up instead with a large field dressing and secure them against the WIA's torso. WIA. That was what we learned to call the patients: wounded in action.

KIA. Killed in action.

Head and face wounds could be tricky, especially if the WIA was unconscious. Ram your two fingers into his throat, if there was enough left of his face, and rake out blood and shattered bone and teeth and flesh. Maybe you'd have to do a tracheotomy to get him breathing.

Now a sucking chest wound, that was really a bitch. Some-thing—shrapnel, bullet, knife—had pierced the lung so it wouldn't hold air. Something airproof had to be slapped immediately over the frothing hole to seal the lung so the WIA could keep breathing. You could use a four-by-four gauze pad impregnated with Vaseline, or you could use tin-foil, a piece of plastic, an M&M's wrapper.

I could take all this. The mulages, talking about wounds, practicing by applying bandages and tourniquets to healthy fellow students. What got to me was the films. I could hardly watch them without running outside to gasp for fresh air or removing my glasses. I couldn't see shit without my glasses.

The first few movies were in black-and-white. They turned to living color during the third or fourth week and became more graphic and bloodier, especially the movie entitled *Vietnam Casualties.*

On the screen a writhing soldier with multiple abdominal wounds was carried into a large tent and placed on an operating table. Although the sound was muted, he was obviously screaming in agony. His eyes looked like two caves with fire flickering and about to die somewhere in their depths.

One stroke of the surgeon's knife opened him up like a melon from his sternum to his left thigh.

"Holy shit!"

I swept off my glasses. That didn't help. I bolted outside. I found shade beneath a tree and sat in the Texas heat with my head between my knees while I struggled to keep from passing out.

How had I gotten myself into this? Why hadn't I listened to Dianne?

On the screen a soldier had been torched with aviation fuel. Doctors were literally skinning him from head to toe.

"Lord!"

I was determined to sit through it. With my glasses on.

On the screen medics tossed a wounded soldier on an operating table. Doctors began to saw off his mangled leg.

I made it all the way through only one casualty movie: the one on how to deliver a baby. It had a certain erotic appeal.

We would see these wounds, instructors lectured, but we would spend most of our time as medics on more mundane procedures and treatments.

"You will be treating everyday maladies," they said, "such

as trench foot, skin infections, gastrointestinal problems, fevers, pulmonary infections, cuts, bruises, sprains, and socially contracted diseases. The jungle will rot your feet off, and Asian VD will rot your dick off."

I was Honor Grad out of a graduating body of 604 students. Of these, 530 received orders to Vietnam. FTA—"free trip to Asia." I looked at my orders. Dianne was going to be pissed and scared to death.

"It's too bad you didn't get me pregnant while you were on leave," she said as she kissed me good-bye before I reported to Fort Ord for departure to Vietnam.

I looked at her.

"Then I would at least have something to remember you by," she said.

4

As the war had intensified in 1965, U.S. bombing, shelling, and defoliation of rural areas had driven peasant refugees thronging to the fringes of cities and towns like Saigon, Da Nang, Vung Tau and Bien Hoa. Four million men, women, and children, roughly a quarter of South Vietnam's population, were shunted into makeshift camps of squalid shanties whose primitive sewers bred dysentery, malaria, typhoid, and other diseases. The cities were almost medieval, with beggars, hawkers, whores, and drug sellers roaming the streets, whining, and tugging at Americans for money.

By the time I arrived in Vietnam on October 7, 1968, Bien Hoa, north of Saigon, had degenerated into a sleazy tenderloin of bars and brothels. In the middle of all this sat a gigantic American air base. A stewardess added her bit to the continuing unreality of the Twilight Zone as the airliner carrying its human cargo soared on to final landing at Bien Hoa.

"On behalf of the captain and crew," she announced cheerfully, "we would like to thank you for choosing Flying Tigers Airline. The approach to beautiful Bien Hoa will be steeper than normal to avoid attracting ground fire. Chances of a sniper attack or mortar fire are twenty percent. The temperature at destination is one hundred degrees Fahrenheit with one hundred percent humidity.

"On behalf of the pilot and crew, I would also like to say that we would like to see each and every one of your smiling faces when we return to pick you up in exactly one year. May God keep you all safe."

As I stepped out through the door of the air-conditioned plane into the blazing sun, the heat and smell of the country hit me like a blast furnace blowing across a sewage pit. From then on, every time I smelled shit—human shit—I thought of Vietnam.

I squinted through the blinding tropical sunshine and drifting dust. I saw sweating GIs hustling around unloading supplies while others loaded stacks of six-foot-long metal boxes onto a C-130 Hercules. I looked twice and realized they were caskets. A cheering crowd of GIs dressed in khaki uniforms waited to board the airliner as soon as we deplaned. Their tour of duty was finished. It was back to the land of round-eyed women, indoor plumbing, air-conditioning, and automobiles.

The air base was a patchwork of wooden buildings and Quonset huts, parking ramps for aircraft, and dusty roads. Various military vehicles loaded with troops and supplies scurried about like ants. Jet fighters loaded with bombs and rockets took off with thunderous roars, climbing straight up, trailing black smoke as they went. Helicopters—Hueys and Chinooks and Jolly Green Giants—choppered about like bumblebees. A school bus with screens fixed over the windows drove up to haul us to the reception center. The next day, after the roads were cleared of mines, it would take us to nearby Camp Bearcat, where all FNGs—fucking new guys—received their in-country indoctrination.

Accommodations were air mattresses spread in a building whose lower half was wood and whose upper half was bug screen with a corrugated metal roof. The heat reached down into my guts with a scalding fist. Then dark clouds rolled in and dumped a Texas year's worth of water on us in less than an hour. The red dust that had caked buildings and Jeeps and soldiers was now replaced with red mud. I was meeting the two entities that troops in Vietnam hated even worse than they hated the enemy and the mosquitoes and the leeches and the screaming shits. The heat and the mud had both been invented, patented, and perfected in Vietnam just for the war.

Artillery batteries fired intermittently from the air base all night long, flashing up the horizon like lingering sheet lightning after the departure of the monsoon. I sat in the dark of the hooch to which I had been assigned and let the feeling of war permeate my cells. It was scary and unreal. It was also exciting.

"I hear the war starts at sunset each day and ends at sunrise," whispered the FNG who had spread his air mattress near mine. "I heard some of the men talking. They call the nights VC nights because the nights belong to the Vietcong."

We both stared past the bug screens into the darkness.

"They'll issue us live ammo if the base comes under attack," he said. He had been assigned to Vietnam as a meteorologist, a weatherman. "Otherwise, they don't issue new guys ammo until after we finish indoctrination. I guess they think we're so scared we'd shoot each other."

"Wouldn't we?"

I missed Dianne. I had written her a letter earlier telling her how much I missed her and how much I loved her. I told her I had been assigned to the 9th Infantry Division, which I would be joining at its base camp in Dong Tam on the Mekong Delta as soon as I completed in-country training. I was a replacement for some other medic who had either bought the farm or DEROS'd (date eligible for return from overseas) back to the United States after his tour. I hoped he had DEROS'd.

At this point, I still looked upon the war as a great adventure. I was too green to understand that when old men send young men off to fight accompanied by the beating of drums, what begins as a noble crusade often loses its glamour in the mud and blood of the battlefield.

"No great dependence is to be placed on the eagerness

of young soldiers for action," wrote Vegetius, a military scribe in ancient Rome, "for the prospect of fighting is agreeable to those who are strangers to it."

Military units come with their own histories and legends, which are passed down and enhanced through the generations. Perhaps because of my father's participation in his war, perhaps because of the legends of famous outfits like the Big Red One and the Screaming Eagles, immortalized in movies and books, I had developed in childhood a fascination with combat and the men who fought wars. Characteristically, as soon as I received my assignment to the 9th, nicknamed the Old Reliables, I eagerly read every word of the indoctrination literature passed out to the newbies. I hoped the division was heroic and honorable, worthy of my participation.

It was.

The 9th Infantry Division, I learned, was organized on July 18, 1918, at Camp Sheridan, Alabama. World War I ended before the unit saw action. It was demobilized, then reactivated again as a division on August 1, 1940, at Fort Bragg, North Carolina, with units drawn from those that had seen combat action during World War I.

The 9th took part in the fierce fighting of World War II in North Africa, with landings at Algiers and French Morocco. It blitzed north to Tunisia to help smash Hitler's Afrika Korps, and then fought in Sicily.

On June 10, 1944, the division landed at Normandy. It battled its way across France. On September 3, elements of the 9th entered Monignes to become the first Allied unit to begin the liberation of Belgium. The division moved into Germany and beat back the Germans at the Battle of the Bulge. After a forced march, the 47th Infantry Regiment of the 9th deployed over the bridge at Remagen to become the first infantry regiment to battle across the Rhine barrier since the Napoleonic Wars.

The 9th received its present nickname, Old Reliables, for its capture of the Schwammenauel Dam on February 12, 1945. No advance over the Roer was possible without the dam. After the battle, V Corps commander, General Huebner, commended the division commander with a letter that included the phrase, "The old reliables of your command have again proved there is no substitute for a battle-hardened and experienced combat division, that no army has ever known better soldiers than we are now privileged to command, and that the 9th Division is of this distinguished company."

The division saw no action in Korea. The latest chapter of its history opened February 1, 1966, when the Old Reliables became the first division since World War II to be organized, equipped and trained for deployment to an overseas combat theater. It was to be a new kind of war in Vietnam, dominated by helicopters, airpower, and armored assault boats. The 9th Division, preparing for combat in Vietnam, encompassed ten maneuver battalions attached to three brigades, the 39th, 47th, and 60th. Also included in its ROAD (Reorganization Objective Army Division) were Division Headquarters Company; three brigade headquarters; 3rd Squadron of the 5th Cavalry; 15th Engineer Battalion and Division artillery with four organic artillery battalions; 9th Aviation Battalion; 9th Signal Battalion; 9th Administration Command; 9th Medical Battalion; 9th Supply and Transport Battalion; 709th Maintenance Battalion; and the 9th Military Police Company. Additional support for the division included two engineer battalions and an aviation battalion.

The 15th Engineers became the first echelon of the 9th to arrive in Vietnam on October 19, 1966, to set up base camp at Bearcat, near Long Thanh, twenty miles northeast of Saigon. General Westmoreland himself welcomed Major General George S. Eckhart and the main body of the Old Reliables on December 19 when the division landed on the beaches of Vung Tau. The 9th was the first American infantry unit to establish a permanent base camp in the VC-infested Mekong Delta at a place called Dong Tam.

Almost immediately the division began making contact. During Operations Colby, Junction City, Paddington, and a dozen other similar operations, the 9th left in its destructive wake a 1967 body count of over 1,500 VC KIAs. A six-hour battle in the predawn hours of March 20 pitting the 3/5 Cavalry against the 273rd VC Regiment near Bau Bang was the division's first important battle. Enemy losses were 230 dead compared to 4 friendly U.S. KIAs and 67 WIAs. October 1967 was highlighted by the largest arms cache ever seized in the Vietnam War. Elements of the 9th uncovered a massive subterranean tunnel system thirteen miles southeast of Bearcat and captured 1,140 weapons, 95,000 rounds of small arms ammo, 3,634 grenades, 2,273 recoilless rifle shells, 452 mortar rounds, and enough drugs and medical supplies to treat 1,000 patients for a month.

During the 1968 Tet offensive, VC troops attacked all over South Vietnam in the biggest Communist push of the war. Soldiers of the 9th achieved decisive victories all over their TAOR (tactical area of operations), accounting for some 1,625 VC and NVA KIAs. The rest of 1968, prior to my arrival in October, had consisted of clashes on the treacherous Plain of Reeds (225 enemy KIA); Cholon, the Chinese community in Saigon (200 enemy killed); and Fire Support Base Jaeger, ten miles west of Dong Tam (100 enemy KIA). Two days before I arrived in-country, division units fought a fierce two-day battle west of My Thuoc Tay in which 138 VC died.

By October 1968 the division was using helicopters and its joint army-navy Mobile Riverine Force in extensive combat operations throughout the Mekong marshlands. It had even penetrated the previously secure U-Minh Forest.

I had reported to the right unit for action.

"You're a medic?" my meteorologist bunkmate asked.

I nodded.

"I'll be assigned to the rear area," he said. "You will too, if you're lucky."

I hadn't volunteered to come to a war to watch it from the bleachers. It was like sex in the backseat of a car. After you went so far, you had to go all the way.

"I'm a *combat* medic," I said.

"You mean going out in the field? Going into battle?"

I squared my shoulders.

"You're crazy," the weatherman said. "You could get yourself killed."

5

It was scary, like any situation that involved one or more possible outcomes, some of which could be fatal. After indoctrination at Bearcat, a muddy deuce-and-a-half truck and driver showed up to transport FNG replacements to the 9th Division base camp at Dong Tam. A low gray ceiling had grounded helicopter flights. We were about to travel through enemy-held Vietnam in a one-truck convoy full of scared green rookies led by a single veteran driver.

We piled into the truck. The canvas top had been stripped off for safety purposes. The truck driver explained that we'd be desiring to unass the thing over the sides in the event somebody tossed a grenade among us. He issued each replacement one magazine of 5.56 ammo for our M16s and warned us not to chamber rounds yet. "I don't want anybody getting nervous," he said.

Getting nervous? I piled into the back of the truck with the other new guys and knew what the old combat veterans of my father's generation meant when they talked about getting so uptight they couldn't have driven a ten-penny nail into their assholes with a sledgehammer. We new guys stared at each other. We stared around us at the hostile land as the truck rumbled out the gate. I thought I could hear the dry crackle of tongues trying to moisten lips. I felt like nothing but eyeballs and an asshole.

The truck took Highway 15 to Highway 1, which the French during their long war in Vietnam had called The Street without Joy. We passed bright green rice fields bordered by fringes of impenetrable jungle and lined with great, beautiful palms as tall as three-story buildings. Farmers toiled in the fields with flat-horned water buffalo. Young kids rode the beasts and sprawled across their backs.

The warning about grenades fresh in our minds, we watched with suspicion the pedestrians in cone-shaped straw hats who thronged the little grass-hut villages and formed walking ant lines along the road. A cacophony of engine sounds and blasting horns filled the air in the towns as bicycles, Honda motorcycles, three-wheeled Lambrettas, old Ford trucks and psychedelic-painted school buses maneuvered for clearance and advantage. Kids shouted at us.

"Buy Coke-Cola, Joe? Gimme chop-chop?"

The women in Saigon, much prettier than the peasant women in the countryside, wore colorful *ao-dai*s. Saigon was a modern city with tall buildings, pastel shops, sidewalk cafés, and traffic jams. Some of the buildings were pockmarked with bullet holes. I recalled there had been fighting in Saigon during the Tet offensive in January and February.

The land was flat south of Saigon. It was green-squared with rice paddies and dikes, through which cut numerous muddy streams bordered by thick growth. Along Highway 4 many of the bridges had been blown up and were being repaired by U.S. Army engineers. ARVN (Army of the Republic of Vietnam) checkpoints and security camps built of dried mud and barbed wire squatted alongside the road. The South Vietnamese ARVNs looked like little children garbed in oversize helmets and baggy uniforms, like kids playing war in a vacant lot. Few of them weighed much more than 100 pounds. They held hands, as was the Asian custom, and waved at the truck.

I was starting to control my fear and enjoy the Kiplingesque adventure of my first trip through the exotic Orient when the driver pulled the truck over to the side of the road. He looked tense. We were in the heart of the Mekong Delta.

"Get out a minute and stretch your legs," he said. "We're about to enter Ambush Alley."

What?

"You can load a round now. Squat down below the level of the seats and keep a sharp eye out on either side. If anyone shoots at us, return fire. I'm not stopping for nothing from here on until we reach Dong Tam. So suck it in and let's go."

I didn't relax again—maybe I didn't even take another breath—until the truck jounced speeding through a small hooch city filled with whorehouses, souvenir shops, Coca-Cola and beer stands, and laundries, echoed across a bridge, and entered the front gate of the 9th Infantry Division's base camp at Dong Tam.

In the language of the Vietnamese, Dong Tam means "united hearts and minds." The camp had originally been a 600-acre swamp. Soil dredged from the My Tho River, which flowed alongside the base, had been used to fill in the swamp and level it out. The camp was surrounded by a high dried-mud berm, barbed wire, concertina wire and cleared fields of fire in which all cover and concealment for an enemy approach had been cleared. The truck ground its way along a road off which stretched row after row of two-story barrack buildings. Everything looked neat and orderly, like a stateside military post. The barracks were better than those I'd lived in at Fort Knox during basic training.

The truck let me off in front of the 9th Medical Battalion Aid Station, a long, low frame building with a covered walkway running along its front. I reported for duty immediately. The duty NCO explained that I was being assigned to the 9th Med instead of to one of the infantry companies as a line medic. It was rear-echelon noncombat duty. Jesus. I was a REMF—rear echelon motherfucker. To the combat troops, a REMF was one of the lowest forms of life, superior only to most officers.

"I thought I was going to be a combat medic," I complained mildly.

The NCO looked at me with some sympathy. "The gooks mortar us every few days," he said with a tolerant smile. "Will that help?"

How was I going to prove myself if I was kept safe in a city protected by barbed wire, claymore mines, and artillery batteries? I owed it to myself to experience *real* combat, not the sterilized version of it at a secure division base camp.

"You're in Vietnam," the NCO said. "You're just as vital to the war effort here as you would be in a combat unit. Consider yourself fortunate. Not everyone can be a hero."

I ran into Dave Krogan, a medic from my training class at Fort Sam. He had arrived in-country a week earlier. He filled me in on the battalion skinny.

"Whale shit floats higher than morale in the 9th Medical

Battalion," he said. "The CO is Colonel Robert S. Arnold. The man is the head chickenshit of all REMF chickenshits. We have in-rank personnel inspections once a week and formations every morning. You wear starched jungle fatigues and spit-shine your boots. You're confined to the battalion area and the PX—that's it. He's placed the Enlisted Men's Club off-limits because of racial violence. There's not that much work to do—we have so many surplus medics—but we're on twelve-hour shifts seven days a week. Arnold says if the infantry works twenty-four hours a day, so do we, whether we have anything to do or not. Welcome aboard, Evans. You're gonna *love* this chickenshit outfit."

He showed me my barracks and helped me find a bunk on the second floor. Ground floors were always full because they were safer when the gooks mortared the base.

Krogan lowered his voice. "There's a lot of talk going around," he said. "Some of the guys are talking about fragging Colonel Arnold."

"Fragging?" I had never heard the word. More army lingo.

"Offing the bastard. Giving him the DX. Slipping a grenade into his pocket."

If that wasn't clear enough, he added bluntly, "Killing his ass. He's making life miserable for everyone. I guess they figure if anybody deserves fragging, it's that son of a bitch."

6

Assholes like Colonel Arnold turned the base camp into Riker's Island. Life at Dong Tam, at least life with the 9th Med, became a tedious routine of chickenshit rules and regulations and even more chickenshit jobs. Sarcasm sneaked up on me like a sapper through the bush. I thought of all the lectures at Fort Sam about how important medics were, how we were essential to the great GI fighting spirit, how the troops depended on us.

I learned a new meaning for FTA: fuck the army.

As a PFC, a private first class, I found myself low-ranking man in the battalion but high-ranking man when it came to shit details. I was assigned along with other surplus medics to build a morgue attached to the 9th Med clearing station. The clearing station handled minor wounds and medical problems. The more serious cases went directly from the chopper pad to the 3rd Surgical Hospital next door. The morgue was just a square wooden building filled with long shelves on which to stack the full body bags when they came in.

Nine GIs at once broke the morgue's cherry. Almost an entire squad had been wiped out because some dumb-ass lieutenant gave the wrong map coordinates when he called for artillery fire. The nine dead GIs arrived in olive-drab bags, along with a new term: "friendly fire." That was what it was called when your own people wasted you.

"It happens a lot—friendly fire," Krogan explained. "Christ. This war goes on much longer, we'll kill ourselves off."

Then I was issued a deuce-and-a-half truck and appointed, quite against my will, as the 9th Med's new sanitary engineer. Every morning following formation, I drove around picking up all the trash and garbage in the battalion area and hauling it to the dump outside the main camp. The little kids and the women from the village were always waiting for me. The women were sullen and suspicious; they weren't hookers. The scruffy little ragamuffins tugged at my jacket.

"*Donnez-moi* chop-chop."

"What, baby-san?"

The boy left, received some advice, then returned with a translation: "Gimme chop-chop."

I gave him a Tropic bar, chocolate that wouldn't melt in the tropical heat.

The kid sniffed it. "Number ten, GI!" he scolded and wouldn't eat the bar. I didn't blame him.

The villagers were like pack rats. They salvaged everything we threw away. Leftover food became stew in their kettles. Flattened Coke cans made passable shingles for their hooches. Old Jeep and truck tires were turned into Ho Chi Minh sandals for the Revolutionary Front. While kids back in the States were learning the alphabet and the multiplication tables, Vietnamese kids scrounged for chop-chop at foreigners' dumps and learned to beg.

"What did you do during the war, Daddy?"

"Oh, I hauled garbage to make sure we had an orderly war."

Picking up garbage required little attention to uniform. I soon stopped spit-shining my boots and having my fatigues starched at the post laundry. The flies at the dump didn't seem to mind.

Sergeant Shelby, my section leader and an understudy for Colonel Arnold, stopped in front of me at formation as if he had run into a trip wire. He lifted his lip and sniffed the air. "What's that stink I smell?" he inquired.

He knew damned well what it was.

"Garbage! Evans, you're a dirtbag. You'd better get yourself squared away, boy."

I requested transfer to a line unit, or at least to the MEDCAP (Medical Civic Action Program) missions, which were a part of the civic action programs and went outside the wire to treat the Vietnamese villagers. Shelby blocked the request.

"Haul your garbage, Evans," he sneered. "You don't have enough experience to treat the Vietnamese."

Chickenshit was contagious. It was something inherent in REMFs, especially lifers. Troops who stood down from the field for a few days and came to Dong Tam to get away from the war liked to go around in shorts and sandals so the sun could dry up their fungal infections. The army didn't give a rat's fuck if fungus ate out a grunt's crotch just as long as he wasn't out of uniform. MPs were required to give out clothing-violation tickets to anyone not in proper uniform.

Word went around that some general was coming to inspect the base. That made the REMF brass go ape-shit, as if they'd never seen a general before. In the field, it was "If it's alive, kill it. If it's not, burn it. If it won't burn, blow it up." With the REMFs, it was "If it moves, salute it. If it don't, paint it." Privates were out lining walkways with painted stones. Colonel Arnold ordered four soldiers to go into the nearby jungle, dig up palms, and transplant them in the company area. A little wartime landscaping. Better living through *Vietnam Homes & Gardens*.

It took the troops two weeks to transplant the palms. Since the monsoon rains were ending, the trees had to be watered every day. Potable water became so scarce that soldiers couldn't take showers. The palms all died after the inspection. Troops had to dig them up again and return them to the jungle.

Occasionally, in between shit details, I received some medical practice working at the 9th Med clearing station. All the clearing medic did was take the patient's history, temperature, and blood pressure and send him on back to the doctor. Routine cases. Boring. A trained ape could have done it. Colds, skin infections, cuts, bruises, sprains, and respiratory problems. The important combat cases went next door to 3rd Surg.

The 3rd Surg got the sucking chest wounds; 9th Med got the Vietnam flu, as the clap was called. Plenty of cases of that. Prostitutes had set up shop right outside the gates. They were welcome everywhere there were soldiers, GI or NVA. The fleshpots of Sodom and Dong Tam.

"Men," we were told at in-country indoctrination, "you've all heard about that little island off Japan and the black VD?"

What island?

The one where incurable cases of VD went to rot away and die in quarantine. The big crud. Your dick turned green, and then it fell off. You became a walking bag of pus. "If you're not careful . . ."

Most of the doctors didn't go along with the scare story. "The men have got a raw deal," they said. "If the only way they can have fun is to consort with whores, then we can cure anything they get."

So the men groveled in the dung and came to us with the VN flu. Only enlisted men were ever treated for gonorrhea, according to their medical records. The officers had their careers to protect; they were treated for "nonspecific urethritis."

"What did you do in the war, Daddy?"

"Oh, I treated VD to keep the real fighting men fighting."

7

I volunteered for Vietnam. I did not volunteer for *this*—hauling garbage and replanting palm trees, spit-shining boots and standing formal in-ranks inspections. I figured most of the guys at the 9th Med put up with it because it was safer here than in the bush. Krogan thought I was crazy to want to go with an infantry platoon. But that was where the war was being fought. I was a combat medic. At least I wanted to be a combat medic. Never mind that the sight of blood made me nauseated. I was sure I'd get over it.

I felt like a real grunt, as if I might be in a real war, only during the deuce-and-a-half journey over from Camp Bearcat and during the intermittent mortar and rocket attacks on Dong Tam.

I lay sleeping in my bunk in the barracks the first time the mortar rounds came over. First an eerie whistling sound jarred me awake. I lay wide-eyed in the dark listening to it and hearing the peaceful snoring of the other men in the bay. The whistling sounded high. Then it got louder and louder. It sounded like a Volkswagen being hurled through the air as it streaked above the barracks.

I thought about jumping up and yelling, *"Incoming!"*

I didn't dare. Krogan told me the gooks hadn't shelled the base in over three months. I'd never live it down if I was wrong. FNG afraid of the dark.

Some other troop in the barracks did it for me: *"Incoming!"* In a voice that might have been used to herald Armageddon and the Second Coming. I didn't realize my muscles were stretched so taut until they propelled me out of my bunk and onto my feet before the base sirens started wailing and mortar rounds landed with sharp, crumping bangs.

I was scared worse than when I was a kid and tornadoes

23

used to spin their way across Ohio in the spring. But I also felt a certain smugness at having been the first to recognize and detect the incoming rounds, even if I hadn't announced them. Somehow I found my glasses in the dark and managed to jerk on my fatigues and boots. The men sounded like cattle stampeding down the wooden stairs as they scurried for their assigned bunkers. I grabbed my rifle, for which I had not been issued ammo, and joined the flight.

Red flares streaking across the sky illuminated throngs of half-dressed GIs darting wildly in different directions. I was relieved not to see any green flares. Red signaled a rocket or mortar attack; green meant a ground attack.

We huddled in the sandbag bunkers in the dark, as if we were in a storm cellar. I felt overdressed for the occasion. Everyone else, including Krogan, wore either underwear or civilian pajamas. One man was stark naked. I was the only one who had taken the time to pull on a uniform and grab a weapon.

"What if they attack us?" I whispered to Krogan. "Nobody has a weapon. How are we supposed to fight 'em off?"

"Do you have any bullets for that thing?" Krogan asked with a sarcastic sneer. "What are you gonna do, beat 'em to death with it?"

The naked man flinched every time we heard the distant bang of a mortar round exploding. He bent over and held his ears and closed his eyes as the base artillery opened up answering fire. Incoming mortars ceased.

"Charlie was just letting us know he's still out there," Krogan said, whispering, as though afraid of being overheard outside the bunker. "It's Charlie's way of saying he cares."

Finally I received the opportunity I'd been waiting for—a chance to go outside the wire to where the real war was being fought. It came about one morning while a bunch of medics were policing up cigarette butts in the company area. Important job. MEDCAP needed an additional medic for the day. Needed him right away for a mission. Needed a man with a weapon. I was the only one in the group who had his M16. The others had their weapons locked up.

"You've volunteered, Evans," Sergeant Shelby said.

DOC: PLATOON MEDIC

Hallelujah!

MEDCAP was the acronym for Medical Civil Action Program—winning the hearts and minds of the natives by providing them with medical treatment. Each AO (area of operations) had at least one team that tramped around from village to village. The team consisted of two medics, a Vietnamese interpreter, a security element of MPs, and two Military Intelligence spooks who wore no markings on their uniforms, not even their names. Medics treated the villagers while the MI interrogated them about VC activity.

It was the first time I had ever prepared an aid bag for a real mission. The other medic was a speedy four, a specialist fourth class, named Fenderbender. I barely contained my excitement as he helped me select medications. Darvon 65 was a favorite painkiller among the villagers. Robaxin helped papa-san relax his muscles after a dawn-to-dusk day bending over in his rice paddies. Diarrhea was a common ailment, so I took Kaopectate. Penicillin and tetracycline would cure everything from infected teeth to foot sores.

"Take twenty bars of soap," Fenderbender recommended. "It's almost nonexistent over here. Most of the kids have terminal cradle cap, a psoriasislike disease. Just washing with soap and water cures most of their problems."

Except for my less than glamorous trips to the garbage dump, this was my first excursion outside the wire since my arrival. The patrol climbed into Jeeps and passed through the gate. My senses came alive, like those of a deer thrown into a field with a pack of wolves. This was Indian country. I locked and loaded.

"MEDCAP rarely runs into problems," Fenderbender said reassuringly. "We only go out during the day, and Vietnam is a night war. I'm sure we treat Vietcong now and then and some of our medications end up in VC hands. Besides, it would be bad form for the VC to ambush us, since we're treating people for free."

After a short time, with the MPs running point down a well-worn trail, I lost my fear and became immersed in the beauty of the countryside. Banana and grapefruit trees grew wild alongside the pathway, and coconut palms rose fifty feet into the air. Rice paddies glowed in vibrant hues of green. The scenes of peasants working in their fields with their dark water buffalo and women squatting with their cone-shaped hats in front of palm frond-and-tin huts came right out of photos in *National Geographic*. I was thrilled and amazed by it all. I felt a trill of pride that my country and I were helping these simple people protect their freedom from the evils of communism.

Vietnam looked like a paradise when you observed it from afar. It could be deceiving. Vietnam, I was soon to discover, was like a beautiful woman you spotted at the far end of the street. Then you came close to her and found her to be a scabby old hag covered with warts.

The people of Vietnam had been at war with somebody—the Japanese, the French, the Americans, the Chinese, one another—for most of the twentieth century. Many of them were born in war, lived in war, and died in war. They knew more firsthand about war than any other people in the world.

The path we followed led into a village and became a dusty road lined with hooches made of clapboard, palm thatch, and rusted tin. Swaybacked pigs, bare-assed chickens, and half-naked children rooted among the hooches and darted around us. I was amazed at how old women could squat on their haunches for hours chewing betel nut, a mild euphoric that dribbled red juice and helped dull the pain of lives inured to labor. Women of thirty looked sixty.

I realized that what I saw, these few bare necessities, was all these people possessed. They had no TVs, radios, refrigerators, washers, or cars. No pillows, blankets, or nightstands. No electricity. Families slept on mats spread across a low table or on the floor. Their only light came from the cooking fire or an oil lamp. The village smelled of burning bamboo. The kids collected it. It was plentiful and made a good starter for heating water to cook rice. They had rice for almost every meal.

When I left Dong Tam, I had crossed the line between the First World and the Third World. I had left canned food behind, along with clean water, electricity, literacy, radio, TV, air conditioning, and iced tea. I entered a world where people still believed in witchcraft. I thought, I'll go home in a year, if I'm lucky, but these poor people *are* home.

Children wanted soap and chop-chop, something to eat.

People too old to work in the fields placed their palms together in a praying position and bowed. They were ugly and withered, with eyes squinted to knife slits. Their toothless, red-stained mouths resembled soft, mysterious caverns. They offered bitter tea without sugar as a token of their appreciation for medical treatment. They had nothing else to offer.

"Bac-si," they chattered. *"Bac-si."*

Fenderbender told me that meant "doctor" in Vietnamese. Doc. I knew that the grunts out in the field called their medics Doc. It was the first time I had been called that. I liked the sound of it.

I wrote Dianne a long letter telling her of the terrific day I'd had in the field and how my heart had gone out to these little people. Being a medic wasn't half as bad as I expected. I didn't have to use the radio or call in air strikes. I hadn't seen blood either, just ulcerated skin, infections, toothaches, and cradle cap. I could be comfortable with this.

It had been weeks since I'd received a letter from my wife. Krogan offered little sympathy. "Guys over here get Dear Johns all the time," he said. "It doesn't take long for women back in the world to forget about us. Why shouldn't they forget us? Everybody else has."

Sergeant Shelby and Colonel Arnold blocked my permanent transfer to MEDCAP, but I volunteered to accompany the team every chance I got. Fenderbender and the other MEDCAP medics liked having me. It gave them a rotating break from the field. I was eager to learn, and I genuinely enjoyed helping the Vietnamese. Out past the wire, forging rivers and wading through rice paddies, I felt like a real GI. A true Doc. I returned to base camp exhausted and caked with mud and reeking of sweat and jungle decay—but happy. If you could be happy under such circumstances.

I'd had this John Wayne fantasy ever since I arrived in-country: I would drag half my platoon out from under enemy fire and save their lives with expert medical treatment, maybe blast away a gook with a machine gun, receive a wound—but not too serious a wound—win the Medal of Honor, and rotate home to a hero's welcome. Working with MEDCAP, I had almost forgotten my fantasy. As Fenderbender said, it wasn't to the VC's advantage to ambush us. Which suited me fine. Although I still wondered how I would react under fire, I wasn't *that* eager to experience it. Not yet.

When the MPs from MEDCAP asked if I would accompany them on a mission one morning, I replied immediately, "Is the pope Catholic?" Fenderbender laughed. He said I was the only medic he knew who could slip *out* through the wire faster than a VC sapper could sneak *in* through the wire.

The MPs' objective was a whorehouse a few klicks—kilometers—up the My Tho River near Kim Son. A boat transported the raiding patrol through enemy country and dropped us off in tangled underbrush. I was starting to get excited. Enemy soldiers as well as GIs frequented the whorehouse. That was the main reason the MPs were on their search-and-destroy mission. GIs could use the steam-and-creams on post or they could slip out to see mama-san outside the gate, but houses like this were dangerous and off-limits. What if GIs and Charlie both had a romantic yen the same night?

This was a *real* combat operation. As the patrol approached the house of ill repute, the sergeant in charge posted a security element in a circle around the hooch while the raiding party prepared its surprise. We were stationed at fifty-meter intervals along likely escape routes. I crouched among thick underbrush and waited expectantly for the action to begin. The vegetation was so dense I visually commanded a radius of only about ten feet. I had only a general picture of where the other men were located.

After a few minutes of waiting and listening, I heard a rustling noise in the bush ahead of me. I shrugged it off as just my imagination at first, recalling how a tree had kept moving in my mind one night during in-country indoctrination at Camp Bearcat.

The rustling continued, sounding furtive. Someone *was* coming toward me, slipping through the brush. I dared not breathe. Slowly, my thumb found the selector switch on my rifle and eased it to semi. Tension sweat burned my eyes and fogged my glasses.

The man was moving stealthily nearer. A branch cracked. Leaves shook.

Oddly enough, I wasn't frightened. I was excited. Adrenaline pumped concentration into me like a predator poised on a limb overlooking a primitive jungle trail. I could do this thing. I could do whatever was required. My life or his. A man could do anything, I was discovering, when it came down to his survival.

Then I remembered. Oh, Jesus, Lord and Christ! I had not loaded a round into the chamber of my weapon when the mission started. *You stupid shit.* I faced an enemy coming directly at me, would be on top of me within seconds, with what was essentially an unloaded rifle.

I dared not chamber a round now. He would hear it and blast me.

I felt for the charging handle. My only option lay in waiting until the last instant. As soon as the VC showed himself, I would yank back the charging handle, chamber a round, and fire at the same time.

I drew in a deep silent breath. My eyes were riveted on the rustling jungle where the enemy soldier would emerge. My muscles were so taut I felt as if I would explode as soon as the guy showed himself.

The jungle whispered and fluttered. And then he appeared. There were *two* of them.

Ducks. *Big* ducks.

I stared. Tension drained out of me like air from a punctured tire. I understood from that moment that I *could* fight and I *could* kill if it became necessary.

Those ducks—VC ducks, no doubt—had almost become dead ducks.

8

The post quartermaster laundry misplaced my clean uniforms. The only fatigues I had to wear to Colonel Arnold's formation and inspection were filthy from a MEDCAP in the field. I had no choice. Standing orders said every swinging dick attended the colonel's personnel inspections. I stood at attention in ranks in my funky jungles and watched Colonel Arnold and Sergeant Shelby work their way toward me. The colonel resembled some prissy storeroom clerk with terminal hemorrhoids. Shelby's head and his neck were the same size. They were going to go ape-shit when they saw me.

They executed their crisp military facing movements and stood in front of me. I looked straight ahead. I saw the red creep up from the colonel's heavily starched collar, followed by the same red creeping up from Shelby's equally heavily starched collar. It was said that every time the colonel went to shit, Shelby carried the toilet paper.

"Have you been living with the Vietnamese pigs, shitbird?" Shelby growled. "The condition of your uniform can get you an Article Fifteen."

An Article 15 was nonjudicial punishment for common infractions of rules and regulations.

"Deplorable," said the prissy colonel.

I should have kept my big mouth shut and let them chew ass and then forgotten about it. As the field troops put it, "Don't sweat the small shit; it don't mean nothing." But I had been fed so much chickenshit I could almost taste it.

"Maybe you should give the quartermaster an Article Fifteen," I suggested. "It's not my fault the laundry lost my uniforms."

Shelby's starched blocked hat almost popped off his head and went into orbit.

"Evans, that's an Article Fifteen for that wiseass remark."

"The way I understand it, Sergeant," I replied calmly, "I have a right to refuse an Article Fifteen and request a general court-martial." In a combat zone, court-martial officers were required to be drawn from the infantry branch. "I'll enjoy seeing what three combat officers think about being pulled out of the field to try a man for a dirty, unstarched uniform," I added a little too smugly; I couldn't help myself.

"Evans, you're nothing but fucking trouble. If you're not careful, I'll have you transferred to the field so fast it'll take a week for your ass to catch up with you."

The colonel nodded.

But of course, since I *wanted* to go to the field, I couldn't. That was the way the army worked.

Shelby stayed on my ass after that, no doubt encouraged by the colonel. In my locker he found a few rounds of M16 ammunition left over from a MEDCAP mission. Surprise barracks and locker inspections were another way of harassing the troops.

"Look, I just forgot to turn them back in."

"It's against regulations. You can get an Article Fifteen."

It had worked before, so I tried it again: "Three infantry officers will find it amazing that I'd be court-martialed for having ammo in a combat zone."

Shelby and the colonel were on to me. "It won't be for possessing ammo," Shelby said with a predatory grin. "It'll be for disobeying an order to turn in weapons and ammunition."

He had me there.

No one knew exactly how common fragging officers had become in Vietnam. There was always talk about it. If some asshole who was making life miserable for his troops caught one in the skull during a firefight, who was to say if it had come from enemy or friendly fire? Such a thing would have been unthinkable in normal society. But here in this strange environment where society's normal rules of decent conduct had been suspended and death tiptoed through the night, fragging an asshole seemed both plausible and natural. Being an asshole in a combat zone was an unsafe thing to be.

"It's *us* or it's *them*," went the argument as discussions of fragging Colonel Arnold and Sergeant Shelby intensified in the 9th Med Battalion. "A couple of guys have already committed suicide just to escape them. They're going to kill us all with their chickenshit rules and regulations. We have a right to defend ourselves."

It wasn't like the medics were hot in the middle of firefights every day. Colonel Arnold's untimely journey on a slab to our newly constructed morgue could hardly be blamed on enemy fire. Conspirators gathered in tight, whispering clumps of secrecy throughout the battalion area and mulled over elaborate plots. Suggestions ranged from hotshotting the tyrant with drugs to arranging a Jeep accident. "Frag the bastard" became a rallying cry that united the men of the 9th Med like never before. Sex fell to a distant second as a topic of conversation. Gonorrhea cases declined significantly two weeks in a row.

If these had been normal times, I would have been appalled at my participation in the endless intrigues—Dan Evans, who almost fainted at the sight of blood—but these were not normal times. I wanted out of Dong Tam, no matter what it took. But if I couldn't get out, I could at least, for my own sanity, help eliminate the source of all our misery.

Several plans were considered and rejected. The plan had to be perfect. It must cast suspicion on no one in the battalion. The CIA would have been inspired by the design and clandestine nature of the plot my little group concocted.

It was built on the premise that many of the gooks who worked on the post as janitors and caretakers and laundresses and scullery help were VC agents and spies. We would simply contact one of them and pay him to have the mortar crew zero in on Colonel Arnold's sleeping quarters the next time the VC shelled Dong Tam. Foolproof. The VC got the blame; we received the benefits.

"How are we going to contact a VC?" someone asked.

"Simple," came a reply. "We start asking around among the gooks."

The next few days were a hubbub of furtive activity, clandestine rendezvous, and hushed expectations. One of the conspirators went around humming "The Big Bad Wolf Is Dead." Others paced off the precise distances between the wire and the sleeping quarters of our prospective target, then triangulated them against the POW camp whose location the VC undoubtedly knew. We drew secret maps.

Then everything went to shit. A grenade booby trap exploded underneath Shelby's bed, planted there by another group of fraggers, no doubt. Sergeant Shelby didn't happen to be in his bed at the time. Shrapnel peppered his bunkmate's legs, but he was not seriously injured.

I first heard about this fruition of one of the countless schemes webbing the 9th Med when the MPs came storming up the barracks stairs like the gestapo. We were all jarred out of bed in our underwear and lined up while the MPs went through our lockers searching for contraband and evidence. I hoped I hadn't left a map among my socks and skivvies. I chanced a glance at the guy next to me. He stared straight ahead. His face was the color of a fish's belly.

"Somebody up here knows who did this!" the MPs shouted. "CID'll get it out of you. You'll talk. Some of you will talk. You'll get out of Vietnam all right, but it'll take you about twenty years to get out of the federal penitentiary."

I thought one of the guys was going to vomit. The guy next to him was shivering. CID questioned every enlisted man in the 9th Med for about a week while Colonel Arnold and Sergeant Shelby holed up out of sight somewhere. Then the investigators gave up, went on to investigate some other fragging elsewhere. When Colonel Arnold ventured back into daylight, he seemed somewhat less the asshole than before. He held an in-ranks inspection, but he threatened no one with an Article 15.

9

The medical company commander summoned his surplus medics to his office. Eight or ten of us filed inside and stood at uneasy parade rest in front of his paper-cluttered desk. Electrical wires, fixtures, and wall studs stood out in relief. The office looked temporary, but it had been temporary for nearly two years. The CO was slightly overweight with white paper-shuffling hands. REMF. He cleared his throat and stood up. His eyes avoided ours. When he spoke, he sounded as though he were signing our death warrants.

"Uh-oh, shit storm," someone whispered.

"Men," the CO said, "I want you all to know that if I had a choice, this wouldn't be happening. But I don't." He paused, took a deep breath. "Men, the 4/39th Infantry Battalion has come up short on field medics." He didn't explain the shortage. "The 9th Med has been tasked with supplying the 4/39th with four medics. It'll only be for a two-week period. You'll be going into combat with the platoons. First, do I have any volunteers?"

My hand shot up independently of my brain. I stood there among the little group adjusting my glasses with one hand while the other hand reached for the ceiling. It was the only hand up. Me, me, teacher. Choose me. I felt a little foolish. What'sa matter with you, Evans? Ain't you learned you don't volunteer for nothing in the army? The army'll fuck you every time. But I'd have done anything to get away from the Dong Tam chickenshit, even if only for two weeks. Besides, I still had that John Wayne fantasy.

"You *want* to go into the field, Evans?" the CO asked. He couldn't believe it.

"Yes, sir." That was why I volunteered for Vietnam. I

had to prove myself. God, help me meet the challenge. I had been in-country two months.

"You're down for it, Evans. Get your combat gear and report back to my office in one hour. Do I have any more volunteers? If not, I'll have to select from among you."

I wanted to write Dianne the exciting news. A macabre thought struck me. This could be my last letter, and I didn't know my own wife's address. The last I heard, she had moved out of my parents' house and they hadn't heard from her since. I hadn't heard from her either. I'd left for Vietnam feeling secure in my marriage. Doubts were now starting to creep in. I ended up jotting a quick note to my parents and my kid sister, Patty:

> Dear Mom, Dad, and Patty,
>   Sorry to inform you but I am leaving in an hour to go on a two-week mission with the 4th and 39th Infantry. . . . I just found out about it at 1:30 P.M. and it is 2:15 now. . . .
>   I don't know how much I can write in the next two weeks, so if you don't hear from me, don't worry.
>   I got to go now. Love, and don't worry because my guardian angel will look after me.

I signed the letter "Doc."

10

The 4th Battalion of the 39th Infantry was working out of a small fire support base at the nearby village of Vinh Kim. Its primary mission was to provide security for the 9th Division's base camp. It had established four platoon patrol bases (PPBs) scattered throughout AO Kudzu surrounding

Dong Tam. Platoons switched off with each other in patrolling out of the PPBs.

Laden with weapons, helmet, and other field gear, I reported to the battalion aid station at Dong Tam to catch a deuce-and-a-half out to Vinh Kim. With me was another medic named Ramsey, who had not volunteered for the mission; he had been selected. He looked pale and nervous and kept licking his lips. I dropped my gear just inside the wooden door of the aid station and blinked behind my glasses while my eyes adjusted after coming in out of the bright sunlight.

Captain Byron Holley, the battalion chief surgeon, and a tall medic named Benny Fontenot rushed to pump our hands as if we were manna from heaven. I liked them both immediately, Holley especially. He was slender and tanned and wore dark glasses. He didn't appear to be that much older than I was. I stood grinning in surprise like some tall, gangly, good-natured hayseed. I suddenly felt happy to be needed, wanted. No more building morgues and hauling garbage and in-ranks inspections. I was a combat medic. A Doc. I felt important at last.

I was sure no one in the 4th and 39th had ever even thought about fragging Dr. Holley.

He explained that I was to be assigned to First Platoon, Bravo Company. Ramsey would report to Charlie Company. Fontenot led us to the supply room and helped us select and pack field medical supplies. He was about my age, maybe younger, but he had already experienced being a platoon, company, and now battalion medic. I held open my ruck and shuffled awkwardly as he went through the medications and supplies, explaining the value of each item and the reasons for including some and excluding others. I felt so damned green.

"Pack only the bare necessities when you go out," he advised. "That ruck'll get damned heavy. Fast."

Twenty bandages of various sizes and five cravat bandages disappeared into the ruck. Penicillin and tetracycline followed. Then cough medications, I.V. fluids, malaria pills. Iodine. Kaopectate and Lomotil for dysentery, better known as the GI runs or Ho Chi Minh's revenge. Darvon-65, the wonder drug of the Vietnam War. I had to sign for five morphine Syrettes.

"Don't leave the morphine in your ruck; somebody'll steal it," Fontenot advised. "Keep it in your pockets. You have to account for them all. Dr. Holley won't tolerate any of his medics becoming addicts."

I asked for Vaseline gauze.

"What do you need it for?" Fontenot demanded.

Didn't he remember medic school? "It's great for treating sucking chest wounds."

He gave me a dozen packages of it. I gulped. I hoped I wouldn't need even *one* packet.

I was actually preparing for combat—this green FNG doc who couldn't even sit all the way through a casualty movie. I would be the only thing out there between the wounded GIs and Almighty God. Each combat grunt eventually had to face his trial by fire. Combat medics faced trial by death. No doctor could save a wounded man unless the medic could keep him alive long enough to reach a field hospital. Deep down, I knew men died in battle and that I couldn't save them all, no matter what I did. Other medics had told me this. People *died* out there.

I wondered if I could handle it. Could I do my job? Could I save *some* lives?

Fontenot must have seen the anxiety in the muscles of my face. He paused. "Evans?"

I jumped, startled.

"This your first time going to the field?" he asked.

"I've gone out with MEDCAP a few times."

"You'll do all right," he said.

I drew in a deep breath. "God, I hope so."

Doc Holley took Ramsey and me aside before we loaded onto the deuce with our gear.

"Forget all the heroics you've read and heard about," he advised gently. "No one is going to think any less of you if you can't get to a wounded man because of enemy fire. Don't get yourself killed trying to prove something."

11

Vinh Kim smelled of vegetation and sweat and cook fires fueled with bamboo and human excrement. Passing from the hamlet to the fire base was like going from a shady, quiet green town to a plowed, unshaded, flat, noisy frontier fort surrounded by Indians. The sun beat down hard and fierce on the bunkers and tents. The Vietnamese lived in harmony with the land; we Americans came in and knocked the top off the land before we built our bases. The base smelled of insecticide, burning feces, urine, cordite and men.

Three infantry platoons and an artillery platoon worked out of the camp. It was a squalid, irregular-shaped compound of sandbagged Quonset huts, bunkers, and trenches surrounded by wire and razor concertina. Trash dumps contained everything from expended artillery-round casings to half-empty C-ration cans. The C's bred rats as big as possums. They showed no fear of America's finest fighting force, would stand up on their hind legs and challenge anything that came near them.

Green as I was, I liked the relaxed atmosphere in comparison to the 9th Med at Dong Tam under Colonel Arnold. I didn't realize then what a sorry outfit the 4/39th really was overall. Command post groups slept on cots inside tents. They had stateside footlockers, folding chairs, portable radios, and plastic coolers filled with beer and Coke. Amid the shit and the toilet paper and the live ammo lying trampled in the mud were troops who wore love beads and peace symbols. They looked more like hippies than soldiers. They bitched constantly and seemed low in spirits.

No one appeared to be watching the perimeter. A trooper walked along, dragging the stock of his M16 on the ground.

Few others even carried weapons. Many ran around bare-chested, wearing cutoff fatigue trousers and shower shoes. Grenades hung untaped from the load-bearing equipment of a squad preparing to go out on patrol. The machine gunners wore their ammo Pancho Villa–style.

I found out later that VC "harassment" had virtually gutted the battalion both physically and emotionally. The battalion operations sergeant charged with keeping track of casualties tallied that the dichs (one of many names for the enemy) suffered zero KIA and zero WIA while, during the same time period, the 4/39th took something like 20 KIAs and 400 WIAs. Rockets, mortars, booby traps, and even friendly fire had imposed a deadly attrition upon the battalion. First Platoon, Bravo Company, to which I was assigned, was down to half strength, two squads instead of four, with a staff sergeant instead of a lieutenant as platoon leader.

Jim Whitmore, the platoon medic I was replacing, greeted me with a broad grin. He wore glasses and had a wide black mustache. Black hair grew on his shoulders and down his back. He finished packing his ruck—he would catch the next truck back to Dong Tam—and then escorted me along planks laid around during the muddy monsoons as walkways to the long, sandbagged Quonset hut that temporarily housed First Platoon.

He filled me in on conditions as we walked. "We never see them," he said. "They're like ghosts, the enemy is. Most of our casualties have been from booby traps. But we were ambushed three days ago. Terry Weaver had a sucking chest wound. Harry Fullmer and Eusebio Fernandez took some shrapnel. Dave . . ."

He paused on the boardwalk, blinking rapidly.

"Dave Gardner was my best friend. He was from Walpole, New Hampshire. After the ambush, he lay flat on his back. He wasn't moving. He wasn't bleeding or anything. There didn't seem to be a mark on him. But I couldn't find a pulse.

"I opened his shirt. There was a . . . a small hole the size of a pencil eraser directly over his heart. Dave was dead. He died and he didn't even know when he died. We found out later that a ten-year-old boy had blown up two claymore mines against the platoon."

Whitmore adjusted his attitude. We continued walking. "Evans, don't trust even the baby-sans," he said. "They're *all* the enemy."

A cold gray pall seemed to flatten out the searing sun and settle around me like a wet shirt in January.

"You're a cherry and the men are going to give you all kinds of advice," Whitmore said. "Listen to them. Most of it'll be good. Let me give you my advice now, the best I can. It's this, Evans: Don't get personally involved with the men. Be friendly but not friends. You're the one who's going to have to patch them up, and you may have to watch them die. Catch my drift?"

The rough young men of First Platoon gathered around to get a look at the new doc when Whitmore introduced me. They looked more like a gang off the streets of L.A. than a platoon of American GIs. They shook hands with me solemnly, the platoon sergeant first.

Sergeant Jim Richardson stood over six feet tall but looked even taller because he was so thin and young. I expected a combat platoon sergeant to look something like Brian Dennehy or Richard Widmark or maybe John Wayne—older and tough-acting with big hands and steely blue eyes. Something like a father figure. Instead, what I got was my brother. Richardson was not much older than I was. The tropical sun had burned him like rawhide and bleached brittle his shock of short hair. His thick Oklahoma accent eased out soft and hill-country dry.

"We need you, Evans," he said simply, then withdrew.

The squad leaders were even younger. Sergeant John Svatek was handsome, blond, and tan; he would have looked more at home on a surfboard in Malibou than on a patrol in the Mekong Delta. He was maybe twenty, twenty-one years old at the outside. He said he had been wounded twice during the last six months.

"I hope you're a good medic," he said.

I hoped so too.

Second squad leader Sergeant Don Wallace was short and swarthy with big ears and large features. He moved up to squad leader when the previous leader and two others hit a booby trap and were medevac'd. He had been in-country less than three months. He had already collected one Purple Heart.

That was the primary leadership of the First Platoon—as young as or younger than I was. I did not feel that I was in particularly good hands with Allstate. I wanted to be secure in the knowledge that my leaders were highly skilled and carefully trained. Instead, young noncoms were given crash courses in leadership and combat tactics, then shipped to Vietnam for postgraduate training in navigation, jungle warfare, artillery support, and small unit tactics. Those who survived went home as staff sergeants. Those who flunked went home in body bags; they often took others with them.

I looked over the other grunts as they introduced themselves. I was a kid, but these were *kids*—teenagers who less than a year ago had been riding bicycles and going out on dates and fixing up their first cars. Dale Gass, a blond hick farm boy from southern Illinois who carried around photos of the prize Chester White hogs he and his dad raised back on the farm; skinny little Arles Brown from a town in West Virginia so small that he received his draft notice while he was still in high school; Marty Miles with his horn-rimmed glasses and mischievous dark eyes; long, tall soul brother Joe "Slim" Holleman; Harry Fullmer the radiotelephone operator, or RTO; the tall, skinny black kid from Texas, L. J. Henderson, whose first advice to me was to get rid of my underwear and socks.

"Underwear stays wet all the time, man," Henderson said, "an' it give you jungle rot. It'll rot off your dick, an' I want to keep every foot of my own dick, don't know 'bout you. Same goes for your socks. Jungle rot is some bad motherfucker. Hear what I'm sayin'?"

All in the platoon offered guidance to the FNG: Don't march too near the radiotelephone operator, because his antenna attracts enemy fire like a lightning rod draws lightning; put a condom over the muzzle of your M16 to keep rain and trash out of the barrel; always carry a poncho; find a utility net to use as a hammock; carry plenty of Kool-Aid to kill the taste of the water; place one P-38 C-ration opener in your helmet and the other on your dog tag chain.

"And don't try to collect no hero badges," Henderson concluded. "Hear what I'm sayin'?"

The doc got to go to the head of the line to make the first C-ration selection.

"You can move into Whitmore's bunk," Sergeant Richardson said. "You'll be a combat veteran in no time, Doc. It doesn't take long to lose your cherry in this shitbag country."

12

Since the war in Vietnam was largely a night war, First Platoon soldiers had it easy during the day. They lolled half dressed around the fire support base, or FSB, writing letters home, dealing cards, grab-assing, and listening to the Armed Forces Network radio station out of Saigon. A truck from Dong Tam rolled in every day about noon to deliver hot meals. Meals on Wheels. The rest of the time we ate C's.

A certain restlessness took over as nightfall approached. Sergeant Richardson called the squad leaders in for their briefings on the night's mission; First Platoon went out almost every evening. Henderson or Gass or one of the others strode out to the wire and stood silently looking out across the wide cleared field of fire past the rice paddies toward Vinh Kim. Life seemed so goddamn *normal* out there, picture-postcard normal, with papa-sans and water buffalo working the rice crops, traffic heavy and rumbling on the road, little shops and markets conducting a brisk trade, whores and kids waving at passing GIs and shouting, " 'Meli-can GI numbah one!" There might not have been a war at all, from the look of things.

Henderson noticed me watching him at the wire. He angled toward me, all long legs and arms and white teeth against a heavy black jaw made darker by constant tropical exposure.

"See that mama-san?" he asked, pointing to a young girl in black PJs and a cone-shaped hat lolling in the red sunset on the back of a water buffalo. "She just waitin', watchin' for us to haul our exposed asses out through the gate so she can go tell it to Charlie. Charlie know every move we make, man. He know when we wipe our ass an' what it smell like when we fart. One of these days he gonna kick our asses, Charlie is. He gonna hurt us bad, Doc. That's when I want you to keep your eye on this soul bro' an' patch up his black ass quick."

As the sun went down, dying, troops hid in their bunkers and trenches and silently hoped the war would take a path around them until the sun rose again. I would get used to the routine, but now everything was so fresh and strange and scary that I missed nothing. First Platoon was about to introduce me to the war. I spent an hour packing an aid bag, trying to think of worst-case scenarios and be adequately prepared. I didn't know what to expect, other than that the war would start on time out there.

Sergeant Richardson apportioned equipment among the platoon members—claymore mines, extra 7.62mm machine-gun cartridge belts, C4 explosives, additional radio batteries. He handed me a one-pound block of C4. It looked and felt like hardened Silly Putty.

"It's safe," he said, "as long as it's not subjected to heat and concussion at the same time. You can burn little pieces of it to heat your C's. Just don't try to stomp it out when it's burning. It'll blast off your toes. You want to carry a few rounds for the machine guns?"

Anything for the war effort. I draped a heavy belt of M60 ammo across my chest Pancho Villa–style, the way I'd seen the other grunts doing. I hoisted my ruck and my aid bag, rifle, and LBE (load bearing equipment) as the platoon saddled up in the gathering darkness. I tried not to look too green. The others behaved as though they had been doing this kind of shit—shooting and getting shot at, dying and killing—all their young lives. I supposed you could get used to anything.

The platoon moved out of the fire support base against a

bruised pink-and-purple sky. A long green broken-backed caterpillar creeping across the surface of the earth. Wasn't this what I wanted? To be tested? To face my moment of truth?

Could I hack it?

I stuck with Sergeant Richardson and his RTO, trying to stay as close to the sergeant as I could without getting too close to the radio antenna. I felt important as part of the platoon's command element. Harry Fullmer, the RTO, made love to his radio; he didn't merely talk into it. He was about five-ten with curly brown hair and a smooth puggish face, and his lips remained constantly near the radio transmitter snapped into his LBE at the shoulder. He spoke in an odd code.

"Charlie Charlie, Hotel Romeo? Over."

"Lima Charlie. Hotel Mike? Over."

"Same same. The Papa has left the Whiskey. Out."

Translation: "Communications check, how do you read me? Over."

"Loud and clear. How me? Over."

"The same. The patrol has left the wire. Out."

Missions were assigned from company level or above. Most of the time the grunts in the field had no idea how any particular mission fit into the overall scheme of things. We followed orders. We went out and did what we had to do and hoped we all got back with the same number of arms and legs and heads we'd started out with. Then we did it all over again the next night. Grunts called it KITDFBS—kept in the dark, fed bullshit.

The platoon moved cautiously along a trail bordered on one side by a thick forest and on the other side by a field that gradually disappeared as the last of the sun's memory faded. My imagination ran wild. I visualized man-eating tigers, bloodsucking insects, and VC crawling toward us on their bellies or waiting ahead, alerted by the mama-san on the buffalo. Deadly devices awaited our approach—trip wires attached to grenades or mines, shit-smeared punji stakes, spike-filled foot traps. Out of the darkness charged buzzing black clouds of mosquitoes, surrounding the outside of my head the way black clouds of impending evil filled the inside of my head.

The platoon entered the forest, then split into two squads. Sergeant Wallace and his squad veered to the right to set up on a ville where VC were known to recruit replacements and collect taxes. They vanished into the night jungle like ghosts. Sergeant Richardson moved the rest of us to a tiny grassy clearing next to a river. The heat was so intense it seemed to drug even the mosquitoes. He posted security and ordered everyone else to chow down, as there would be no eating once we moved into our ambush position.

"Aren't we at the ambush position?" I asked the sergeant.

"We passed through it about three hundred meters back," he replied, whispering, even though every Vietnamese within ten kilometers knew we were out here. "We'll ease back into it after full dark. That way Charlie won't know exactly where we are if he's been watching."

I remembered an old movie title: *The Night Has a Thousand Eyes.*

I ate canned turkey loaf and fruit cocktail in the dark. I was halfway through my meal when gunfire filled the air. It came from the direction of Wallace's ambush position. Men hit the ground and crawled into a hasty 360-degree perimeter. During in-country orientation and training, instructors had demonstrated the difference between the short, guttural bark of the Communist AK-47 and the sharper popping of the American M16. This was the first time I had ever heard small arms being fired with deadly intent, but it sounded like M16s to me.

Sergeant Richardson and I crouched in the center of the perimeter and watched Fullmer make love to his PRC-25 radio. It was pronounced "Prick-25." He seduced the damned thing in the darkness, whispering into its open mike mouth over and over again, trying to raise Sergeant Wallace.

"Bravo Five-two, this is Bravo Five-six. Bravo Five-two, this is . . ."

Wallace's RTO finally came up on the air. "Bravo Five-two, do you need assistance?" Sergeant Richardson asked him.

"Negatory on that last transmission," Wallace answered personally, as calmly as though on a Ma Bell line. He explained that his squad had been moving through a cemetery when it received fire and returned fire.

"No Whiskey India Alphas," he said: no WIAs—no wounded.

I let out a sigh of relief.

Sergeant Richardson and Sergeant Svatek saddled up our squad, and we moved back the way we had come to the ambush site on a high bank overlooking a bend in the river. The squad sent out flank security, positioned claymore mines facing the stream, and settled down in thick vegetation to wait. VC used the rivers as arteries along which to move troops and supplies.

"You want to be included in the guard roster?" Richardson asked me. Medics were not required to stand guard duty.

"I'll take my share."

Richardson nodded his approval and eased his lanky form on down the ambush line. Each man would take two one-hour shifts on watch during the night.

It took a while for me to settle down after Wallace's little firefight. I kept hearing the stealthy dipping of sampan paddles into the river, seeing shadows forming into human shapes. After a while, when nothing happened, my heart slowed to its normal rate. A full moon bloomed and turned the river into a silver pathway fringed by low undergrowth and nipa palms. It was such a lovely night that it reminded me of a Boy Scout camporee. Except that Boy Scouts never set up ambushes to slaughter other Boy Scouts.

My thoughts, troubled now, turned unwillingly toward home. I had finally received a letter from Dianne. She requested I not pass on her new address to my parents. I couldn't figure it. She had always gotten along well with Mom and Dad. She once said they made her feel like their own daughter.

So what had happened to change that?

In what was almost a postscript at the end of the letter, she causally mentioned that men were already asking her out on dates. "I haven't accepted any invitations yet," she added.

Yet? *Yet?* A little comment like that could drive a man crazy. Ten thousand miles from home and men were trying to get dates with your wife, and you couldn't do a damned thing about it except live with the ache in your guts and hope the next letter brought better news.

"I love you," Dianne had said before I left. "I'll always love you. I'll wait for you as long as it takes."

Sounded to me as if she was already getting tired of waiting. I had only been gone two months.

In-country training sergeants had warned us about women and the dangers of letting our thoughts dwell on home.

"Don't think about home, pussy, or your 1957 Chevrolet," they'd said. "Think about your job here, and think about your buddies. That's what will keep you alive to go home in one year to your pussy and your 1957 Chevrolet."

That first ambush patrol, for me, turned out to be a dry hole. I was almost disappointed. One of the ambushers snored so loud that Sergeant Richardson appointed a man to pinch his nose every time he started. The sun was already up and sucking steam out of the rice paddies around Vinh Kim by the time the platoon reconsolidated its two squads and straggled back through the gates at the fire support base.

As the troops yawned and lighted pieces of C4 over which to heat cocoa and Ranger coffee, Wallace gave an after-action on his encounter last night in the graveyard. This morning, his squad had gone online and swept the area. Later they came across a single hooch perched at the edge of the cemetery. Wailing came from the hooch. Some of the GIs went inside to check it out. They found a Vietnamese family in mourning over a dead man laid out on a low table for burial. A stray bullet had killed him.

Wallace looked uncomfortable with this, but he said, "At least they won't have to carry him very far to get him to the grave."

I hadn't personally seen the dead guy, so I thought little of it. Hot cocoa from my canteen cup, plus meatballs and beans heated over C4, tasted especially good this morning. I removed my jungle jacket and settled back to enjoy breakfast and the sunrise. I had survived my first combat mission.

If this was all there was to war, I thought, it wasn't nearly the hell it had been made out to be.

13

Word came down from higher-higher that Bravo Company would assemble at Dong Tam for a company-size search-and-destroy sweep along the My Tho River. VC had been spotted near the wire at Dong Tam and the post had received increasing mortar fire. VC were fucking up the general's golf game or something.

Most of us in the field looked forward to the mission. It would break up the drudging routine of nightly dry-hole ambushes, plus, even better, it would give us a free night in the country club atmosphere at Division to catch a movie and down a few beers at the Enlisted Men's Club. Morale peaked as though a bunch of poor farm kids had been promised a night out at McDonald's and a Walt Disney film. Like a Saturday night in town. Slim Holleman wondered if he could sneak away for a quickie outside the gate.

"That nigger is growin' *horns,* he so horny," Henderson gibed. Henderson was black, too, but he was always telling "nigger" jokes. "Wonder if he knows gook snatch grow sideways?"

"I don't care if it grow behind the bitch's ear, I'm gettin' some," Holleman vowed.

Doc Holley summoned me to the battalion aid station as soon as Bravo rolled through the gate. I grabbed my rifle, helmet, and aid bag and trotted over to the long wooden building with the makeshift porch running along the front, wondering what I'd done wrong. Nine times out of ten, when an officer sent for an enlisted man, the EM was in deep shit. It was a fact of army life. Officers got the medals; privates cleaned the latrines.

"Evans, I'm assigning you an assistant for this mission," the doctor said. I relaxed. "His name's Private Browner. I want you to make life miserable for the poor bastard. Fill his ruck with enough medical supplies to treat the entire division."

He explained: Browner had been with the First Platoon before. He and Fabrizio had been assigned to a listening post while on an ambush position. When it came Fabrizio's turn to catch a few winks, Browner shot himself in the foot in the hope of getting shipped home. The report from the gunshot triggered a response from the ambush site that damn near got both Fabrizio and Browner tagged and bagged.

Browner healed and was afforded the opportunity of either returning to duty or pulling a tour at LBJ, the Long Binh jail. He decided he was a conscientious objector and refused to carry a rifle. Battalion made him a medic's aid.

"Fuck all them motherfuckin' lifers in this motherfuckin' army," Browner said later, as Bravo prepared for movement. Then he sulled down inside himself like a stunted black ferret with darting eyes as I loaded his ass down like a pack mule. Liters of Dextran and other I.V. fluids went into his ruck, followed by tubes and bottles. He was a walking pharmaceutical warehouse.

"What you doin', man?"

"We're expecting contact," I said.

"I ain't goin' out there an' lettin' them assholes kill me."

"You *are* going," I said.

He made my skin crawl with his cowardice. Then I thought, Hold on, Evans. It was easy enough being *bac-si* to the villagers, treating cradle cap and handing out malaria pills to the troops every Monday. What happened when the real war started?

Maybe I was a coward too.

The thought disgusted me.

I assumed Browner piled out of the deuces with the rest of us when the trucks offloaded a high-strung Bravo Company at the basin on the My Tho River that sheltered the River Assault Group and the Brown Water Navy boats. Four LCMs (landing craft, mechanized) were tied up at the docks, waiting to be loaded. In the carnivallike atmosphere of troops with rucks and weapons piling into the boats, I failed to check on Browner. Each LCM as it became loaded snarled deep-running away from the docks and slowly circled on the mud-brown waters, waiting to get into formation for the daylight push upstream. Sampans and junks laden with produce, livestock, and people sailed past the mouth of the basin.

I crowded into the hold of the LCM designated for First Platoon.

"Keep your heads down and don't be peeping over the gunwales, people," Richardson warned. He rode up on the foredeck with the coxswain. "Snipers would love to use you for a bull's-eye."

I didn't have to be told twice. I hunkered down in the boat, which quickly became an oven. The sun burned down on us, turned up to Broil. I looked up and watched scattered white clouds and an occasional waterbird flapping overhead. KITDFBS—kept in the dark, fed bullshit. LCM engines throbbed and vibrated like a platoon of tanks somehow gone amphibious.

I wondered if Dianne would come to my funeral if my guardian angel failed me. Maybe—if she didn't have a date.

"Where's that shitbird assistant of yours?" Harry Fullmer asked, looking up from fine-tuning his PRC-25.

That was when I missed Browner. He was carrying most of my medical supplies.

"He must have climbed into one of the other boats," I replied. God, I hoped he had.

"I didn't see him on the docks," Fullmer said. "Maybe he shot his other foot."

Nothing I could do now.

All we had been told was that we were headed for the Kim Son area. It was supposed to be full of little yellow men with big guns.

I braced myself on my M16. Listened to the river humming and slapping against the boat's hull. Tried to keep my thoughts compact and simple. Mario Sotello crouched across from me with his M16 and a belt of shining brass M60 ammo crisscrossed on his chest for the machine gunner. Mario was over six feet tall, with broad shoulders and thin hips and a dark chiseled face like that of an Aztec. The other guys called him one tough motherfucker.

"I hate this shit," he murmured. "Stuck in this coffin like

a trapped rat. Look out when they lower the door. One RPG fired in here'll get us all."

As if I didn't have enough to worry about.

Soon the LCMs nosed hard onto the mud-crusted beaches, slamming us against each other. I had seen the landings under fire made by John Wayne in *The Sands of Iwo Jima*. As the troops were vomited out of the landing craft onto typical lower-delta terrain or stubby intertwined jungle, I locked and loaded and darted for the cover of the nearest vegetation. Mud sucked at my boots before I reached the tree line. I expected all hell to break loose. Instead, I got silence. Not even the sound of birds. The air felt cool compared to the boat. I looked around, wide-eyed, waiting for something to happen.

It was what the army called a clusterfuck. Sergeant Richardson was shouting and gesticulating and trying to restore order. I still didn't know much about infantry, but I instinctively knew this ratty bunch would have been dog meat had the VC been waiting on us with a reception party ready.

"Don't bunch up like geese, goddammit," Richardson shouted. "Sergeant Wallace, get your squad over there and set up security. Sergeant Svatek, get 'em ready to move out. Holleman, what the hell you doing standing around with your thumb up your ass?"

Browner wasn't on any of the other boats. He had most of my medical supplies in his ruck, items like I.V. fluids I'd need if we were hit and took casualties. I had bandages and morphine for battle wounds but little else. How could I have been so damned stupid?

I reported the AWOL to Sergeant Richardson. I was scared to death, and now that asshole Browner had run off with my medical supplies.

"He must have missed the boat," I said.

Richardson bit off an obscenity. "He's a worthless turd anyhow," he said.

Leave it to a cherry like me to fuck things up.

14

Shouting officers sorted out the company and got it lined out. First Platoon was tasked with left-flank security. Bravo stretched out for nearly a half mile when it got started. The giant mottled green sweat-soaked, fear-smelling caterpillar crawled through the rice paddies and stretches of jungle and forded muddy canals and clambered over dikes at a forced-march pace. Clusters of hooches perched on the high ground between rice fields. Living bamboo fences surrounded some of them. Potbellied pigs, bare-ass chickens, and half-naked kids scurried out of our way.

We paused at the hooches while search teams probed baskets of rice with their knives and jabbed at the floors, looking for tunnels and concealed caches of VC weapons and food. Officers went back and forth to make sure none of the troops got overzealous and used BIC cigarette lighters on the hooches or shot at anyone unless we were shot at first.

"Fucked up," Fullmer said between orgies with his radio. "They can shoot us, but we have to ask for their IDs and get permission from the president of the United States to shoot *them*. We should bring in the fast movers and bomb 'em all the way back to their ancestors. Napalm sticks to kids."

Sergeant Richardson's command post element, me with it, marched near the rear of the column, where we were pretty much kept in the dark about what was going on toward the point. It wasn't long before my 40-pound ruck dug into my back and started painful saddle sores. The M16 threatened to drag my arm out of its socket. My jungle fatigues turned black with sweat. I nursed my canteen, not wanting to have to drink out of the paddies and streams: the locals squatted right in the water to relieve themselves, then dipped out a bucketful of it in which to boil their rice. A 100-pound Vietnamese could live with a 40-pound tapeworm that would kill the average American.

In spite of the advice my predecessor, Whitmore, had offered about not getting involved personally with the men, I felt myself being drawn to them. Dad always said men in war formed brother bonds that nothing could sever. The more I learned about the grunts of the First, the more I liked them.

Big Sotello, whose weapon looked like a toy in his thick brown hands, had once jumped into a flooding river to save a comrade, even though he couldn't swim a stroke. Svatek surprised a VC squatting to take a shit only fifteen feet away from him; the VC fired a full magazine at Svatek and missed every shot. Will Stevens waded into a river to brush his false teeth just as a sniper opened fire; confused, teeth in hand, he charged directly at the sniper by mistake. "Gonna chew that yellow man's ass," Henderson had ragged him. Harvill had a short-timer's attitude: "Man, I am so short that I'm afraid to go to sleep and let the Freedom Bird leave without me."

The sun climbed high over the caterpillar, then inched lower toward the west, lengthening the shadows, before the local VC responded to the intrusion. They began gathering to harass the advancement, like wolves along a caribou migration. Most of the action occurred forward. News worked its way back mouth-to-mouth to explain the occasional crackle of gunfire or the periodic shouting and halts. Fullmer eavesdropped on the company radio net and tried to keep the platoon informed.

Three VC carrying stretchers were seen moving east, as if they might be preparing for a battle. Point shot at some VC running into a wood line. Snipers pinged at GIs, then withdrew. Bravo slowed to a snail's pace, starting and stopping as it coped with each new challenge.

I hit the ground the first time or two that gunshots clapped in the air. Buried my face in the dirt.

Richardson knelt beside me. He grinned. "You'll get used to it," he said. "They're not shooting at us."

"They ain't shooting at us *yet*," Fullmer corrected him.

Suddenly I felt hundreds of sinister unseen eyes watching from the dark forest, waiting for nightfall.

"It's quiet out there."

"Yeah, too quiet."

Older hands amused themselves by telling FNGs horror stories about how VC captured Americans and tortured them for hours by pulling out their fingernails, slicing off their testicles, cutting out their tongues, gouging out their eyes, and finally skinning them alive—all within hearing distance of their comrades.

Contact continued to pick up as the afternoon wore on like a bad movie. Third Platoon, on point, wounded a VC carrying a syringe and other medical supplies. I heard the muffled crump of an M79 grenade exploding. Then I heard wailing as the emotionless caterpillar crawled on. A woman hiding in a hooch had been killed by the blooper grenade. Her family's keening sliced into my guts like a razor. Vietnamese stared at us as we slogged by. Most of us did not look back at them.

A young girl was next, shot, followed by the M79 grenading of another woman for standing in the door of her straw hooch. All the VC activity had stretched everyone's nerves. Fuck 'em. Shoot first and let God sort 'em out.

Word came back: "Medic!"

Bravo had four medics. The other three were more experienced than I.

"Medic!" The others must have been busy.

Richardson lifted an eyebrow. "They've got a gook needing treatment," he drawled.

What else could I do except swallow the dryness in my throat and make a show of it? I shed my ruck and sprinted forward with only my aid bag and M16. I hoped I didn't need an I.V.

Three or four GIs stood around the door of the woman's hooch keeping other villagers at bay. They made a pathway to the door as I arrived. I was panting from the run. The grunts looked at me with stony faces as I bent over a tiny woman in bloody black PJs writhing in pain on the dirt floor. She was about the size of a ten-year-old American girl, but her face looked as old and corroded as the Buddhist temples in the jungle.

"Is she going to be a body count, Doc?" one of the young soldiers asked with all the emotion of someone back home ordering an ice-cream cone.

All that gore. What a mess. Right thumb blown off; gleam of white bone, stringy red sinews hanging. Mouth gaping in fear, filling the air with the stench of *nuoc mam*, the half-rotted-fish sauce the Vietnamese ate with everything. Splatters of blood on her cheeks. Black blouse ripped and shredded by shrapnel. More blood. Dozens of punctures and tears in breasts and neck and belly. I remembered Whitmore telling me about his buddy dying from a single puncture the size of a pencil eraser.

"Doc? Are you all right?"

That snapped me out of it. It was as if I shifted into automatic mode. I hadn't known I could do that until now. It surprised me. The side of me that longed to be "Doc" overpowered the squeamish side of me. I opened my bag and surprised myself again with the efficiency and detachment with which I tended the woman's wounds. She uttered no sounds, but her suffering eyes never left mine.

I felt pretty good about myself by the time the dust-off chopper flew in to transport her to the surgical hospital at Dong Tam. Her family and my own platoon soon dampened my spirits, however. Vietnamese surrounded our interpreter like squabbling geese. The family wanted compensation. Lieutenant Bob Knapp, the company commander, finally forked over 5,700 piastres, about $50 U.S. The family insisted on more. Lieutenant Knapp rummaged up another 5,700 piastres. Free enterprise in action.

Sergeant Richardson's Okie accent rumbled across the flats: "First Herd, saddle up. Come on, people. Let's move out."

"You should have shot the bitch full of something to kill her," a GI said. "Sooner or later she'll repay you by killing one of us."

Treating a gook, I deduced from all of this, wasn't the same as treating one of our own. I handled her all right, I thought, but could I take care of business if it was Richardson or Svatek or Henderson? I figured I hadn't proved anything yet.

15

AK-50 machine-gun fire from a wood line directly ahead caught the company in the open. The hidden gun ripped off a long burst, dot-pluming the open rice field with geysers interspersed among the scattered troops. GIs dropped wherever they were, as if God had reached down and tapped them with a Louisville Slugger.

Surprising how long it took to get from a standing position to flat on your belly in a foot of smelly polluted water. Fullmer dived for me. We fell together behind a low dike. Fullmer's face was in the mud not six inches from mine.

"Doc, you gotta get down faster," the RTO lectured. He bent down his antenna to keep it from waving at the VC gunners. "Bullets ain't got eyes, and they ain't discriminating. They kill the good and the bad, the pretty and the ugly, the bright and the stupid, without preference. Bullets are equal-opportunity killers."

He laughed. The curly knob of hair sticking out from under his helmet made him look like a little boy playing at war.

Friendly artillery pounded the hell out of the wood line, detonating in short, overlapping strings of explosions. Small fires started; smoke oozed out of the jungle and settled, caught in the upper palm fronds. That silenced the machine gun. Soldiers stood up across the width of the field, hesitantly at first, then with more confidence as the purple shadows of night drifted in above the emerald green of the rice to conceal them from enemy observation. The curtain of the Vietcong night was coming down.

The RTO was always first to get the word. Grunts lived and died by the word. The word said Bravo would dig in for the night in this open rice field where the gooks couldn't sneak up on us. The low dikes that gridded off the field offered as much cover from small arms fire as trenches did. Sergeant Richardson positioned his men to defend Bravo's left flank at the front. Wallace and Svatek oversaw the placement of claymores, trip flares, and the platoon's two machine guns manned by Gass and Henderson and their assistant gunners.

I stayed with the RTO and the platoon sergeant in the command post—the CP—located behind a dike to the rear of the platoon's outer defensive line. Richardson made his quiet rounds, constantly checking on things, stopping to offer a word of encouragement here and there. The men would remain on 50 percent alert all night. Fullmer kept his ear to his radio handpiece while he squatted on the lee side of our dike and opened an OD can of beanie-weanies.

I felt exposed, under the scrutiny of a thousand hostile eyes. I crouched lower. I saw a man out on the line trying to read a letter in the last light of the day.

"It don't mean nothing," Fullmer said, pausing with a spoonful of beans halfway to his mouth, his head cocked to one side with his ear against the radio handpiece attached to his shoulder.

"What?"

He swept the spoon of beans across the scene of rice field, GIs cowering behind dikes in the water and darkness, first stars coming out.

"It's the Vietnam soldier's philosophy," he explained. "It don't mean nothing. That's how you live with it all."

It *had* to mean something. Otherwise, why were we over here?

No time to ponder such questions. A sudden whooping mechanical scream echoed from out of the darkness. A single shrill alarm repeated itself in rapid echo from one side of the rice field to the other: *"Incoming! Incoming!"*

Fullmer dropped his beans.

"Over the dike!" he yelled, grabbing my sleeve and yanking me with him.

He had survived mortar attacks before. The sound of the shell shrieking through the night told him which quadrant it had targeted. I sprang with Fullmer to the other side of the dike, flattened myself underneath my arms, would have crawled into my helmet if I could have, just as the explosion flash-banged in the night, sending mud and debris erupting and raining down on us. Hot shrapnel hissed as it hit the water.

More shells followed. Each began with a faint distant whisper, then expanded into a nerve-shattering scream just before it landed and opened up a blinding hole in the night. Closer and closer the screaming came until the expectation of its landing made you feel as if *you* would explode before *it* did. Fullmer, lying breathless next to me, called the rounds. I didn't know how he did it, just from the sound, but when he said, "Stay put!" I stayed put. And when he said, "Over the side!" I went over the side to keep the dike between us and the violent crashing mushrooms of light, noise, smoke, and deadly shrapnel.

Men all over the field were doing the same thing, playing leapfrog with the mortars. Viewed objectively, it could have been comical. Green-clad GIs hopping around in the water like giant bullfrogs trying to escape firecrackers thrown at them.

Among the alarms of "Incoming!" I now detected even more chilling cries: "Medic! Medic!" First Platoon was getting the shit blown out of it.

"Medic!"

That was *me*. Doc. That was my cue.

Just before I switched my mind into automatic mode, as I had done with the wounded female, I cursed Browner for having run off with my supplies. Then I blocked all thoughts of what I might encounter out there. I snatched my aid bag and charged splashing across the field in a crouch. Mortars walked on through the rest of the company, flash-banging and flash-dotting the landscape.

As I scurried along First Platoon's defensive line, checking on the men, the mortaring ceased as suddenly as it had begun. VC never wasted ordnance. Most of the troops were splattered with mud, but only Sergeants Richardson, Svatek, and Wallace were actually wounded. Platoon and squad sergeants' lives were apt to be nasty, brutish, and short. The leaders had to be up and checking on their men and the situation while everyone else tried to play mole and burrow to the center of the earth.

The silence that followed the shelling seemed alarmingly empty in comparison. I played a red lens beam from my flashlight on the sergeants' wounds. To my great relief, I found them all minor. Thank God I didn't need I.V.'s. Band-Aids and antibiotic ointment took care of Svatek and the platoon sergeant. Wallace had a large chunk of red mud stuck to the back of his neck. I removed it and located a tiny laceration. I cleaned it with Betadine, covered it with a Band-Aid and then issued penicillin all around to fight infection. The slightest break in the skin could turn ugly in the tropics.

"That's number two," Wallace said. Two Purple Hearts in less than three months. He was becoming a walking magnet for enemy detritus. "Thanks, Doc."

He said it quietly and sincerely.

"That'll be twenty dollars for a house call, Sergeant Wallace." Amazing. I could even joke about it.

"I'll buy you a beer when we get back to Dong Tam, Doc. You're people."

"People" was the highest compliment one grunt could pay another.

I stumbled over Fullmer, who was on his hands and knees fumbling with something.

"Fucking slope-headed, squint-eyed, fish-breathed gooks," he raged. "The little bastards fucked up my beans and got mud all in 'em."

I rode back to the command post on ten feet of air.

16

Fullmer shook me awake for radio watch. I couldn't believe I had been actually sleeping after all that had happened during the day.

"All's quiet," Fullmer said. "The gooks have packed up their rice and fish heads and gone home to watch *Gunsmoke* on TV. All you have to do is call Company CP with a sitrep every fifteen minutes."

"Uh, what's a sitrep?" Damn, I was green.

"Situation report. Just key the mike and say, 'Bravo 46, this is Bravo 56. Sitrep negative at this time. Out.' Got it?"

Sounded simple enough. Fullmer wrapped himself in his poncho liner and was soon asleep on the dike at water's edge. The night was purple and quiet. After fifteen minutes I called in my first sitrep: "Bravo 46, this is Bravo 56. Sitrep negative at this time. Out." By the book. I felt a little smug. I was getting this infantry shit down.

My eyes swept the night. Each time a thought of home tried to intrude, I scolded it soundly and dismissed it. Sergeant Richardson had cautioned me to keep my thoughts focused if I wanted to go home in one piece.

"This," he drawled, "is your real world for the next ten months."

A few minutes after I called in my next sitrep, Company buzzed me back: "Bravo 56, this is Bravo 46. Sitrep? Over."

I keyed the mike and repeated my rote message. That still wasn't good enough.

"Bravo 56, sitrep? Over."

Okay. I gave it again.

"Bravo 56, sitrep?"

This time a third voice interceded. "Bravo 46, Bravo 56 must have fallen asleep."

Asleep? My eyes were so wide a platoon with full battle gear could have marched through them. I thought the radio must be malfunctioning.

Sergeant Richardson relieved me. When my second watch came up, the same thing happened whenever I tried to call in a sitrep. At dawn I complained to Fullmer that I couldn't have reported an attack if I had to, because the radio was out. He stroked a radio check out of the PRC-25 like it was a woman. Worked perfectly. I watched him with the thing. Then I saw. *I* was the malfunction. Instead of pressing the mike button when I wanted to transmit, I had been pressing the clip used to snap the handset to your web gear.

Maybe I should have been kept at the 9th Med after all, driving ambulances, hauling garbage, and building morgues. At least Browner knew and accepted his limitations.

Word came that that day's mission was canceled. I celebrated by drinking the rest of the water in my canteen. Bravo caterpillared back to the river and loaded into LCMs. First thing I intended to do when we got back to Dong Tam was find Browner and kick his ass. Then I intended to drink a whole case of cold Coke.

As the boats approached the basin at Dong Tam, I chanced a peek across the gunwales. We steamed right on past Dong Tam and kept going. We left my case of cold Coke in our wake.

"Welcome to the real army, Doc," Sergeant Richardson said. "Change four hundred twelve. Word says we've been rerouted to sweep the area between Dong Tam and My Tho."

Someone began singing a mournful rendition of the Mickey Mouse theme song: "F-u-c-k-e-d a-g-a-i-n, fucked again . . ."

It don't mean nothing.

17

The next sweep consisted mostly of a short walk in single file on a trail through jungle so thick I thought the sun had gotten fed up with the human race and committed suicide. Again, VC sniped at the head of the caterpillar and there were the ubiquitous booby traps, which took their toll in lost toes, blown-off kneecaps, punctured eyes and such, tended to by the platoon medics. My platoon was riding a streak of luck. No new casualties.

A muffled explosion ahead was almost a welcome relief; it meant a few minutes' break by the side of the trail until the medevac chopper arrived. My canteen was empty. I split open a coconut, drank the milk, and ate the meat. So what if it gave me the shits? I could deal with that when it happened.

Bravo—and indeed the entire 4/39th—was taking an inordinate number of casualties while inflicting few on the enemy. I hadn't even *seen* the enemy yet. I knew he was out there only because I heard his mortars and snipers and our dust-offs flying in to take the mangled bodies back to Dr. Holley. It was as if we were fighting ghosts. The men bitched and tried to make up excuses to stay behind when the missions went out, but few were as bold as Browner to disappear from ranks at the last moment.

To say morale was low was like saying the bottom of the South China Sea was low.

"We have to take off our boots to shit, this raggedy outfit is so low," was the way the farm boy, Dale Gass, put it.

"The missions are simple and easy to understand," said RTO Fullmer, who had taken it upon himself to break in the FNG medic and keep him alive. "We go *here* where they tell us to go—and get shot. We go *there* where they tell us—and get shot. We're targets. That's all we are. The VC practice on us."

Henderson snapped up his machine gun and point-swept it at the jungle that closed dark and moist around us. "Just once," he said, "I'd like to get them motherfuckers in my sights. This Texas black boy would raise some mean stuff."

"Why can't we find them and make them fight us?" I asked.

"You don't understand," Fullmer said. "This is a paperwork war for the politicians. On paper we're kicking shit out of the North Vietnamese. Look around you, though. Who's kicking shit out of who? They take us out one by one, and our generals stand around with their thumbs up their butts and doctor up the paperwork to make themselves look glorious. Somebody is making money out of this war. They don't want us to win, and they can't let us lose. They want it to just keep going on and on. At this rate, someday our grandsons will be over here fighting."

"If we live long enough to have grandsons," skinny Arles Brown said, peeping out from underneath the helmet that seemed to settle down on his shoulders.

"One thing I want out of this war," Slim Holleman added. "I want to go home where the real war is startin'. Black people ain't gonna take this shit much longer. There's gonna be a revolution of color all over the racist U.S. of America. I gonna be a general in the revolution."

"Talk that shit, man," Henderson scoffed. "Your buds is right here in First Platoon, no matter what color they is."

Holleman was the only radical black in the platoon; back at Dong Tam, black REMFs pushed their weight around in loud gangs. MPs had to be called a number of times to quell mini-riots. Color didn't matter that much in the boondocks. Holleman talked his racist shit, but I figured he was a guy who'd be with you when you needed him.

Sergeant Richardson came riding his long legs down the spread-out relaxed length of First Platoon. "Saddle up, people. Can the crap and saddle up."

The word had come.

"Tell 'em to call off the war for lack of interest," Sotello suggested.

Boonie rats grumbled and bitched, but we clambered to our feet.

The fucking snipers. They were an annoyance, like the leeches that tried to crawl up your anus, the clouds of mosquitoes each individual carried with him around his face, and the stink of your own foul body. In Germany and in Korea, GIs at least *saw* the bad guys and stood toe-to-toe with them to slug it out. But this was a war of attrition here in this shitbag country that most of us had never even heard of before 1965. VC picked us off one by one. One by one. Day after day.

A feeling started growing in the pit of my stomach. I felt its claws sharpening themselves against the lining. The 4/39th, First Platoon with it, was helpless and demoralized against a superior army of ghosts that could do to us what it wished. Heavy shit would come down sooner or later. I could feel it.

Still, considering my only other option—Colonel Arnold's chickenshit at the 9th Med—First Platoon came out aces up as the better choice. Back at Dong Tam I drank everything I could find that was free of iodine and then paid Doc Holley a visit to explain Browner. The MPs had picked him up and were holding him for shipment back to Vinh Kim with the platoon.

"I'll never let anyone carry my supplies again," I vowed. "I want them with me so I'll know where they are when I need them."

Dr. Byron Holley was a dedicated surgeon who had taken no R&R leave in all the time he'd been in-country. He ventured away from station only to visit one of the fire support or platoon support bases in the boonies. He smiled at me in a different way than before, as if we were colleagues rather than superior and subordinate.

"I've heard good things about you, Dan," he said, using my first name.

I had not yet seen real combat and real wounds. But at least I hadn't reacted like one former medic whose disgrace still stained every other doc in the outfit. The guy had frozen under fire. The platoon sergeant had to literally drag him to the wounded man, stand over him, and force him to render medical aid.

"My two weeks with the 4/39th are almost up," I found myself saying. "Doc Holley, I want to stay with my platoon."

He gave me a long, solemn look. "There are guys who would give up a leg in order to ride out their tours in relative safety here at 9th Med."

I couldn't explain to him that I felt *needed* by the First, that I felt *important.* I'd never have to explain to my son that I had hauled garbage to the dump and treated VD during the war. Besides, I hadn't been tried yet.

I flashed the doctor what I hoped was a reckless grin. "I guess I'm getting used to drinking water filled with chemicals and Kool-Aid so you don't taste the feces the Vietnamese dump into it," I said.

Holley's look said he approved of me. "Doc Evans, you'll stay with your platoon until we find a replacement for you. That may be two days, two weeks, or a month. Here."

He handed me a badge to wear on my uniform—a little silver litter surrounded by a wreath. The Combat Medic Badge was the equivalent of the Combat Infantry Badge awarded to grunts. It signified that I, as a medic, had provided medical aid in support of an infantry unit under fire.

"I-I don't know if I deserve this yet," I stammered.

There would be no question about it in the weeks ahead.

18

First Platoon was tasked with manning Platoon Patrol Base Cougar over the Christmas holidays. Cougar was a mini-frontier fort about two miles from Vinh Kim, in the middle of a rice field off a road the infantry working the area of operations, or AO, called Widow Maker Alley. Hooches lined the road. Naked children with smudges and grins on their round, squint-eyed little faces ran out with their aunts, mothers, and older sisters to souvenir us and beg for chop-chop.

A secondary dirt road junctured off Widow Maker Alley and narrowed between palms and forest before it ended among three hooches surrounded by living bamboo fences. A wizened woman too old to work in the rice fields squatted outside over a cook fire. Red betel juice oozed into the spiderwebbed crevices around her mouth. She watched without change of expression as the GI platoon filed onto a narrow path that snaked through thick forest.

After less than a half mile, the path opened onto a wide, flat rice field. PPB Cougar occupied the center of the field, like a giant crayfish berm. It was no more than a hundred feet across, with three mud- and sandbag-reinforced sides and razor concertina outside. Inside was a command bunker as well as a bunker in each of the three corners. Brackish water from the rice field flooded inside the platoon patrol base. Built-up walkways of sandbags connected the bunkers.

"Honey, we're home!" Mario Sotello sang out.

Fullmer explained to me that Cougar was an OP/LP—observation post, listening post—for the 9th Division base camp at Dong Tam, which lay over the horizon a few miles away. "If a large enemy force were to start marching to attack Dong Tam," he said, "they'd have to hit us first. That would give Dong Tam time to prepare."

Skinny little Arles Brown grinned. "History would record us as a speed bump," he said.

"Expendable," said L. J. Henderson, getting in his opinion. "Eleven bang-bangs, the infantry grunts, have always been expendable, man."

Browner, who had been returned to us under threat of the Long Binh jail, sulked. I refused to accept him back as an assistant, and he refused to carry a rifle. "I'm a conscious objector," he protested.

"Conscientious," I corrected.

The man was worthless, like many of "McNamara's 100,000 boys." By 1968 the draft pool was being pushed to its limits, what with college deferments, the National Guard, and eligible men running off to Canada. Project 100,000 drafted men who would otherwise have been ineligible—guys with low IQs and criminal records, those who were unable to read or write. And people like Browner, who just weren't able to handle the stress of battle. Cannon fodder. They got themselves killed in Vietnam at twice the normal rate and were almost always discipline problems. Some of them went over the edge, bugfuck. Browner was a sterling example of McNamara's 100,000. His favorite expression was "Fuck all y'll lifer motherfuckers."

It did no good to explain to Browner that most of us were draftees too, like him. So mostly we ignored him and let him sulk. Someone voiced the common opinion that maybe some gook sniper would do us the favor of pinging his ferrety ass.

PPB duty was lazy duty. Almost downtime. Combat duty in the field was the only place a soldier could go to get away from the army's pervasive chickenshit rules and regulations. First Platoon followed the example of its higher-higher and played it lax. More lax than most infantry outfits. Leave the chickenshit in Dong Tam. We played cards, passed around crotch novels, wrote letters, and generally fucked off during the day. Every day at noon, half the platoon walked out to the secondary road where it ended at the three hootches to wait for the Meals on Wheels truck from Dong Tam. They ate a hot meal there, then brought back food for the rest of the platoon. The VC could have set their watches by the truck's arrival. In fact, as we were to find out, they *were* setting their watches by it.

We rotated guard duty at night and listened to transistor radios, since we had no light by which to do anything else. We sat in the dark at rifle slits and listened to Nancy Sinatra and Dean Martin and the Beatles over the Armed Forces Radio Network. Someone popped a handheld parachute flare every so often to illuminate the rice field so we could see if Charlie was sneaking up on us.

The annual holiday truce would start at 6:00 P.M. on Christmas Eve. The U.S. forces didn't mind that the VC and NVA used the truce to move men and matériel. It gave the GIs a legal opportunity to stay out of the field.

The annual VC resupply stand-down, Sergeant Richardson called it. "Charlie must not be too low on supplies this year, since the truce is only for twenty-four hours."

First Platoon quit the war a little early. I caught the meal truck back to Dong Tam on December 22 with half the platoon to pick up supplies and goodies for a holiday cele-bration at Cougar. Showers and a movie, cold beer, hot chow, and a little holiday R&R. We rode Meals on Wheels back to Cougar on December 23 to permit the other half of the platoon to ride in for a short stand-down. As part of his punishment, Browner had to stay at the PPB throughout Christmas. Fuck him.

I had a bunch of mail waiting for me at 9th Med. Mom, Dad, and Patty had sent me enough treats to share with the entire platoon. There was nothing from Dianne, however, not even a Christmas card.

Slim Holleman suggested I sneak off with him to get some "gook pussy" and forget about the bitch. Gass the farm boy said, "Hogs, now, you can always count on hogs. Put 'em inside a fence and keep 'em there. Doc, you wanna see the picture of our shoat that was grand champion at the state fair?"

The atmosphere at the three hooches had changed over-night. As the squad, laden with care packages and other supplies, piled out of the Jeep quarter-ton and trailer, I no-ticed that the Vietnamese kids were strikingly truant. They were an enterprising lot, yet there was no "Amelican GI numbah one!" and no "Coke-Cola, GI?" No begging, no boom-boom girls. Even the chickens and pigs seemed to have gone into hiding. The fire tended by the familiar old woman had gone out.

"What the fuck, over?" Henderson said, looking around. He checked the feed tray and ammo feed on his M60.

Fullmer stroked a sitrep out of his radio from the PPB. Snafu came the reply: situation normal, all fucked up. Other-wise, five-by-five: all quiet. I could just hear John Wayne, "Yeah, *too* quiet." Only the hum of insects vibrated the heated air.

Sergeant Miles looked around, then sent Gauerke down the trail ahead with a point element.

"Keep fifteen-meter intervals," he barked as we entered the jungle with our fingers on triggers and our eyes darting like those of kids on Halloween night.

The Jeep's driver and assistant driver didn't like the idea of being left alone for even a few minutes. "Tell the rest of your platoon to haul ass, else we're leaving without them. This shit is too spooky, man."

We felt a little foolish when we broke free of the shadows and the sun still shone brightly on Cougar. Marty Miles or somebody issued a nervous little laugh of relief, and the holiday mood re-descended upon us. All that spooky shit must have been in our imaginations.

19

Creech and Sotello and Forte and the others had their rucks packed at the PPB and were waiting their turn to go to Dong Tam. Since last year's Tet offensive remained too fresh in the military mind to let all the experienced vets take time off during the Christmas truce, Sergeants Richardson and Svatek asked Wallace to stay behind at Cougar. Just in case. The men would enjoy their one-night stand-down, but the leaders stayed behind. Clearly, the unnatural atmosphere along the road bothered the platoon sergeant.

Wallace placed his assistant squad leader, Bauer, in charge of the eleven-man R&R party. The men were on a high and not about to let the possible threat of a few scroungy little VC rob them of a holiday. Rumor had it that Bob Hope might give a holiday show for the 9th Infantry Division at Dong Tam. Bob Hope meant round-eyed girls from back in the world.

"Don't let 'em bunch up," Sergeant Wallace lectured Bauer. "Keep alert. Don't hitch a ride on the chow wagon until you get to Vinh Kim at least. Walk Widow Maker Alley to Vinh Kim. *Walk,* don't ride. Is that clear? I want you to stay on the radio until you reach the FSB."

The grunts left Cougar in holiday spirits. Sergeants Richardson and Wallace watched them file past the walls and wire and enter the jungle. Then the sergeants returned to the command bunker with the RTO, Fullmer, who radio-checked the detail twice before it reached the waiting Jeep and trailer. I hung around at the command post as well, feeling uneasy. I was still green, but I was starting to get a handle up on how things should operate. Instinctively I knew that you asked for trouble when you established a routine in a combat zone, as we had done with the Meals on Wheels truck. I was also beginning to make a vague correlation between the abnormally high number of casualties suffered by the 4/39th and the lackadaisical way the platoon worked. Colonel David Hackworth would point that out with unbridled fury when he took over command of the battalion a few weeks hence.

Overcome with holiday spirit and their eagerness to reach Dong Tam, the eleven grunts of the R&R party ignored the change of atmosphere at the three hooches and piled cheerfully onto the waiting Jeep and its tiny trailer, jammed in so tight they could barely free an arm or a leg. Grunts hated to walk when they could ride. Besides, the sun was shining, and everyone knew the VC fought mostly at night.

Sotello rested his M16 across his compressed knees and opened a can of peaches as the Jeep and trailer, carrying thirteen crowded soldiers, motored to the end of the narrow lane and turned toward Vinh Kim and Dong Tam on Widow Maker Alley's narrow macadam surface. That was when the sky caved in.

An American-made claymore mine triggered the ambush. The world in front of the Jeep blew up suddenly in smoke and fire. A wall of supersonic steel balls blasted into the Jeep and its passengers, shredding metal and flesh.

RPG rockets hissed viciously from the foliage on either side of the road. Contrails of smoke ended in violent explosions that lifted the vehicle and trailer into the air in the center of an expanding fireball and shook mangled soldiers all over the road.

Automatic rifle fire stitched every square foot of macadam as those few GIs still able made a run for the water-filled ditch that bordered the road. Those left behind screamed and wailed and cried out. They crawled and pulled themselves around in the middle of the road like crushed bugs with limbs and pieces of their bodies missing. The hellish sounds of their terror and torment diminished even the staccato grinding of rifle fire.

"Mommy! Mommy!" someone shrieked.

Tall, lanky Teddy Creech used his elbows to claw his way across the road like a mangled worm. His hands were mutilated beyond recognition. His leg had been severed from his hip, except for a tether of bloody skin and flesh. He dragged his leg like an anchor. The jagged end of the detached bone kept digging into the road and staking him in place. He fumbled out his knife and, in the way that a trapped animal will gnaw off its own foot in order to escape, cut himself free of his leg.

Then he passed out near Forte, who was either dead or unconscious.

Bauer regained consciousness and found himself lying in the road with bullets splatting all around him. He jumped up and scrambled for the ditch, shouting, "I'm coming! I'm coming! It's me! Don't shoot!"

He dived into the water directly behind Fitzpatrick, whose eardrums were ruptured and oozing blood. Fitz whirled and rammed the muzzle of his .45 pistol into Bauer's face, a heartbeat away from squeezing the trigger. He pulled the muzzle off at the last instant.

"Damn you, Sugar Bear! Damn you!" he raved. "Don't ever sneak up on me like that."

Fletcher, Stevenson and Abrahamson, the supply sergeant, all made it to the ditch. The water was stagnant and about waist deep, turning red now from the blood of the wounded men tumbling into it. Fletcher's elbow was blown off. Bone gleamed from where the flesh of Abrahamson's right arm was laid wide open from elbow to wrist. Stevenson contorted to bring his belly wound out of the water, trying to get a look at it.

Steve Seid held on to Eugene Harvill to keep Harvill from drowning. One of the lenses in his glasses was shattered and smeared with blood. Mario Sotello splashed over to help. Blood from a nasty cut streamed down his brown cheek. The lid of the open can of peaches he had been eating had slashed his cheek open to the bone.

Seid screamed at the ambushers who had them pinned

down: "Motherfuckers! Motherfuckers! Why are you trying to kill us? We ain't done nothing to you!"

Those who were still able made a fight of it from the water-filled ditch. Sotello and two or three others blasted away with M16s they had either held on to or commandeered from the wounded. Sergeant Fitzpatrick still had his .45 pistol. It bucked in his hand as fast as he could snap the trigger. Although wounded, Ed Hogue popped out 40mm grenades from his M79 launcher. They exploded in the thick foliage with sharp bangs and dislodged showers of leaves and twigs.

Fullmer at the PPB gripped his radio with white-knuckled hands as the blasts of man-made thunder reverberated from the direction of Widow Maker Alley, and the first message blasted through to us: "Help! Help! We've been hit! I don't know how many men are hit. Bodies all over the place!"

Wallace lunged at the radio as if he meant to grab it and shake it. The rest of the platoon burst into the bunker.

"That was *Fitz's* voice!" Wallace exclaimed. "The gooks have hit my squad! They've hit the chow wagon!"

Didn't the fucking gooks know about Christmas, peace on earth and all that?

Pandemonium erupted in the command bunker. Everyone wanted to go on the rescue. In spite of the laxness, the outfit was tight when it came to the platoon. Only Browner remained sulking and afraid in his corner as men snatched up their M16s and fighting harnesses. Sergeant Richardson grabbed them and jerked them back.

"Goddammit, you *all* can't go!"

"It's my squad," Wallace cried. "I'm going out there!"

I had no choice; I was the Doc. "I'm going," I snapped. "I'm the medic."

I had known this day would come sooner or later. I remembered what we had been told in medic school about triage—the sorting of casualties to decide who was treated first. "In a mass casualty situation," the instructor had said, "it is your job to decide who will live and who will die."

Richardson's lean young face beneath the thatch of sun-bleached hair looked suddenly old but nonetheless determined. He was the only enlisted man in the battalion acting as a platoon leader, such was higher-higher's trust in him. His finger began stabbing out those who would go: "Wallace, you. Doc Evans, you. You, Svatek. Miles, you. You and you . . ."

He selected nine of us.

"The rest of you are on full alert," he barked. "Cougar could be next. Man the wall."

Wallace led the mad charge from the compound. We rushed across the rice field and into the jungle while small arms fire from the road rattled like angry lawn mowers. I lugged my M16 in one hand and my aid bag in the other. Medic school warned us that docs in Vietnam had better be as good with a rifle as with an I.V. unit.

We could be running directly into a trap, a secondary ambush. Charlie wasn't stupid; he knew the round-eyes always sent help. But we charged on anyhow, like trying to break a four-minute mile, cross-country runners overdressed in green jungle fatigues, helmets, and combat boots. Shadows along the trail swelled with potential threat as we bounded over obstructions and over log bridges like a troupe of Flying Wallendas.

It was a rule: You never let your buddies down. If your buddies needed help, you *went*.

God sometimes smiled on idiots and fools.

Tall and long-legged, I easily replaced the shorter Wallace on point. My body felt electrified. I felt invincible. Reality had not yet set in.

Momentum carried me ahead of the others and down the road toward the firefight on Widow Maker Alley. I shot out of the narrow road into a scene of unbelievable carnage. The high-pitched crack of a bullet passed near my head—rude awakening. Bullets spanged and geysered in the road around me. Overturned jeep and trailer, smoking, leaking fuel. Mangled bodies. Wallace shouting behind me.

"Doc! Doc! You goddamn idiot! Get your ass down!"

They needed me. My guys needed me. I was the Doc.

I heard a fresh outburst of firing as Wallace's rescue party laid down suppressive fire. I subconsciously adjusted my horn-rimmed glasses, which had come loose during the heart-pumping run. That was my only hesitation. I lurched forward, combat-running across the violent field of death. My reaction surprised even me.

Guardian angel, you'd better be on duty.

20

Maybe it was my guardian angel. Maybe it was blind fool luck. Maybe it was the suppressive fire laid down by Wallace's men. Whichever, I reached the ditch miraculously untouched by the rainfall of enemy fire. Running through the rain drops, as it was called. I dived and rolled, and I was in the water. Came up sputtering.

Sotello's desperate shout: "Doc, you idiot! You'll get yourself killed."

Fetid water waist deep, chest deep in places. Studded with evil-looking black-crusted reeds and grass. Faint pinkish tint to it now, after all the blood. Heads and shoulders and weapons stuck up from the surface as if they'd been planted there. My stomach rolled over like a squirrel in a cage. Stench of cordite, diesel fuel, coppery blood. Fear and death.

Total chaos. Carnage. It awed me. Sickened me. I was the medic trainee who couldn't watch the Vietnam casualty movies at Fort Sam. Giving a hypodermic injection nauseated me. But this was no longer training or a movie. It was real, and I was stuck square in the middle of it.

Injured, wounded and dying men called for me.

"Doc, help me!"

"Medic!"

"Doc! You'd better take a look at Harvill's leg."

"Doc! Doc, Stevens is bad hurt!"

"Doc! Doc?"

Death. I had seen it neatly encased in body bags back at the morgue I helped build for the 9th Med. I had not seen it like this—waiting to strike in a blinding flash of light or the split-second impact of a bullet screaming into flesh. Death both of terror and of morbid fascination. Death as the star of a living nightmare from which none escaped.

They're gonna die, I thought. These men are gonna die if I can't help them.

"Medic!"

I switched into automatic mode, just like that, just like before. A part of me detached itself from the rest. The detached part of me shrugged its shoulders and watched me go to work as in the drills in casualty exercises back at Fort Sam.

Seid was still holding Harvill's head out of the water. I fished up his right leg. Ligaments and tendons dangled ragged from the raw hamburger mass of his thigh. The water was bright red around him. He was losing a lot of blood. Artery severed. I ripped the sleeve off my uniform and used it as a tourniquet. Slapped field dressings onto his other wounds. All I could do right now. I moved on.

A geyser of water exploded a foot ahead of me.

Treatment on the fly. Everyone had some type of wound. I soon ran out of bandages. I ripped up my shirt and cut off my trouser legs to use as tourniquets and bandages. I treated the men in the ditch, then crawled out onto the road to make house calls on those too sick to come to me.

I didn't mark the passing of time, but it suddenly came to me that the wounded men were no longer fighting. They were crawling out of the water like primordial salamanders. The rescue party's withering fire had driven off the ambushers. Only one sniper remained behind to cover his comrades' withdrawal. He plinked at us to make us keep our heads down.

Fuck him.

Other rescue parties were also responding, including additional medics. Jim Whitmore, the medic I had relieved at First Platoon, and a grunt named Ron Miller grabbed their aid bags and jumped aboard one of two Jeeps laden with volunteers the battalion commander and the operations officer assembled. The loaded Jeeps recklessly tore up Widow Maker Alley to get to us.

Lieutenant Bob Knapp, the Bravo Company CO, had been in a meeting with the head province chief when he heard the ambush. He dispatched Second and Third Platoons double-timing it down the road from Vinh Kim. A nervous VC security element blew a sixty-pound Chicom claymore at the leading platoon, but it blew too soon to cause damage. The platoons rushed right through the smoke and kept coming.

I overheard Sergeant Wallace shouting, "Pinpoint that fucking sniper. Waste his ass!"

I looked up and saw Whitmore and Miller ignoring the sniper, as I was. I had already lost my helmet and rifle and used up most of my uniform. Whitmore dropped down next to Teddy Creech and flung open his medical aid bag. "A dust-off is on the way," he shouted to me.

Creech's left leg, still wearing its combat boot, lay discarded in the road next to the mauled Jeep. His other leg was twisted like that of a cloth puppet without joints. Blood and gray ooze gushed from his many wounds.

Whitmore started to move away. "This one's dead," he announced.

Creech's eyes slowly opened in the bloody mask that was his face. "I ain't dead yet," he croaked. "Give me a shot of morphine."

The bullet hole in Richard Forte's abdomen had sealed itself. His bloated belly told me all the bleeding was internal. There was little I could do for him. His face was the color of old ivory.

"It's all right. I'm okay, Doc," he groaned. "Doc, the others . . . they need you. Go help my buddies, Doc."

Where did the army get such men—thinking of others while they themselves were dying?

When the medevac chopper arrived, it skimmed in low over the trees, dragged its tail, and sat down on the narrow road in an explosion of dust and sniper fire. Dust-off medics leaped out to assist with the evacuation while the crew chief knelt on the roadway with an M16 across his knees.

"Get 'em aboard! Goddammit, load 'em!" the pilot roared above the whumping of the blades and the engine that he kept revved at full rpm, ready to bolt. An AK-47 round bored a hole through the chopper's thin skin.

"We're lifting off. We're going!" the pilot threatened.

We medics were feeding torn bodies into the chopper's belly as fast as we could. The bird's floor was slippery with blood. The chopper kicked in even more rpm. Its skids bounced lightly on the road, kissing it, like a racehorse trying

to bolt from the starting gate. The pilot was going frantic
on us.

"Fuck it! Fuck it! We're outta here!" he bellowed.

"All the wounded aren't aboard," Lieutenant Knapp
shouted at the chopper pilot.

"Get out of the way. We're lifting off."

Knapp shouted something to a sergeant named Sinclair.
Sinclair leaped onto the side of the helicopter like a fly and
thrust the muzzle of his M16 through the open side window
and hard against the pilot's flight helmet. Whatever he said
to him had the desired effect. The bird remained nested on
the road until it was full of mutilated young Americans.
Sotello and Seid and one or two of the less seriously injured
men were loaded onto the battalion commander's Jeep for
transport to Dong Tam. Third Surgical Hospital was going
to be busy.

Afterward, stunned and emotionally spent, I stood wearily
in the middle of the road and stared without seeing the
splotches and puddles of thick blood left around the smoldering Jeep. Patrols out sweeping the area had driven off
the sniper. I was glad someone had thought to toss Creech's
severed leg aboard the chopper. I don't think I could have
checked my gorge otherwise.

"What happened to your clothes, soldier?" one of the
battalion leaders demanded.

I wore only my boots and the remains of my jungle trousers. I had ripped off the legs for bandages and tourniquets.

"Where's your helmet and weapon, GI?"

I was too spent to answer. I stared at the blood on my
hands. Red gloves. I fixated on them. I guessed I was qualified now to wear my Combat Medic Badge. A sinking hard-
knot feeling formed in the pit of my stomach. This is only
the beginning, the feeling seemed to gloat. You ain't seen
it all yet.

As if from a distance at the end of a pipe, I overheard
someone explaining to the officer that I was the medic and
I had used my clothing in treating WIAs.

Someone nudged me. A gentle voice. "Doc? Doc, here.
You can have my shirt."

21

Somehow, something fundamental changed in me after Widow Maker Alley. I knew without knowing exactly how I knew that I would never be the same again. In the space of one hour I had aged twenty years on the inside. I had become a veteran, like Sergeants Wallace and Svatek. Like L. J. Henderson and Sergeant Richardson and the others. I had come to war to prove myself. Now I wasn't exactly sure what it was I proved.

It don't mean nothing.

The grunts who had come to the rescue at Widow Maker Alley were raging for enemy blood in retaliation for the ambush. They raided every hooch in the vicinity, bursting in, fingers on hair triggers, while old men and women and children cowered in the corners. They ripped apart sleeping mats and dumped baskets of rice into the dirt, searching for weapons or signs of VC presence. It took officers yelling and shouting threats to keep GIs from torching every little grass shack they came across. Any resistance at all, however slight, would have resulted in a massacre of every Vietnamese within reach.

"They *all* knew an ambush was coming down," soldiers raved. "Not one of these slant-eyed little cockroaches warned us. Kill 'em all and let God sort 'em out."

One of the VC who had ambushed our squad surrendered to the ARVN under the Chieu hoi program. *Chieu hoi* means "to come over." He brought with him a Chicom—Chinese Communist—mine, three U.S. claymores, and two Chicom grenades. He received payment for the weapons and immunity from prosecution. He would end up a Kit Carson or Tiger Scout for the United States. He revealed that the ambushers were VC from the hamlet of Long Hung. The information used in staging the ambush had come from the girls who laughed and sold Cokes and souvenirs to us at PPB Cougar. MI—Military Intelligence—arrested some of them. I would never again regard the Cokes and boom-boom girls with the same benevolence as before.

Surviving members of First Platoon, now down to an all-time low of fifteen men, counting Browner, reacted each in his own way to the tragedy. It was a silent and morose band of boonie rats who filed back behind the walls at Cougar. Everyone except the sentries gathered around Fullmer while he stroked bad news out of the PRC-25 for the rest of the day. He turned up the volume so everyone could hear. I collapsed on an ammo crate with my head and spirits down.

Sergeant Wallace coiled up around his anger like a dark, wiry spring. "I should have been with them," he agonized. "It's my fault. If I had been there, I wouldn't have let them ride in the Jeep."

John Svatek looked as if something had taken a bite out of him.

"The *bastards,*" he said, pounding one fist into the palm of his other hand.

Whitmore had warned me not to get personally involved with the men when I relieved him at First Platoon. I'd ignored him, as he must have known I would. I was starting to pay the fiddler now. Making friends on the line carried a high price.

I always thought door-to-door salesmen must have had it rough during the Vietnam War. The military sent representatives to the family's house to make the notification whenever a GI was killed. My mother refused to answer the doorbell or a knock on the door as long as I was in Vietnam. I wished I had a door now that I could refuse to answer. I wished I had a door I could slam in the face of reality.

Instead, I huddled with the others around the radio in a sandbagged bunker deep in the bloody heart of the Mekong Delta and waited for news. From time to time one of the men patted me on the back or shoulder. "Doc? Doc?"

What else could be said? I had done the best I could to save them. Hadn't I?

Anger turned to sadness, sadness to a deep melancholy as word of the condition of the wounded platoon members gradually trickled into Cougar. My first Christmas away from home was going to be a long Christmas.

We learned about Richard Forte first: he was dead from the tiny bullet hole in his abdomen by the time the dust-off unloaded him at 3rd Surg in Dong Tam—dead from a tiny hole, just like Whitmore's friend. Forte had been popular in the platoon. His dying affected everyone. Although Jim Whitmore helped treat the WIAs on the road, he had somehow not realized Forte was among them. Forte and he were close friends. Learning of Forte's death was the only time Whitmore ever cried in Vietnam.

Svatek and Forte had feasted together on pepperoni and cheese that Forte's mother sent in a Care package for Christmas. James Fabrizio and Forte had arrived in-country about the same time. Fabrizio was going to be best man at Forte's wedding after the war. Sergeant Richardson radioed Battalion's commander in Dong Tam and requested that a letter he had seen Forte write to his fiancée be removed from the dead soldier's shirt pocket and mailed. I wondered if Richard's body lay bagged in the morgue I had helped to build.

Someone walked by Browner, who huddled apart from the others, his eyes round and white and frightened. "Why couldn't it have been your sorry ass?" the soldier complained.

Sergeant Wallace rose so slowly with the weight of all the guilt he carried that he staggered as he escaped out the bunker door. Sergeant Richardson went to him where he sat on a pile of sandbags gazing out across the rice field. They sat together, shoulder to shoulder, without speaking as the sun turned red and the red deepened into the purple of another Vietcong night. Then they silently returned to the bunker ready to face the news about the other casualties.

The man riding shotgun, Gene Abrahamson, lost an arm. Eugene Harvill and Teddy Creech each gave up a leg. Surgeons stitched 500 sutures into Creech and removed three inches of the bone in his remaining leg. Going home, Creech was three inches shorter than the six-four he'd been when he arrived in Vietnam.

Albert Fletcher was blind; doctors didn't know if he would ever see again. Hogue and Sugar Bear Bauer would be away from the platoon for about a month recuperating. Sotello and Seid would be back on duty within a week.

Although I mourned the loss of men who were becoming my friends, in that secret place in my heart that a man never shares with others I was thankful that if someone had to get it, that that someone was not me.

Third Platoon relieved First at Cougar on Christmas Day. The battalion commander must have figured we needed the stand-down. On Christmas Eve the platoon patrol base had been the loneliest place in the universe. The next day we combat-marched down the road to Vinh Kim. We had learned a tough lesson about riding. Blood still stained the road at the ambush site. The Jeep and trailer were gone. We marched past the blood and, one by one, stared at it, then looked quickly away.

We cleaned up at Fire Support Base Moore and ate a hot holiday meal. A Catholic chaplain celebrated Mass. First Platoon attended to a man. Only one man had gone to confession.

"Why is it that everyone came to Mass, but there was only one for confession?" the chaplain asked Sergeant Wallace.

"He's the only Catholic in the platoon," Wallace explained, "but you offered the only service. We figured we can use all the help we can get from God."

22

LBJ and the other politicians sent Americans to Vietnam to win the hearts and minds of the people, pacify the villagers, defend the oppressed, rehabilitate the deluded, bolster the economy, neutralize communism, and only then, after all that, run up a good body count. All the VC had to do, on the other hand, was to shoot, maim, and kill round-eyes. Everything considered, the enemy had the easier job of it.

A platoon from Alpha Company out on a security patrol encountered an armed squad of VC twenty-one minutes before the Christmas truce ended at 1800 hours. The American brass went ape-shit and threatened to court-martial the platoon leader because he fired first, an instant before the VC opened up. I felt certain the VC platoon leader faced no similar action; he would probably have been court-martialed if he *hadn't* tried to open fire first.

Rain fell for three days following First Platoon's return to Cougar, further dampening our spirits.

"It's raining," an acute weather observer said.

"No shit, Dick Tracy."

"It's cold," the observer added.

"Should we put on our ponchos?"

"Hell, even if we wear them, we'll still get wet."

The monsoons brought great billowing clouds rushing angrily in from the South China Sea. Dark grayness covered the land. A violent two-hour torrential downpour, an hour of sun and steam, and then a violent three-hour downpour. It fell in driving sheets that pounded the jungles and rice fields until every stream, every canal, every river, swelled and overflowed. Men and machines bogged down. In some areas of the Mekong, only boats carried on operations.

Rain turned Cougar and our morale into a bog. I treated the men for foot problems, issued tins of powder for trench foot, and placed Ellis on a regimen for a bad cough and sinus problems. Routine dragged. Fullmer's radio was our communications lifeline. We grouped around it like a bunch of bored housewives living our lives through neighborhood gossip and *As the Stomach Turns* on TV. Fullmer was always eavesdropping on the battalion net for us.

The enemy was starting to put the 4/39th's feet to the fire. A main force VC brigade had moved into AO Kudzu. Alpha Company located a VC tunnel complex. Delta Company nabbed a female at the Dong Tam garbage dump salvaging discarded U.S. Army field manuals on booby traps and small unit combat tactics. A scout dog attached to Charlie Company tripped a booby trap and was killed; his handler was wounded. Patrol boats crossing the Kinh Xang Canal took thirty rounds of AK fire. An ARVN company found two graves containing the remains of American GI MIAs.

DOC: PLATOON MEDIC

Captain John Seeker came in as Bravo Company commander. About thirty-five years old, he had previously belonged to the Ohio National Guard. One of his first actions was to send out a cordon-and-search mission to Long Hung to flush out the VC who had staged the ambush at Widow Maker Alley. Third Platoon, finding nothing in the village, swept on through and pushed hard against a platoon of hard-core North Vietnamese Army regulars clad in khakis and pith helmets. The platoon killed one NVA soldier and wounded another before the enemy element escaped across a river and into a wood line. That must have caused a stir back at battalion headquarters.

The 4/39th was about to meet some real resistance instead of the nickel-and-dime snipers and booby traps that had been taking such a toll from the Americans during the past weeks.

"I got this bad, *bad* feelin' down in my guts," L. J. Henderson said.

Seeker, our new CO, lasted exactly one week before he sprained his ankle on a day operation. He hobbled into a sampan to take him to a road bridge spanning the Kinh Xang canal. Charlie ambushed the sampan. Seeker's RTO, Sergeant Robert Sinclair, and a military intelligence specialist named Sullivan were killed. Seeker was wounded in the gut and evacuated. Lieutenant Neumann of Third Platoon advanced to acting CO of Bravo Company.

"Think this CO will last longer than a week and set a new Bravo record?" skinny little Arles Brown asked in his squeaky West Virginia voice.

83

23

Sergeant Richardson moved the platoon stealthily through the purple Vietnam dusk toward another of the innumerable night ambushes. He called a halt, and word filtered back from man to man that the mission was canceled; we were to return to Vinh Kim.

"Bad news, man," Henderson grumbled. "They gonna bring us in an' dump some real heavy shit on us."

To our surprise, Division loaded the decimated platoon into a deuce and transported us to Dong Tam to attend the Bob Hope show while the rest of the 4/39th set up base security. Since the show was going to be televised in the States, it wouldn't do for the folks back home to see boonie rats looking as if they'd been in combat. First Platoon had reserved seats about five rows back from the stage, right in TV camera view. Division issued us all clean new uniforms to replace our rags and ordered us to shave and get our hair cut.

"I shave my balls, they want it!" Henderson exclaimed, shoving out his heavy lower jaw. "One day away from the dinks is one more day this nigger gets to keep all his arms an' legs. Hear what I'm sayin'?"

When the show started, every available aircraft flew the line to protect Bob Hope, Ann-Margret, the Gold Diggers, and the rest of the cast. In the background, Cobra helicopters worked over distant terrain with their rockets and miniguns. The 4/47th Infantry inserted onto an island in the My Tho River to prevent enemy water infiltration while the 4/39th dispersed along a circular perimeter 6,000 meters out.

There were two empty rows in front of us, the best seats in the audience. Walking wounded filed in to take these seats. Three or four mummies had their heads wrapped in bandages. One hobbled in on crutches with a cast on his leg. Another rode in on a wheelchair. Others had casts on their arms or bandages on various parts of their anatomies. They looked pitiful yet heroic, as if they had survived one hell of a battle. Sympathetic TV cameras played back and forth across them.

I did a double take when I recognized Dave Krogan and the other REMF medics of the 9th Med.

"What in hell happened to you guys?" I cried.

Krogan laughed. He had one arm in a sling.

"Bob Hope wanted some wounded soldiers in the audience for the people back home to see," he explained. "The ass-kissing generals ain't going to disappoint Bob Hope, but the *real* wounded at the 3rd Surg Hospital were too sick to come and the 9th Med didn't have any patients. The only thing left to do was make up some of us to look like wounded. Don't we look great? We ride ambulances to the show and get front row seats. That makes everybody happy."

24

Word filtered down that the enemy wanted to declare a three-day truce over New Year's, but the American brass remembered the last truce. Infantry radios all over Vietnam warned the Green Machine: "No—repeat, *No*—New Year's truce has been declared. Operations by units subordinate to this headquarters will continue as scheduled."

Dong Tam celebrated New Year's Eve by firing green, red, and white flares and red machine-gun tracers across the night sky. Henderson, Fullmer, and I sat on sandbags at Cougar to watch the display.

Henderson grinned wryly and took out a cigar. "Let's celebrate," he suggested, firing up the tobacco.

Fullmer looked at the cigar. "Happy New Year, Doc." He sighed wearily and ambled toward the command bunker.

I thought of my folks and of Dianne. I had finally received a Christmas card from her; it was already Christmas Eve in Vietnam when it was postmarked.

"Happy New Year, L.J.," I said to Henderson. I sighed also and turned toward the bunker.

Henderson nodded.

The next day brought more radio drama. All the RTOs were chatting up the air about the miraculous escape of Major Nick Rowe, whom the North Vietnamese had captured and held for five years. Stories of how he had survived the POW camps and then escaped lifted spirits all over Vietnam. Even the First Platoon resisted mutiny when word sent us out on ambush patrols. But something seemed to have died in Sergeant Richardson with Forte's death and the maiming of the others. The fire had gone out of him, at least temporarily.

"I want to get through this without sending another man home in a body bag," he had said after a booby trap wounded Wallace during a short security patrol.

I had heard the sharp crack of the explosion. Then I held my breath and crowded around the radio with the others, until Wallace came up on the air.

"Bravo 52 Actual is hit in the back of the arm and shoulder," he radioed. "Nothing serious. Will return to Cougar."

"If we lose any more guys," Svatek declared without humor, "there won't be enough of us left to have a baseball team."

A couple of Band-Aid patches took care of Wallace. One man had been wounded for each of the nineteen days I had been with the platoon, and Forte had been killed. I still preferred field duty over the chickenshit of Colonel Arnold's 9th Med.

The platoon stayed clear of Widow Maker Alley and its bitter memories whenever we went out at night. We went out only on direct orders, then strived to avoid contact. One night the men declared a bottle of Johnnie Walker Red as a full and respected member of the platoon and stuffed it into a ruck before we departed the PPB.

We set up an ambush near the graveyard where Wallace's

squad had killed the civilian two weeks earlier, at a hooch whose papa-san and mama-san proved to be GI-friendly. After laying out claymores and trip flares, we broke out Sergeant Johnnie Walker and twisted off his headgear. Mama-san boiled rice and *nuoc mam* sauce for everyone. *Nuoc mam* stank of fish heads, eyes, and entrails, but after a visit or two to Johnnie Walker nobody cared.

Party time. FTA. Fuck the army. Fuck the war.

Farm boy Gass was reaching that mellow stage when he was about to take out the photos of his pigs to show papa-san when Sergeant Richardson paused and suddenly held up a hand for silence. Laughter and loud merry voices drifted in on the air, their volume rising and falling with the intermittent breezes. Noise traveled great distances at night.

"Numbah ten VC have potty same-same us," explained the Vietnamese Tiger Scout assigned to us for the mission. A few weeks earlier, some GI had mistaken him for a VC in the dark and grazed him across the chest with a bullet.

"Potty?" Richardson asked.

"Potty. *Potty.*"

"Party?"

"Potty, all same-same. Beaucoup VC have big potty same-same us. We leave them 'lone, them leave us 'lone. No war. Everybody potty, potty, potty."

Henderson grinned around his cigar and mimicked the scout. "Everybody potty hotty," he said and burst out laughing.

The VC were a mile or so away. They partied hardy, we partied hardy. First Platoon declared its own truce for the night.

25

Fortunate was the line unit that managed to keep together a hard core of combat vets for more than three or four months. The insanity of the 365-day DEROS rule made the constant turnover of experienced troops a certainty. FNGs arrived every month while the vets shipped out—sometimes horizontally. Life at the platoon level consisted of an ever-diminishing cadre who knew each other well, who had a history together, who trusted each other in a firefight, and a widening circle of newbies who were not quite trusted by the cadre. A platoon maybe had one or two guys who stuck together for an entire tour.

Charlie, on the other hand, was in for the duration. Some of the dinks had been fighting for Uncle Ho for fifteen years.

After three weeks in the platoon, I was no longer the cherry, the FNG. Fresh replacements from the States straggled in one or two at a time to replace the casualties. They arrived wide-eyed, eager to please, and scared shitless. I took Whitmore's warning more seriously after the ambush and tried to keep an emotional distance. A doc couldn't afford to get too close to his prospective patients. Made it too hard on him to send them home in body bags.

Ron Miller from Saint Louis took Forte's place, the same Ron Miller who had accompanied Doc Whitmore to the ambush in which Forte was killed. He had been a crop duster before being drafted. A deuce drove him and an ROTC lieutenant, Bob Celphane, out to the three hooches, where some of the guys met them and brought them to Cougar. A real officer for a platoon leader, the first since the last one got wounded and shipped out. Sergeant Richardson dropped back into his more comfortable position as platoon sergeant.

Lieutenant Celphane's first announcement was that he hated the fucking army just like everybody else, but the outfit had to be strak, had to be sharp, when it went out on a mission. He wouldn't last long; officers never did. It was good for their careers to get a little trigger time, maybe generate a medal or two, cop some war stories from the enlisted men, and then get back to the States as quickly as they could to parlay the war into bars and stars. Like the grunts said, officers got the medals, enlisted cleaned the latrines. GIs didn't respect the brass; they respected the other guys on the line. It took a lot for an officer to earn respect.

What with enemy activity picking up in the area of operations, Division expected the 4/39th to carry a heavier war load. Get out there and get with 'em instead of hiding behind walls and wire. More patrols, more ambushes, more body counts. First Platoon found itself evicted from PPB Cougar to roam the AO like a band of wandering Gypsies. The platoon paused in the rice field to glance back one last time at the crayfish nest.

"It ain't much," the farm boy commented, "but it was home."

Kicked out for failure to pay rent or something.

"All of y'all know what it feels like now to be a nigger an' a bastard stepchild," L. J. Henderson cracked. Unlike some of the REMF homeboys, Henderson had none of the militancy that separated black from white at the base camps. At least while on the line, there was no color except green, and race could be joked about.

The platoon slogged here and slogged there in pursuit of the elusive Mr. Charles. Browner, as expected, got himself kicked back to Dong Tam while the First bounced all over the AO. The company commander sometimes split the under-strength platoon into two squads. Half of us ran night ambushes, largely dry holes, out of an abandoned two-room schoolhouse on Ambush Alley while the other half pulled bridge security near the front gate at Dong Tam. We slept wherever we happened to be, simply unrolling our ponchos and bedding down like wild animals in the forest, on the floor of the schoolhouse, inside an abandoned hooch, wherever.

The platoon might have been a Gypsy band, but it was *my* Gypsy band, *my* tribe. Each day I expected to receive the word: Report back to 9th Med. Your medical services are urgently needed to make garbage runs, plant palms for the inspection of REMF generals, and build another morgue.

26

Browner, back at Dong Tam, finally went totally bugfuck. The platoon heard about it from some other battalion GIs who had been there when it happened. Word said the platoon's full-time shitbird and part-time conscientious objector finally went for a body count on his own—against American soldiers.

While Browner conscientiously plotted to avoid all Vietnamese with guns, he just as conscientiously contrived to associate with the Vietnamese boom-boom girls outside the gate at Dong Tam. Some other GIs came across him out by the bridge beating the hell out of his whore. When they tried to break it up to keep him from doing to her what he was afraid to do to the VC, he grabbed an M16 and threatened to kill the GIs. He looked wild-eyed and doped up. Desperate sweat sheened his dark ferret's face as he broke into a wild, shambling run toward the wooden transient barracks where he was billeted. "I will kill any motherfucker comes after me," he shouted back over his shoulder.

The deranged GI exploded onto the second floor with a mad look in his eyes, a loaded M16 in his hand, and fierce spittle spewing from his lips.

"Motherfucker lifers!" he roared and sprayed bullets the length of the bay. They punched holes through the thin walls, splintered the floor, and sparked off metal lockers.

Guys lounging around playing cards, reading or bullshitting set a new record for evacuating the building. Even Charlie's mortars couldn't have cleared the building faster. GIs outside took cover behind vehicles, buildings, and whatever else they could find. Someone sprinted to get the MPs.

Svatek, at Division on platoon business, came running. Technically, he was still Browner's squad leader. Dead silence had settled over the barracks. Someone told the young sergeant that Browner was upstairs with an M16: "He is *crazy.*"

Something had to be done. The MPs would kill the poor spaced-out bastard. Svatek took a deep breath.

"You ain't going in there, man?"

Somebody had to. Sergeant Svatek opened the door and started up the stairway.

"Browner, it's me. Svatek. We have to talk."

"Don't you show your white ass on this floor, dude. I'll blast you, Svatek. I swear."

"You know you don't want to do that, man. I'm unarmed. I'm not going to try anything. Look."

Two or three other sergeants followed Svatek up the stairs at a safe distance. Svatek slowly eased upward. He continued talking in a soothing voice. The first thing he saw as his eyes rose above the level of the upper floor was Browner standing spread-legged in the middle of the vacated bay, breathing heavily as though from a run, gripping the M16 hard with both hands. The rifle's muzzle covered Svatek. Browner had his finger wrapped around the trigger. Svatek felt more vulnerable to death at that moment than he ever had in combat.

"Don't try nothin', Svatek, or you goin' home in a body bag, motherfucker. I ain't goin' back out in the field no more."

Svatek displayed his empty palms. "I'm not armed, Browner. This is not going to get us anywhere. Let me have the rifle. Then we can talk about it."

His eyes casually explored the dormitory. There didn't seem to be any casualties lying around. So far, so good. Svatek continued his slow, deliberate advance, talking in a calming voice that he hoped was getting through to the man's befogged brain.

"Stay back, motherfucker. *Stay back.*"

"Browner, I'm not your enemy. You don't want to shoot me."

"I will. I will."

Tension like melted butter made the air in the bay oily and hard to breath. Svatek counted on Browner's cowardly nature. Sure, he'd beat up a 90-pound Vietnamese whore, but shoot a man facing him? Svatek bet his life Browner didn't have the guts for it. He hid his contempt as he slowly approached, talking calmly, smoothly, in a tranquilizing monologue. His eyes held Browner's prisoner.

He continued like that, step by step, while the other sergeants watched helplessly from the stairwell. Finally, the muzzle of Browner's M16 was pressed against his chest. Browner looked stunned, confused. Svatek's hand struck like a deadly green tree viper and snatched the weapon from Browner's hands.

Browner stood frozen for a second. Then a keening wail of fury and frustration tore from his throat.

It took a half-dozen soldiers to subdue him and drag him screaming and fighting downstairs. Svatek ordered him locked inside a metal Conex container, like a huge metal shipping crate, until the proper papers could be obtained. Screams from this prime example of McNamara's 100,000 held the post gripped in its intensity for over an hour while Browner clawed and banged and bounced around inside the Conex.

No one from First Platoon ever heard from Browner again. Another casualty for the 4/39th.

27

The village outside the 9th Division base camp extended along the road and past the narrow rickety bridge that spanned the muddy canal. Two brick houses, rare in Vietnam, one at either end of the bridge, were conspicuous signs that their owners were merchants or tradesmen. The houses had other rare features: electricity, radios, TVs, chairs, tables, and beds instead of mats thrown on a dirty floor. During the time First Platoon had been rotating between security at the bridge and night patrols from either the bridge or the abandoned schoolhouse, I gradually made friends with the aging papa-san and mama-san who lived in one of the houses. They often invited me in to watch TV or simply to relax away from the other GIs. I began looking forward to the visits.

I often sat at their table in the two-room house and wrote letters. Long letters home to Mom and Dad and my kid sister helped keep me sane. I hunched over the table and adjusted my glasses. Strange how in such a short time I had grown unaccustomed to electric light. In the same room, my host and hostess watched my favorite TV program, *Mission Impossible,* dubbed in Vietnamese, on their portable black-and-white TV set. They called me *bac-si*—doctor.

Dear Dad, Mom, Pat,   11 Jan. '69
   In my letter yesterday, I said I would probably write today. I have two hours free before this night's patrol. Last night I went on an ambush patrol with the second squad. We had to go a klick. That's army talk for five-eights of a mile or 1,000 meters, which isn't far. Except when you walk in water up to your knees and cross rivers up to your

waist. We left at 1745 hours (that's army talk for a quarter to six). We were going along pretty good, everyone had a two-day rest. At 6:45 P.M. we heard an M79 going off to our right.

We knew that the other squad was in the woods to our right, so Sgt. Wallace called the other group to find out what was happening. The new lieutenant (Lt. Celphane) was with the other squad. They replied that they were reconning by fire, firing their M79 on the path in front of them, trying to blow up any booby traps. Anyway, we started walking again. Just then a command-detonated mine exploded. I saw the mine blow. The point man was blown backwards along with the second man. I figured they were dead. I started to run to their location but stopped. I don't know why, but I did. I yelled to ask the point element if they were okay. They answered "Affirmative." That's army talk for okay. The third and fourth men were okay. I was the fifth man.

The five of us got to the other side of the dike in case more Vietcong were around. I moved to my next position in case a VC was hightailing it out of the area. (I consider myself an infantryman until someone needs a medic.) The sixth man yelled that he was hit. I went to him, and sure enough he was wounded. He had a piece of shrapnel in his arm and was bleeding a little. The seventh man had a piece of shrapnel in his arm too. It was too late to call in a dust-off helicopter. No one was badly wounded. I decided to have the men stay with the platoon and go into Dong Tam in the morning.

Then 51 Bravo (first squad leader) called us to say the new lieutenant got hit in the hand by a secondary explosion. He was not that bad and would stay out in the field for the night. He would go to Dong Tam in the morning with the wounded from our squad.

Keep reading as it gets better as the night goes on. We had to change the ambush patrol because the booby trap went off near the prearranged AP.

(That's army talk for an ambush position). We received permission to go to another spot. Our new location was next to a hooch. Everyone was talking about what happened, especially the first two men that got blown off their feet and backwards.

Just then an artillery round went over our heads and hit just a short distance from us. Sgt. Wallace called Dong Tam to find out what was happening. He was told that an ARVN artillery unit was firing some rounds. Wallace told the person on the other end of the radio to have the ARVN unit add five zero zero zero. I started laughing because this is a very long distance. I laughed all the way to the bunker in the hooch. The mama-san and papa-san were in the bunker. I came in so fast that they were laughing. The artillery rounds stopped.

I came out of the bunker and saw a red light to my NNE, about one or two rice paddies over. I told Sgt. Surletta. When he looked, he didn't see anything. Sgt. Wallace said he saw it also. Wallace called higher-higher for permission to fire the M79 grenade launchers at it. Several rounds were fired. Wallace said he was going out to investigate and needed a volunteer to go with him. No one wanted to go. I volunteered.

The two of us went out looking for the light source. We had only gone a short distance when an artillery unit fired illumination rounds into the sky above us. We had to lie flat on the ground until the flare went out. Flares have parachutes to keep them up in the air for five minutes. The enemy could see us. The night looked like day. The only thing we could do was make like we were a part of the scenery. The wind blew the flares right over our heads. One flare was coming down toward us. Luckily it burned out before it hit the ground.

When the flares stopped, we went back to the squad. The night cooled off. Sleeping was comfortable. I went to sleep at 9:00 P.M. I started my first guard duty at 11:00. At 11:30, Dong Tam got mortared. I watched Dong Tam get hit for twenty minutes. The base fired red flares to signal a mortar attack. I went to bed at midnight. My next guard duty was at 4:00 A.M. Nothing happened on this shift except some friendly artillery was blowing up a wood line about a mile away from us.

At 7:00 A.M. everyone got up, ate C-rations, and returned to base. The American Red Cross girls came by and gave us games and some articles to read. It's four o'clock and I've got to get ready to go on another AP tonight.

Love,
Danny

One thing I omitted from the letter—that I had been wounded. It wasn't much of a wound, and I didn't want the folks to worry. Mom still wouldn't answer the doorbell. I'd sustained a scratch on the arm when the mine exploded. I didn't even know I had it until after I treated the other GIs. Doc Holley was going to put me in for a Purple Heart. I thought of Forte, who had died, and of Teddy Creech and Eugene Harvill, who'd lost legs.

"I don't deserve a medal," I said, meaning it. "It's only a scratch."

"You didn't think you deserved the Combat Medic Badge, either. You did. The only requirement for a Purple Heart is that you bleed from a combat wound."

I'd tell the folks about my Purple Heart later. I finished the letter and folded it into the breast pocket of my jungles for later mailing. Mama-san looked over at me and smiled. She reminded me of my kindergarten teacher.

Now, Dianne. I felt my face stiffen. Her last letter to me, the first since her late-arriving Christmas card, was postmarked January 5. It wasn't exactly a Dear John letter, but it was the next thing to one. She said our relationship was strained. Hell, I'd been in Vietnam for three months, what did she expect? Perhaps, she suggested, we had married in haste. Why did I have this gut-wrenching feeling that she had finally accepted a date with another man?

"I'll wait for you," she had said.

Right. *Xin loi*—sorry about that.

I didn't know what to write to my own wife. I was sitting

there debating it, staring at a blank sheet of paper, when a lovely Vietnamese girl I had never seen before entered the house as though she belonged there. She was about twenty, with black hair that flowed down the middle of her back. She wore a golden *ao dai* and carried a plump baby on her hip.

She made her way directly to me. Without a word, not even so much as a smile, she laid the baby in my lap and started back out the door.

"Wait. Where are you going? What is this?"

She smiled then, but kept going. Mama-san paid no attention. As part of the family, I should be willing to baby-sit if the need arose. I shrugged. What the hell. The kid *was* cute—all round-bottomed and round-faced with black eyes shining through slitted lids and hair as thick and dark as a Vietnam night.

The girl returned shortly with explanations in passable English. She carried a small bag filled with medical supplies.

"Li is my little sister," she said. "I am a nurse."

I shared my supplies with her and talked shop until I grew tired. I stretched out on a plaited rug to catch a quick nap before the night's patrol. To my surprise, the girl and the baby lay down next to me. We soon slept while papa-san and mama-san watched *Bonanza* on TV.

The girl came looking for me the next day. She shyly handed me a Saint Christopher medal on a chain.

"Bac-si," she said, "put it around your neck. You protected now. VC no kill you now."

I wondered what my guardian angel thought about that.

28

Word came. First Platoon was being shipped out of the Dong Tam AO to Ben Tranh for helicopter eagle-flight operations—tagging the enemy from the air in order to fix 'em and fuck 'em over.

"Some deep *kimshi* be comin' down," L. J. Henderson predicted. "Hear what I'm sayin', troops?"

I wouldn't be going along. I had resisted returning to the 9th Med and pleaded with Doc Holley as long as I could. "I *belong* to the First Platoon," I argued. "Doc, do something. Get me permanently assigned."

"You're assigned to Division, Dan, on loan to us," Holley explained. "I'm just a battalion surgeon. I'll do what I can."

Even I admitted I had come a long way in a short time, from a queasy FNG medic to a seasoned doc in about six weeks. Bleeding, wounded men still saddened and horrified me, but I now felt confident that I could handle anything that came along.

Finally, after I ignored a number of radio messages to report back to Dong Tam, the 9th sent out a lieutenant to escort me personally back from Vinh Kim. He said it was the first time he had ever had to force a man off the line. My replacement, a true conscientious objector, was waiting.

"I have explicit orders to take you back to base camp if you're not out on a mission," the lieutenant said.

First Platoon was saddling up. I grabbed my ruck, aid bag, and M16. "You didn't see me, L.T. The guys can't go out without a doc. I'm on a mission."

Sergeant Richardson stepped between the lieutenant and me. "We *need* him," he drawled in slow Oklahomanese. "He's going with us."

The lieutenant left, but he returned the next day. This

time he wouldn't be put off. "You *are* going back," he insisted. "That's a direct order."

Fuck the army. But FTA or not, I watched the platoon, *my* platoon, disappear in the dust of the deuce that was returning me to Colonel Arnold's chickenshit. I might as well have been in shackles. The bond that had formed between me and the platoon had been of a nature I had never experienced before, not even in football. The GIs called it tight.

One way or another, I would go back into the field with First Platoon. I immediately began shooting requests at Colonel Arnold asking for permanent transfer to the 4/39th:

> . . . The month and a half I was with the First Platoon of Bravo Company, one man was killed and 22 wounded. If I go back to the 4/39th, I get to go back to "my" platoon. Also, I was put in for the Bronze Star for Valor and a Purple Heart. Incidents like these tend to make me feel I was part of the platoon and belonged to it.
>
> I have worked just about every job here at the 9th Med Bn and found that the jobs are not challenging, too routine and tend to get boring very quickly. The jobs here cannot keep my interest and do not motivate me. Unlike a majority of the people in my generation that are burning draft cards and showing their discontent of the United States involvement in the Vietnam War, I volunteered for the draft and volunteered to come to Vietnam. I want to do my part to back my government and the ideals it stands for. I feel I can serve my country and be more beneficial to the army as a line medic with the 4/39th. . . .

"You and I are both going to get in deep trouble if I let you put in for a transfer," the company clerk advised.

"*What?*"

"Colonel Arnold thinks it looks bad when personnel want to transfer out of his unit, especially when they try to go into a combat outfit."

Colonel Arnold was still up to his old tricks—formal personnel inspections and chickenshit. Whispers about fragging him still circulated among the enlisted at the 9th Med.

"Keep putting through my requests," I instructed the clerk. "Sooner or later he's going to be glad to see me leave."

As I bided my time, working at the 9th Medical clearing station, I gave more attention to the various medical problems flowing through. I had more incentive to learn this time. I wanted to be better prepared to treat the everyday maladies of my men as well as their wounds when I finally returned to First Platoon. Many of their problems stemmed from simply living in the tropics under less than sanitary conditions. With the guidance of Sergeant Williamson, an older and more experienced lifer medic, I soon learned to recognize and treat most common ailments.

The tropics were full of disease and rot and parasites that consumed human flesh. Every imaginable and unimaginable disease, affliction, and condition hobbled, crawled, or was carried into the Quonset hut, along with, next door at 3rd Surg, gunshot wounds, napalm burns, traumatic amputations, shock, and all the other forms of suffering and agony that accompany war in the tropics. The result to me was a living nightmare of human anguish. The graphic movies I had viewed or failed to view back at Fort Sam Houston paled in comparison. I hardly recognized in myself the Doc Evans who had evolved from the Dan Evans who'd jumped up in the middle of the movies, gasping for fresh air. This Doc Evans could change bandages on *Pseudomonas* burn infections and then eat a hearty meal of chipped beef in tomato sauce at the chow hall.

Tropical skin sores were the most common malady. They started as fungal infections that, left untreated, erupted into bacterial infections. Treatment was so barbaric it reminded me of Civil War surgeons using a hacksaw and liquor as an anesthetic to amputate wounded limbs. "Jungle rot" patients screamed in agony as we used scalpels to scrape scabs off the sores so medication could heal them. Afflicted GIs returning immediately to the field looked at us as if they thought we were crazy when we recommended that they keep their injuries clean.

Venereal diseases, especially gonorrhea, were almost as common as jungle rot among enlisted men. Officers suffered from "nonspecific urethritis," since a case of clap on their medical records could mar their precious careers. But gonorrhea and nonspecific urethritis alike received the same treatment—an injection of five to seven million units of penicillin in the gluteus maximus while Sergeant Williamson informed the victim-patient of the black syph, a potent form of incurable syphilis that VC agents supposedly spread among the ladies of the night in order to infect American GIs. I had also heard stories about boom-boom girls secreting razor blades in their vaginas, but no such injury ever came through the clearing station while I was there.

"This is absolutely the most disgusting dick I have ever seen!" Sergeant Williamson exclaimed over one case. Army medical personnel had no incentive to develop a caring bedside manner. "Evans, take a look at this revolting piece of meat."

The affliction resembled jungle rot gone on a rampage—raw cankerous flesh weeping thick pus from sores in series. The patient was made to suffer further indignities while being ordered to pose his penis for a series of photographs to be used in training medics at Fort Sam.

"You are our VD poster child of the month," Williamson informed the hapless trooper.

Abscesses, parasites, and every manner of infection straggled in for treatment. They came reeking of rot and oozing green-blue slime. One man's face was so swollen from an abscess behind his mandible that it resembled a balloon with eyes, nose, and mouth drawn on it. We incised and drained the abscess and released about a cupful of cottage cheese, then stuffed two feet of iodine packing into the cavity.

Shirkers in the field tried everything they could imagine to get themselves pulled out of combat, from shooting themselves in the foot, as Browner had done, to *eating* C4 plastic explosives. C4 patients were carried in strapped hand and foot to stretchers, screaming and twisting and hallucinating. Some of them died.

We also treated the local Vietnamese indigents who, in the words of the bureaucrats back in Washington, suffered "collateral damage." An MP officer brought in a young Vietnamese girl who had been gang-raped by a squad of GIs. She had to have sutures. Two cooks, a mechanic, three clerks, and a supply sergeant showed up to watch the procedure.

Another Vietnamese girl, one of the civilians hired to work at the Class Six liquor store on post, was brought in DOA, dead on arrival. A pallet of beer had fallen off a truck and flattened her like a pancake.

And the days passed. I continued to request transfer back to my platoon; Colonel Arnold continued to turn me down. I had to get back into the field for the sake of my own sanity. Article 15 threats of punishment were starting to pile up on me again. When philosophers and authors talk about the madness of war, they must have in mind the rear-echelon motherfuckers: the Remington Raiders at their little typewriters with a thousand forms and regulations piled around them, the Colonel Arnold types with their inspections and palm tree brigades. Certainly they did not have in mind the poor boonie rats who worried about only one thing—survival. Maybe there was a certain method to the REMF chickenshit; it made you prefer the insanity of combat over the madness of garrison duty.

As sometimes happens amid the vagaries of war, a chance incident opened the possibility of a way out for me. When Battalion threw a farewell luncheon for an officer about to DEROS home, I volunteered to stay behind with another medic to run the clearing station. I needed to stay as far away from Colonel Arnold as I could. Out of sight, out of mind.

It was a slow afternoon. I sat with my boots propped up on a table thumbing idly through the *Manual of Medical Therapeutics* when two dust-off medics from the 247th Medical Helicopter Detachment rushed in.

"Can you guys give us a hand?" one of them said.

I jumped up, thinking they needed help offloading wounded. Instead, the other clearing medic and I were hustled onto a Huey that was warming up on the helipad. I gripped the built-in litters as the bird shuttered and vibrated, roaring deafeningly, then sprang into the air. I hadn't been informed where we were going or why we were needed, but the thrill of my first helicopter flight left me staring wide-eyed at the terrain below.

It was like a relief map of the entire AO over which I
had slogged with my buddies of the First Platoon. There
was Ambush Alley running straight and narrow through rice
paddies and green undergrowth between Vinh Kim and
Dong Tam, Platoon Patrol Base Cougar looking even more
like a crayfish berm from the air, Widow Maker Alley where
Forte died. There the abandoned schoolhouse. And there
the bridge we had guarded and the brick house where the
pretty girl gave me the Saint Christopher medal that I now
wore on my dog tag chain.

The air smelled fresh and clean and tropic-scented aloft.
The land below was a lovely emerald green, and it held a
bit of my history and the history of the First Platoon and
therefore of the 9th Infantry Division, the Old Reliables.

I missed Sergeant Richardson, Sergeant Wallace, Fullmer
and his PRC-25, Henderson and Sotello and their machine
guns. Svatek, Gass the farm boy, Sugar Bear Bauer, Ron
Miller . . . I missed them. They needed me.

It wasn't until the chopper tail-walked into a clearing that
lay off Ambush Alley near the old schoolhouse that I
learned what our mission was. Colonel Frank Hart, commander of the 4/39th, my old battalion, ran out to meet us.
He looked sweaty and stressed. He pointed toward a wood
line, explaining in phrases that raced tumbling over each
other that one of his companies had walked into some shit
and sustained casualties.

"Bravo Company?" I asked quickly, my throat catching.

"Delta," he snapped with a "Who the fuck is this?" look.
"Alpha has secured the area against further attack, but there
might still be snipers. I need medics to get the wounded out
of the wood line and evacuate them."

We two medics from the bird grabbed litters and sprinted
across the clearing and into the woods. Platoon medics had
gathered the WIAs underneath a tree to the rear of the
action. No hostile fire interrupted us as we transferred
wounded from tree to chopper, although sporadic rifle fire
banged in the near distance.

For my part in this evacuation, the 4/39th recommended
me for the Army Commendation Medal with *V* for Valor
to choke off threats by Colonel Arnold to throw me in jail
and court-martial me for deserting my post in a combat

zone, an offense punishable by death. Colonel Arnold brooked no excuses in the 9th Med.

"If I don't get out of here and back to my platoon," I complained to Sergeant Williamson, "I'll go home either in the brig or as a Private E-1, the same as when I came in the army."

First Platoon had recommended me for Specialist E-4. The 9th Med had put the promotion on hold.

"We count on you here, Evans," Williamson said. "We know you'll do a good job wherever you're put."

I pointed in the general direction of the bush, not trying to hide the exasperation in my voice. "That's *my* platoon out there."

"I really don't blame you for wanting out. If you want out that badly, I'll go to bat for you and see what I can do."

Williamson was a good man, but I had heard that before.

Colonel Arnold threw a surprise barracks inspection. REMF sergeants hit the lights at 0500, startling us awake, then swept through the bay like a patrol through a VC village. I rose on my elbows in bed as a sergeant tore open my locker doors and dumped my gear on the floor. He triumphantly displayed a bottle of sloe gin from my duffel bag. It had been there since I returned from the field. Liquor was forbidden in the barracks.

"What's in the bottle?" the sergeant demanded with a smirk.

I took it, unscrewed the cap, and swigged a nip. "Sure tastes like booze," I admitted.

"That's an Article 15 violation, wiseass," the sergeant promised.

Fuck it. It don't mean nothing.

As if a valor commendation, a court-martial and an Article 15 weren't enough, I then received another letter from Dianne. Holy Christ. Two letters in one month. This one was short and to the point: she wanted a divorce; I could start it at my end or she would at home.

I want a divorce and fuck you and the war very much.

Batting my eyes rapidly, removing my glasses to wipe them, and then replacing them, I gazed out past a dust-off helicopter lifting off the helipad, past the base camp's sandbagged and concertina-wired perimeter, past the cleared fields of fire to where the jungle began. Out there with the platoon, life was basic. Staying alive and keeping your buds alive.

If ever I needed a few vagaries in my favor, it was now. My guardian angel must have been on duty. Quite by coincidence, I ran into Captain Pippin from the 247th Medevac at the chow hall. He remembered me from the mission to evacuate WIAs from the wood line.

"Evans," he said, "we need a dust-off medic for a couple of weeks."

I didn't have to think about it. "If you're asking if I'm volunteering, sir, the answer is yes. *Yes.*"

29

Medevac helicopters in Vietnam were called dust-offs in tribute to Major Charles L. Kelly, a pilot whose call sign was Dustoff when he was killed during a medical evacuation mission on July 1, 1964. The 247th Helicopter Medical Detachment had been formed at Fort Riley, Kansas, in August 1968 and arrived in-country December 21, only a few weeks after I reported to the 9th Med. Fifty-seven hours after the unit landed at Bien Hoa, it moved to Dong Tam and immediately became operational.

The 247th under the command of Major Donald Murphy consisted of twelve pilots, six crew chiefs, six medics, and six UH-1H Huey helicopters emblazoned with Red Cross emblems, which were supposed to prevent the enemy firing on them, but didn't. One "first up" chopper was on call twenty-four hours a day; a backup crew stood by in case of additional calls for service. In support of most of the 9th Infantry Division AO, the detachment typically flew about 1,000 missions a month, 32 a day. The 9th AO Kudzu also included the 7th ARVN Division, the 44th Special Forces Group, and the U.S. Navy Riverine Force.

"We're as busy as a one-legged gook running from napalm," I was assured when I reported to the 247th for temporary duty. One of the crew chiefs escorted me to Supply where I was issued a .38-caliber revolver in a shoulder holster, a flight suit and flight helmet with a built-in two-way communications system, a solid steel bulletproof vest called a chicken plate, and combat boots with zippers on the sides. I looked at the boots.

"Helicopters are made of lightweight magnesium, which burns extremely hot and will even create its own oxygen underwater," the crew chief explained. "If your chopper crashes and catches fire, your boots will stick to the floor. The zippers let you get out of them fast."

If your boots stuck to the floor, what happened to your bare feet?

The crew chief shrugged.

"You crash often?" I asked.

"A medevac pilot expects to crash about ten times during a normal tour. Crashing is just another way of landing. We get shot at a lot."

I fingered the Saint Christopher medal on my tag chain; I hoped my guardian angel stayed alert.

First impressions tend to linger. My initial experience with dust-offs had occurred following the ambush on Widow Maker Alley when Sergeant Sinclair held the pilot on the ground with his M16 while we finished loading the wounded aboard. Not a courageous image of airmen. That picture was to change quickly, however. That pilot must have been having a bad day. I soon conceded these guys had balls as big as basketballs to fly their egg-shelled aircraft into a hail of bullets in order to jerk WIAs out of danger and get them to medical care. The average length of time in Vietnam from when a GI was wounded until he reached a hospital was twenty minutes. Air ambulances made the difference.

My reintroduction to airmobile and chopper pilots came about when a Huey gunship was riddled by ground fire as it flew close-in air support for an infantry platoon in contact. The wounded Huey flew in low and erratically from the southeast, like a bumblebee with an injured wing. It darted above the perimeter wire at Dong Tam and sky-bounced wildly toward the landing pad. Both door gunners, either dead or unconscious, hung by their safety tethers in the open doorways. The copilot slumped lifeless over his controls; the aircraft commander nursed a wounded arm as he fought to nudge the riddled bird to roost. He was the only conscious man aboard.

Quonsets and two-story wooden buildings surrounded the helipad on three sides. Support crews dashed for cover as the helicopter skittered sideways across the sky, listing as if it was about to crash. Its skids tapped the roof of one building. Then it reared back on its tail rotor like a half-wild bronco as the stricken pilot fought with it.

It slid to one side between two buildings, narrowly avoiding a collision. Its thrashing rotor blade created a cushion of turbulent ground air, upon which it rode in a sideslip to the helipad. It dropped heavily to earth on its skids an instant before the pilot slumped forward and lost consciousness.

Officers like Colonel Arnold, I thought, ought to be ashamed to breathe the same Vietnamese air with brave men like those aboard the Huey. My contempt for REMFs, acquired with the First Platoon in the field, grew deeper. Doc Evans would continue to fight to remain a combat medic.

The giant rotor yanked me into the air for my first mission of mercy. I tried to speak but couldn't hear my own voice over the throbbing of the blades. The chopper lurched, and I slid across the seat. The doors were closed, but what if the helicopter did a lateral ninety, the doors slid open, and it dumped us out like pebbles from a tin can? The crew chief and the other medic didn't seem concerned. I tried to relax in the rarefied air above that old-woman country that looked like a lovely young woman from a distance. Beautiful from the air, a shithole on the ground.

Suddenly the landing zone appeared, coming at us fast. I had *Crash!* on my mind. I braced myself. Then the bird pulled up, tail dragging in the air, and sat down normally in a field of rotor-whipped elephant grass surrounded by nipa palms and strangler fig vines. Little ARVN soldiers, looking terrified, charged out of the trees toward us, jabbering and gesticulating and shouting at each other. The elephant grass grew head level to them.

They must have run into some fierce shit. Six of the tiny men were being carried in bloody ponchos, while another four were being half-dragged, half-supported by their comrades. I swung out onto the skids with the other medic and then, dropping into the grass, started tossing wounded into the helicopter's belly. We could sort them out later, get them into the three litters attached in a stack against the back firewall of the helicopter. The litters would hold either three American GIs or six Vietnamese.

I couldn't tell if we were taking fire or not, because of the rhythmic roar of the chopper's engine and blades. But the crew chief was yelling at us. I couldn't hear his words, but I gathered the gist of it was "Get 'em on! Get 'em in here!" He kept a wary eye peeled toward the tree lines.

The four walking wounded huddled together like chickens in the hellhole. I swung back into the chopper, feeling hands grabbing at my legs and having to push two or three ARVN out of the way. ARVN swarmed all over the bird, like ants over a piece of dropped ham, preventing it from taking off again. Pushing and clawing at each other in near-panic, trying to jam an entire company into an area big enough only for a squad—which was about what we had aboard already.

"Get those little fuckers out of here!" the crew chief was shouting. He was kicking them in the face and grabbing them and throwing them back out into the grass. Like trying to remove scared cats from a screen door.

I slipped on blood smearing the floor. Only by grabbing one of the fixed litter legs did I prevent myself from being pulled out onto the ground. I kicked in desperation, aiming for frightened eyes and screaming mouths. I pulled myself erect again, but the weight of the invasion pinned me against the litters.

I don't know how, but the other medic and I managed to stuff the six seriously injured WIAs into the litters and strap them down while the crew chief fought off the horde of ARVN. The chopper's skids broke free of earth, but panicked Vietnamese soldiers trying to escape combat clung to

the skids and brought the chopper back to earth with a
spine-jolting bang.

I heard, "Shoot the bastards if you have to!"

The crew chief brandished his M16, threatened them
with it.

The skids freed themselves again. The chopper lifted into
the air. Most of the Vietnamese lost their handholds and
fell back into the grass, but three or four of them held on.
Their weight made the chopper yaw dangerously to one side.

"They'll kill themselves if they fall!" I yelled.

"Fuck 'em," the crew chief snarled. "Cowardly little mag-
gots. Won't even fight for their own country."

They finally let go, dropping back to earth, before the
bird rose high enough to cause them serious injury.

Suddenly I felt ill. The excitement, the thick coppery smell
and taste of blood in the hellhole, airsickness. I dropped
down and sat in the open doorway, legs dangling in the
turbulent air, holding on with my fingers hooked into a floor
D-ring. I leaned out, gazed straight down into uplifted arms
and frightened faces of our brave allies—and vomited all
over them.

30

The intercom mike in the flight helmet touched your lips to
catch your voice and eliminate background noise. It took
some getting used to, since the Huey's engine, muted by the
padded helmet, sounded far off; that encouraged you to
shout at the mike.

"Tail clear left, sir!" I shouted into the mouthpiece the
first time I directed takeoff.

"*Damn!*" The pilot jerked off his helmet. "Evans, speak
normally into the mike. *Normal* volume. Got it?"

"Sorry, sir."

Seemed I was going to spend the war being transferred around, always being the cherry FNG, pulling dumb stunts.

We evacuated two ambulatory grunts who had sustained minor frag wounds. A cold drizzle was falling. As I jumped back into the chopper for takeoff, I slid the side door closed against the rain. I neglected to buckle my seat belt. The Huey cleared the tops of the trees and was about to beeline it for home when something banged into the fuselage.

"We're taking hits!" the pilot shouted through the intercom. "Hang on."

As the Huey leaped skyward like an elevator, more banging caused my balls to shrink up to about the level of my throat. Most air veterans sat on their chicken plates to keep ground fire from messing with the family jewels. I was wearing my chicken plate. I ripped it off and was going to sit on it when I noticed my seat belt. The buckle had been caught outside when I closed the door. That was what was causing the banging.

Feeling foolish, I quickly retrieved the belt without anyone noticing. The banging stopped.

The pilot and crew chief looked for bullet holes when we landed. They scratched their heads. I pretended to be as puzzled as they.

Most of the flying, I soon discovered, was fairly routine. Picking up minor wounded on secure LZs after most of the danger had passed, transporting patients between facilities, flying blood runs and medication runs. It was exhilarating in a way, flying in the cool rarefied air high above the poor mud-slogging grunts who had to cope with leeches, mind-numbing heat, monsoons, mosquitoes, booby traps, and, especially during the post-Tet offensive, ambushes. About the only time medevac helicopters flew into harms' way was when the mission required them to be sucked to earth to pick up patients still under fire. It was almost psychedelic, sitting in the door high above the emerald-green earth with the FM channel turned to Saigon's Armed Forces Radio Network.

Good morning, Vietnam!

Listening to the Beach Boys or Nancy Sinatra: "These boots are made for walking . . . And these boots are gonna walk all over you."

I loved the long night flights. We flew few after-dark combat medevacs because of the hazards; therefore, the birds made their routine medication and patient runs after nightfall in order to be free for combat when dawn broke. I lay on the bird's cool metal floor and cracked the door a little to let in fresh air and a view. Forced my mind to go blank, up there above the war and all, and let myself become a part of the wonderful sheen of moonlight bathing the peaceful tropics below. Not thinking about Dianne and her divorce. *Her* divorce.

Up here it was hard to imagine a war going on down there. A war in which young men like Teddy Creech were maimed for life and others like Forte ended life halfway around the world from home before life had really even begun. A war in which "peacemakers" argued about the shape of the negotiation tables and protesters back home spat on returning GIs and called them baby killers.

"Don't mean nothing," the GIs said, but of course it meant something. We just didn't know what it meant.

One afternoon we picked up an American USO girl at Can Tho to transport her to Dong Tam. Gorgeous blonde in a miniskirt. Both pilots, the crew chief, the other medic, and I stepped all over each other like a bunch of horny schoolboys, trying to be helpful but also trying to cop an accidental feel or win a quick peek at some cleavage. Round-eyed girls were at a premium in Vietnam. They didn't even have to be particularly good-looking to draw a crowd. Fullmer allowed that if he were an ugly female, horny as he was all the time, he'd be a lifer in the army where simply *being* female qualified you as a beauty queen in a combat zone.

Shortly after we took off, the blonde fell asleep in her jump seat with her short skirt hiked up. Our overheated imaginations could not have created a better fantasy. The crew chief alerted the rest of the crew: "Beaver Alert! Beaver Alert!"

We took turns riding the seat opposite the sleeping girl. Looking right up to the delicious mound of her pink panties. The crew chief imagined he saw hair, and the plane commander ordered him to switch places so *he* could get in some beaver-watching time. The intercom chattered with excitement.

"I can *smell* that sweet pussy."

"Looky, looky, looky. Lordy, it's nooky."

The poor girl never suspected how much pleasure she provided a chopper full of affection-starved, sex-deprived GIs flying high above Vietnam. She smiled sweetly when we landed at Dong Tam. Every airman on the helipad paused reverently in whatever he was doing to watch her wiggle her luscious ass in that short tight skirt out of sight and into the sunsets of our memories. She would be revived again and again on interminable night ambush watches and in lonely outposts. It was around such moments that life sometimes revolved in a combat zone.

First Platoon, *my* platoon, was operating in the vicinity of the schoolhouse when we plucked out some WIAs for Marvin the Arvin. The ARVN were like their national flag, which was yellow with three red stripes. GIs said that the part of Vietnam that was not red was yellow. Out of the field chatter over the radio, Sergeant Jim Richardson's Oklahoma drawl suddenly cut through five-by-five, surprising me. He requested a dust-off for two "Whiskey India Alphas"— WIAs.

We were full and couldn't pick them up; the backup chopper took to the air. Frantic with worry by the time my twelve-hour duty shift ended, I searched the morgue and the 3rd Surg. Hospital before I found Sergeant Wallace and Sugar Bear Bauer at the 9th Med. I could have hugged them, seeing them alive. Wallace, wearing a blue hospital gown, gave me a sheepish grin and sat up at an awkward angle on the side of his bed, one hip slightly elevated. His head was bandaged, leaving his prominent ears sticking out.

Bauer, who had just returned to the platoon after recovering from the wounds he'd sustained on Widow Maker Alley, groaned from underneath sheets in the next bed over. He looked like hell with little but his eyes and mouth showing through mummy wrappings. His short, stocky form looked small and violated underneath the sheets. "Doc . . ." he greeted me in his deep voice.

Wallace had earned yet another Purple Heart. He was

living up to his role as the platoon's magnet for enemy detritus. "They got me in the ass this time, Doc," he said, explaining his awkward sitting posture. "The gooks have no respect."

After so many Purple Hearts, he had the option of going home. I didn't think he would. I was hungry for news about the First. Wallace filled me in.

The 4/39th had been getting the shit kicked out of it during the past two or three weeks. Intelligence reports said that two NVA Main Force battalions might have joined the 279th VC Security Force on operations around Dong Tam. Whatever was going on out there had put the Old Reliables' feet to the fire. Friendly fire casualties were mounting while morale continued plummeting. The battalion's companies and platoons slogged all over the AO chasing Charlie, but Charlie showed himself only when he wanted to be found—generally to the GIs' disadvantage. Word had come down that the battalion was about to get a new commander—a hard-core son of a bitch from the Korean War who, rumor said, was bound for glory, no matter how many GIs he got killed to pave the road for him.

"He's got everybody scared," Bauer said. "Even Sergeant Richardson."

I learned that Lieutenant Bob Knapp was acting Bravo Company commander again. Lieutenant Larry Neumann had replaced Captain Seeker after the Ohio National Guardsman received his wounds and was medevac'd to Japan. Neumann lasted a record twenty-seven days before a booby trap blew shrapnel into his intestinal tract. That put Knapp back in charge.

Lieutenant Knapp was running company-size ops south of An Long, where First Platoon boonie rats tripped four booby traps but were left miraculously unscathed, and along the My Tho River. Gunships chewed over a fleet of sampans that fled an island in the river when Bravo inserted at the other end. Lieutenant Knapp dispatched Sergeant Svatek with a patrol to search for survivors.

The patrol discovered a round metal lid concealed in tall grass on the dike of a rice paddy. The lid to a tunnel. While his soldiers surrounded the tunnel entrance to cover him, Svatek worked his fingers underneath the lid and pulled.

The lid gave a few inches. Then somebody underneath jerked it back into place. Svatek sprang away.

He waited a few minutes, his M16 trained, before he shook off his ruck and approached the lid a second time. This time he switched the selector switch on his rifle to full automatic. If he could pry up the lid one inch, enough to shove the muzzle of his rifle into the tunnel and squeeze the trigger, the hiding VC were in for a big surprise. Honey, I'm home!

The lid again jerked closed before he could ram his gun barrel through the crack.

Svatek crouched to one side, keeping a wary eye on the metal lid. He eased the pin from a concussion grenade and laid it softly on top of the disc, then ran for cover.

The bright flash of the explosion hurtled the lid into the sun. A VC in black PJs popped out of the smoking hole like a dangerous jack-in-the-box. He looked wild and scared, trapped. He took about two steps, sweeping his AK-47 in a wide arc, searching for a target. Svatek stitched him across the middle with his M16, spraying blood and gore and dropping the VC where he stood.

Two other VC lay wounded in the tunnel. Their combined voices bellowed from the hole in the ground as through a megaphone: *"Chieu hoi! Chieu hoi!"* They were giving up.

That was the first time a number of grunts in the First Platoon had ever actually seen a real VC. Until then they could have sworn they were fighting ghosts.

I wanted to know about my replacement and about how Wallace and Sugar Bear had been wounded.

They said the medic who took my place was a newbie named Rick Hudson. He had arrived by deuce to join the platoon the same day I left for Dong Tam. He'd surprised Sergeant Richardson and the others by immediately announcing that he was a C.O.—a conscientious objector—and as such would not carry a weapon. That took the men back a bit, since their only experience with C.O.'s had been through that shitbird Browner.

"I believe in the sanctity of life and will not take another life," he explained. "But I'll do the best job I know how to do as a medic."

"That's what we ask," Sergeant Richardson had said in his understated way.

Hudson came down with heat exhaustion on his first patrol. Then he changed his status as a conscientious objector after the platoon came under fire from a wood line and was driven to cover behind a rice dike. Bullets thumped into the earth around the platoon and screamed overhead. The new medic lay flat clutching his aid bag with both hands.

"What happens," he asked later, "if the VC capture me? Will they know I'm a noncombatant?"

"They don't give a shit, cherry," L. J. Henderson explained, as always direct and to the point. "They will cut your dick off an' stick it in your mouth."

The next day Hudson asked for, and was issued, an M16.

"The kid's turning out all right," Wallace said. I felt a tinge of jealousy.

The night Wallace and Sugar Bear got it, First Platoon had set up an ambush position in a muddy wood line overlooking the river. It looked like another dry hole, until about midnight, when security tugged on the alert cord to bring the ambushers awake and online. The muted thrumming of a small outboard engine gradually grew louder as a sampan pushed upriver against the current.

L.J. lay low behind the trigger of his M60 machine gun. He could have reached out and touched the black water. Next to him sprawled Sugar Bear. It was Henderson who pinned Bauer with that nickname after he playfully intercepted a letter to Bauer from his girlfriend. She had branded her man by addressing him as "Dear Sugar Bear."

Suddenly, as things do on moonless nights, the sampan appeared out of the darkness, already at close quarters. Three silhouettes occupied the boat. Henderson felt as if he could have reached out with the barrel of his M60 and tapped the gooks' heads with it. Knock, knock. Who's there?

Wallace initiated the ambush. A claymore mine set up on the riverbank emitted a deafening clap of thunder. It flashed into momentary relief the dark water, the overhanging trees, and the VC sampan.

Henderson squeezed a long fiery stream of red-gold BBs point-blank into the target. Someone launched a frag 40mm grenade from his M79. The sampan was so near the bank that shrapnel zip-buzzed into the overhanging foliage and into the bushes and ferns where the ambushers hid.

Wallace caught a supercharged hornet in the buttocks. He gave a startled shout and spun around, only to be struck a glancing blow on the head by another hornet. He dropped to his belly, still fighting. He opened up in the direction of the sampan with his M16.

The hornets also attacked Sugar Bear. He had risen to one knee in the excitement. Hot shrapnel cut into his skull while the concussion of the exploding M79 projectile slapped him rolling into the river water. Still yelling savagely at the dying and dead enemy, Henderson fired a final M60 burst, then dropped the gun and dragged his half-conscious friend from the river.

Sugar Bear was raving. "L.J.? L.J., looky at me, man. I ain't dying, am I, L.J.? I don't wanna die like this, L.J."

"Doc!" Henderson screamed over his shoulder, forgetting all about the fight. The three gooks were already dead and in the drink anyhow. Fish food.

"Doc Hudson did *good."* Sergeant Wallace couldn't stop praising my replacement. Maybe the platoon didn't need me anymore. "It was a good thing the ambush didn't last any longer," Wallace said, "else half the platoon would have been in the hospital from our own weapons."

He laughed with a certain suppressed irony.

Hudson treated the wounded grunts as if he'd been doing it since the beginning of the war. He injected Bauer with morphine to ease the pain. The explosions had blasted out one eardrum and filled his cranium with metal fragments. Bauer's wound, combined with his dip in the river, caused his body temperature to drop dangerously. Hudson scrounged nylon poncho liners from the men and wrapped Sugar Bear in them, then crawled inside with him to contribute his own body warmth.

The next morning I had overheard Sergeant Richardson on the radio requesting a dust-off.

"Doc," Wallace said, "Hudson is a good medic. But when are *you* coming back? You're *our* doc."

I had heard through Sergeant Williamson at 9th Med that Colonel Arnold had finally approved my request to return

This picture was taken at the end of February 1969 near FSB Moore. The white bandage on the author's head covered an abscess that the battalion surgeon had lanced just a couple of hours before.

Maj. Gen. Ben Sternberg pinning the Distinguished Service Cross on the author at Schofield Barracks, Hawaii, December 1969. *U.S. Army photograph*

Author giving medical treatment to a local Vietnamese woman.

Tom Smith (left) and Jim Richardson. Smith was Torpie's RTO. Richardson was offered a battlefield promotion but turned it down to remain with the platoon. *Tom Smith*

Joseph "Slim" Holleman (left) and L.J. Henderson. Holleman was wounded on March 25, 1969, and died the next day. Henderson was the platoon's machine gunner.

Sgt. Donald Wallace. Don was nicknamed "the human magnet" for being wounded six times during his tour.

Sgt. Tim "Sugar Bear" Bauer. Wounded twice in Vietnam, he was so impressed with the medical corps that he became a member of his hometown emergency response team.

Lt. Roger Keppel. One of eighteen men wounded on March 25, 1969. He recovered fully from his wounds.

Second platoon medic Rick Hudson (right) is treating a wounded NVA. John Svatek is on the left.

Sgt. John Svatek served with the first and second platoons until he was severely wounded on March 20, 1969. *Rick Hudson*

Arnold "Dale" Gass, author, and Sgt. Jim Surletta (left to right). Dale was a platoon machine gunner until wounded. Jim was so close to the enemy on March 25, 1969, that he could feel the heat from the napalm bombs.

Bernadette Snook and Jackie Hubertus (left to right), Lt. William Torpie's sisters, and Roger Keppel and John Svatek (left to right). They are getting last-minute instruction to lay a wreath at the Tomb of the Unknown Soldier, in honor of all those who died from the 4/39th Infantry Unit.

Richard Joseph Forte, who was affectionately known as WOP #1. His parents religiously sent Italian food, which he shared with the platoon members. He was killed December 23, 1968. *John Svatek*

Actor Ricardo Montalban entertained troops in Vietnam with the USO organization. This photo was taken at FSB Danger in April 1969.

Chinook helicopter is extracting the helicopter in which Roger Keppel, Don Wallace, Ron Miller, Tiger Scout Doi, and author crashed on March 23, 1969.

Dong Tam, the 9th Infantry Division's base camp. The name in Vietnamese means "united hearts and minds."
Don Wallace

Jim Whitmore. Author replaced Whitmore as first platoon medic. Jim then became battalion medic with the 4/39th. *Rick Hudson*

Glenn Ellis, Bill Gregory, Glenn Smith, L.J. Henderson, and Larry Faulkenberg (left to right). Five platoon members taking a refreshment break from a work detail. *Dale Gass*

Lt. Robert "Bob" Knapp. He was the type of officer you would follow through hell without a canteen of water.

to the 4/39th. But since the transfer hadn't been confirmed, I said nothing about it.

"Perhaps soon," I said. "I hope."

My last mission with the 247th couldn't have provided a more satisfactory conclusion. As "first up" chopper, we responded to a call to evacuate a soldier wounded by another damnable booby trap. Shrapnel from the mine had tattered his jungle fatigues and his body, leaving him speckled from head to foot with scores of tiny bleeding flesh wounds from nails, pieces of metal, and whatever else the VC could stuff into the bomb. Ugly wounds, painful, but probably not life-threatening.

Once the chopper was aloft and whop-whopping toward Dong Tam, I hit the red-lensed cabin light, used forceps to pluck out some of the metal parts, and disinfected the wounds. An open injury treated quickly in the tropics was less likely to breed infection.

After I freshened the soldier's bandages, he lay quietly on the litter staring up at nothing. Most likely he was gazing deep inside himself. I fingered my Saint Christopher medal and rested my free hand on his chest to let him know I was there, that he was not alone.

It was important in war not to be alone.

31

While I was waiting to rejoin First Platoon (Rick Hudson had been reassigned as Second Platoon medic), Doc Holley burst into the 4/39th's aid station wearing filthy fatigues and a two-day beard. I had never seen him coming out of the field before, other than his regular day excursions to the FSBs to hold sick call. The on-duty medic had advised me with an uneasy grin that the new battalion commander, a lieutenant colonel named David H. Hackworth, had issued an order that *everybody* in the 4th Battalion was to go to the boonies. There would be no more skylarking and goldbricking in *his* battalion, which he now referred to as the Hardcore Battalion. The troops had been renamed Recondos.

"This is becoming hell," Doc Holley ranted. He was a draftee doctor who took shit from no man. "That GI Joe lifer bastard is going to ruin us all."

Jesus. I might have screwed up asking to get transferred back to First Platoon. Everyone at Dong Tam was talking about the new gung-ho colonel. Doc Holley even went so far as to pull Hackworth's personnel file to check up on him. It turned out he really *was* a war hero.

Hackworth had joined the army before his sixteenth birthday, lying about his age, and had fought in Korea, where he earned a battlefield commission. It was said he'd earned more medals than Howard Johnson's had flavors of ice cream: Distinguished Service Cross, a handful of Silver and Bronze Stars, countless Army Commendation Medals, four Purple Hearts from Korea and one from Vietnam.

Before I left Dong Tam, I jotted a quick letter to my parents, expressing my uncertainty:

> Dear Folks,
> . . . I go to the field tomorrow. I will be about eleven miles away from Dong Tam. The company is making Eagle Flights, which I told you about in another letter. . . .
> I might not be able to write for a week or so. The new commander is a little crazy and I think he will be relieved of his command shortly. He is pushing the men too hard. . . .
>
> Love,
> Doc (Dan)

In my absence from First Platoon, the battalion had been jerked off Division security duty and reassigned to AO Wagon Wheel on the Plain of Reeds, a flat, sprawling expanse of tall elephant grass and little else. This area of operations was called Wagon Wheel because five canals converged there, which, from the air, looked like the hub and spokes of a wheel.

When I got back, I dropped my ruck and aid bag to the ground from the Huey that had transported me, then clambered out myself. I found myself in the middle of an anthill of frantic activity. The 4/39th was building itself a new base camp. It was instantly obvious that the battalion was under new leadership. Most of the men were sweating in the hot sun, sandbagging bunkers, constructing fighting positions, emplacing artillery, laying wire, and clearing fields of fire; the others were on security duty or on patrol. The battalion's new mission was to prevent enemy infiltration from Cambodia, which lay to the west beyond the reeds.

No one was lying around listening to transistor radios or swigging Coke purchased from Vietnamese kids and boom-boom girls. The nearest village was several klicks down the road. The men seemed to have *purpose*. Nothing like the slack routine I had gotten used to the first time—Meals on Wheels every day at noon, nightly dry hole ambushes, half-assed patrols that started at daybreak and ended at dusk. Those routines, I was beginning to understand, had gotten Forte killed, along with twenty-four other GIs in the battalion, and had resulted in lost legs for Creech and Harvill and 485 other wounded Recondos. These figures represented a 100 percent casualty rate in an outfit that had not yet met the enemy in open combat.

That was going to change. I heard that Hackworth could barely restrain his disgust and his temper when he first inspected his new command of love bead–wearing and peace symbol–wearing troops who wallowed in their own laxness and sloth. There was a story going around about a battalion clerk who had inscribed "FTA" on his helmet.

"FTA? What does that mean?" Colonel Hackworth had asked him.

"It means 'Fuck the army,' sir."

Hackworth transferred the REMF soldier immediately to a line company and issued an order that no slogans would hereafter be written on any piece of military equipment. It was now back to basics and sleeping on the ground for support troops as well as for the grunts in the field. The colonel vowed that Charlie would feel the 4/39th's revived presence in cold steel and hot lead. The Hardcore Battalion was going to kick ass.

As I looked for First Platoon among the hardworking soldiers, I saw a soldier salute an officer. That was something new in the field.

"Hardcore Recondo, sir," the soldier chirped.

"No fucking slack," responded the officer.

I turned and watched them in surprise. A troop staggering under the weight of a sandbag sniggered cynically. "Chickenshit," he sneered. "That's the required salute and response in Hackworth's hard-luck Hardcore Battalion. A sergeant in Charlie Company came back from R&R and lost a stripe because he didn't know he was supposed to salute. Chickenshit."

I finally located my platoon working with the rest of the battalion. The men broke to welcome me home. There had been visible changes. Sergeant Richardson, thin to begin with, looked as if he had dropped ten pounds he could ill afford to lose. Sergeant Sugar Bear Bauer was back with a new scar at his hairline. Sergeant Wallace was also back, as I'd thought he would be; his ribs showed bony and corrugated through the sunburned skin of his torso. The entire platoon looked meaner, leaner.

Fresh meat had filled in the ranks. We had lost Svatek to Second Platoon and gained a new platoon leader. Slim Holleman said, "He's a white boy Yankee lieutenant. The Soul Patrol ran him out of Third Platoon. Now we stuck with him."

Lieutenant Celphane had lasted hardly long enough to get acquainted with the platoon before he was transferred out and Lieutenant Roger Keppel transferred in. Officers rarely lasted long. Keppel was lank and boyish and looked as if he might one day be a college professor, if he lived through the war. An OCS Shake 'n Bake lieutenant from New York's Columbia University, he was surprised to find himself a combat infantry leader. OCS had told him he could serve in something safe, like Intelligence.

Bravo Company had picked him up in early February and assigned him to the Third Platoon, or Third Herd, as the rest of the company derisively called it. In a battalion low on leadership and morale, Third Platoon was at the bottom.

One NCO refused to lead a squad; one squad, the Soul Patrol, was made up entirely of blacks who openly defied orders and fell asleep on watch. The only sergeant the green Lieutenant Keppel could count on, Sergeant Tom Diveley, stepped on a mine and was evacuated. Keppel's RTO had a nervous breakdown. Things got so bad in the platoon that the lieutenant himself, the patrol leader, was reduced to walking point.

The company commander, Lieutenant Knapp, took mercy on the FNG lieutenant and switched him over to First Platoon, which was comparatively well organized under Sergeant Richardson. Lieutenant Keppel was still considered an outsider when I hooked up with the platoon again. All officers were pricks until they proved otherwise. The men continued to look to Richardson for their orders.

There were four other cherries in the platoon. Larry Faulkenberg and Larry Fentress were both from Indiana and had been drafted the same day. Because their last names were so close alphabetically and their first names the same, they had gone through basic training and advanced individual training together and then had been shipped to Vietnam together and assigned to the same platoon.

Charles Reese was from Zanesville, Ohio. "Zanesville is so poor," he cracked, "it can't afford to pay attention."

Jim Sweeney, a natural to carry a machine gun, stood over six feet tall and had shoulders as broad as a door. He was a double volunteer—volunteered for the army and then volunteered for Vietnam. He was one of only three soldiers in the platoon who were not draftees.

L. J. Henderson's bare torso glistened silky black with sweat. His white teeth flashed when he saw me. "Hear what I'm sayin' to you, Doc?" he greeted me. "Did I tell you when you left they was some big shit comin' down the road? We fixin' to get screwed, blued, and tattooed. You shoulda kept your white candy ass in Dong Tam."

The men, all eager for a new audience upon which to air their gripes, crowded around me. Everybody had his Hackworth horror story.

"This is probably the lowest point of morale in the battalion," the headquarters company medic said, summing up the new command. "Not only have we been taking a lot of casualties, but now it looks as if somebody is going to come in and kick ass and make career soldiers out of us."

"The bastard's killing us all." That was the common lament.

"No more gravy missions," Harry Fullmer groused, stroking and cleaning his radio. "We are now out in the bush constantly, hunting for the enemy. We've been humping fifteen klicks a day in this shit. There's three or four rivers every *mile* out there. We don't get fresh water brought in. We drink from the rivers, like fucking animals. Put enough halazone tabs in it, I guess, and nothing can live. Including us."

Five new rules a day, every day, came down from the madman. They were posted on bunkers and latrines. Everyplace we looked, new rules. No one had an excuse for not obeying them when he got nailed.

> Wear your steel pot at all times.
> Clean and carry your rifle at all times.
> Ammunition will not be worn Pancho Villa style.
> After darkness every night the fire base perimeter will pull back 300 meters.
> Anything you personally cannot carry with you twenty-four hours a day is gone on the next chopper.

We were going to be soldiers in Colonel Hackworth's image or he'd kill us all off—or let the enemy do it. We were looking for Charlie, and the colonel wanted Charlie to know it. We were in a *war,* goddammit, he was saying. We weren't waiting anymore for Charlie to come to us and pick us off one at a time like helpless geese. The 4/39th was no longer *only* the 4/39th. It was the Hardcore and the men of the Hardcore were dangerous badass bastards from hell.

"Right," Holleman sneered.

Each morning at 0600, the listening posts came in to join the platoons already rolled out of their blankets and bags. Everyone in the base camp fired off a magazine into the air on full auto, a mad minute that got the adrenaline pumping and let the VC know the Hardcore was ready to do business.

"Reveille for Charlie," Henderson called it.

Everyone cleaned weapons after that, had them inspected, and then reloaded before anyone went to morning chow. C-rations were now normal fare in the boonies; no more Meals on Wheels. We were lucky to eat twice a day. We worked harder than anyone in the battalion could ever remember. I was always hungry. I started dropping weight like everyone else.

After breakfast, an air cavalry troop from the Black Hawk squadron whoppered in across the wet grass plains and flew observation and air cover for rifle companies methodically scouring the sea of elephant grass. The choppers looked raw and ready with the image of a black hawk and crossed cavalry swords painted on their noses. They probed and swept the skies until they located movement. Then the platoons were "jitterbugged" in a series of helicopter insertions until contact was made, or they were "eagle-flighted" in helicopter raids directed at specific targets.

The days were still hot and humid, but the nights had gotten cold. Exhausted, always soaked from wading through swamps and rivers, our feet starting to shrivel and rot, our tempers frayed, we crashed wherever and whenever we had the opportunity. We simply rolled into our ponchos and thin nylon liners and went to sleep. Our empty guts growled and our mouths tasted as if the entire U.S. Army's 9th Infantry Division had marched through and left their dirty latrines.

And then, as soon as we finished getting one fire base dug in, we moved it. We moved every three days or so. One or two companies were always filling sandbags and digging fighting trenches while the other rifle companies went looking for Charlie.

"One of these days," Henderson predicted, "we gonna find ol' Luke the Gook. We gonna find Charlie in a big way."

32

Rotary-winged aircraft played a multitude of roles in Vietnam. They were used in reconnaissance, often locating the enemy by intentionally drawing fire; they delivered ammunition, food, water, and other supplies; they lifted artillery batteries across the landscape; they functioned in battle as airborne observation and command posts; they rescued downed airmen and evacuated wounded soldiers; they swiftly delivered riflemen to battle; and they were awesome, armed with rockets, machine guns, and mini-guns, in close air support of ground troops. "Airmobile" was the military term for air cavalry planes in Vietnam.

The 4/39th with its supporting helicopter fleet of slicks (troopships) and hogs (gunships) operated within M16 range of the Cambodian border, jitterbugging or eagle-flighting here and there in Hackworth's determined but largely unsuccessful pursuit of the enemy. While out-of-country operations were specifically forbidden, there were times when we knew we had crossed the line. During those episodes, even the platoon leaders were not issued maps. KITDFBS—kept in the dark, fed bullshit.

"Hackworth, that crazy bastard," someone would explode. "The son of a bitch has put us down in Cambodia."

On almost every mission we came upon old half-eroded fighting trenches left over from the French-Vietnamese wars, occasional stone watch towers, and other debris from the historical past. Made you realize just how long the Viets had been fighting their wars. The more things changed, it seemed, the more they remained the same. Word had it that we were searching for signs of massive enemy troop build-ups. We sometimes located abandoned camps, the larger of these in Cambodia, we suspected, but Charlie seldom left even a scrap of paper behind.

Heat, humidity, water, mud, checking one wood line after another—all of this contributed to chronic fatigue among the troops. The men were wearing down and wearing out, I thought. Immersion foot was a big problem. Skin on the soldiers' feet and lower legs was wrinkling, flaking, and starting to peel off. Before Sergeant Wallace was flown home for his father's funeral, he was starting to limp so badly I threatened to medical-profile him to the 9th Med in Dong Tam. I missed him now that he was gone. For his sake I hoped he would be allowed to stay home, but for the platoon's sake I hoped he returned.

I ordered First Platoon soldiers to double the required dosage of water-purification tabs in their canteens as they stood knee deep in sun-hot water on a waving prairie of water grasses and filled their canteens. Treated water tasted a bit like kerosene, but the tablets made it pottable and prevented dehydration and heat stroke.

Most patrols were long, tense walks in the sun, broken by occasional spurts of adrenaline, as when Marty Miles, who had broken or lost his glasses and was, like me, damn near blind without them, spotted movement in the weeds. It turned out to be a snake fifteen feet long and as big around as my thigh. Miles wanted to shoot it, but we weren't allowed to fire our weapons except in self-defense without permission from the C&C—command and control—chopper.

"Leave the snake alone," Sergeant Richardson drawled. "Snakes you don't have to worry about. VC you do."

"VC," agreed Slim Holleman, adding, "an' that crazy motherfucker Hackworth."

Exhaustion. Total exhaustion. I had never endured such bone-deep, physically and emotionally wrung out, strung out, zomboid fatigue. Six helicopters flew close air support. Tiny mosquito-like observation Loach choppers buzzed around at treetop level trying to entice the enemy to give away his position while lean, predatory Cobras with sharks' teeth painted on their noses hovered and dashed here and there seeking a target for their formidable armaments. Huey hogs worked over tree lines with their machine guns. Recon by fire, trying to get the gooks to show themselves. Puffs of gunsmoke dotted the sky around the Hueys.

"Kill me," Fullmer begged, "and give me some relief and put me out of my misery."

Still we found nothing but old VC signs and empty bunkers. Even the four VC graves we found were empty of both corpses and weapons. Sergeant Richardson broke the platoon for C-rats in the jungle alongside a canal.

"What you having, Fullmer?"

"Rat entrails in monkey-blood sauce. What you having, farm boy?"

"Leech puree over pig assholes."

The grunts started in on Colonel Hackworth, as they did at every opportunity. Soldier morale was at that point in the war when every problem with an officer called for but one solution—frag the bastard. Someone in the company was supposedly offering an $800 bounty for the commander's head, no questions asked. A boonie rat had thought to collect it by shooting down the C&C chopper, but was admonished for it because innocent crew could be killed.

"It's a matter of survival, *our* survival," went the argument. "Someone is going to shoot him. Hackworth is going to be dead meat within the next week or so."

Gass the farm boy spotted a grenade trip wire stretched between two trees almost in the center of the platoon's perimeter. Cold silence descended. Everybody stared. Sotello continued eating, too tired and hungry to care, like everyone else.

"It has to be disarmed," someone finally pointed out.

Excuses started.

"I ain't paid to do demolitions," the farm boy alibied.

"I don't have no demo MOS either," L.J. declared. He had set in his machine gun and was digging into his C-rats.

Skinny little Arles Brown, acting as Henderson's assistant gunner for the day, lay back exhausted with his head resting on L.J.'s knee. "It's against my religion," he said, although he probably hadn't been to church since he was eight years old.

"I disarmed the last one," Hogue said.

Mario Sotello summed up the consensus: "I do not give a shit. It is not hurting me. I will not hurt it."

The damned thing could have disabled half the platoon if it had detonated. We couldn't leave it there to tag the next platoon that came along. I clambered slowly to my feet. "If no one else has the balls . . ."

"Doc—" Sergeant Richardson began.

"I can handle it, Sergeant."

The platoon stopped eating, stopped moving, stopped talking, as I squatted warily to look the trap over. Nothing complicated about it: Grenade secured about knee high to one tree with a nearly invisible wire tied around the spoon and stretched to the next tree. Pull the wire, the wire released the spoon. *Boom!*

Carefully I grasped the grenade and spoon before freeing the trip wire.

Arles Brown's canteen froze halfway to his mouth and remained there. Tension sweat beaded cold on my forehead, even though I now had the spoon trapped so that, theoretically, the grenade could not explode. But gooks could be tricky with secondary timing mechanisms and other evil devices that would detonate when disturbed.

The grenade came loose easily enough. So far, so good. Guardian angel, were you watching? I eased out of the perimeter, walking slowly, holding the little bomb out at arm's length and averting my face, sweating while at the same time icicles seemed to form on my skin.

I walked toward the canal, intending to pitch the grenade into the water.

I failed to see the hole in the ground. I plunged forward.

"Oh, *shit!*" someone bellowed.

Even as I went down and buried my face in the wet humus, I hurled the grenade as far as I could across the canal. GIs dived for earth.

Nothing happened. A dud.

I got up, brushed myself off, and sauntered back into the perimeter. "Dale, you eating your pound cake?"

"Take it, Doc. Take anything you want."

Just before dawn, I stood on the pickup zone at base camp and waited for the helicopters to eagle-flight us in to intercept five VC sampans that had been spotted on a canal. All around me small groups of restless, voiceless men were yawning, coughing, shuffling their feet, adjusting their gear, checking equipment, counting grenades and magazines. Far off, I heard the stuttering noise beating toward us as the slicks rushed in like bumblebees in a panic, darting down to us.

They touched. I sprinted forward with Sergeant Richardson, RTO Fullmer, and three other grunts and clambered on board. The door gunner hung over his slung M60 with bloodshot eyes, clenched teeth, and shaky hands. Doors had been removed to make the aircraft lighter. Each bird held six infantrymen. I sat on the floor.

The rotor yanked us into the sky. Rushing through the cool predawn air in a bouncing helicopter, among armed men, toward a hot landing zone filled with machine-gun fire and falling artillery. Moonlight reflecting off rivers and canals produced an exotically beautiful spiderweb below us. Thin layers of shimmering silver mist and fog lay in the low spots.

Suddenly the choppers dropped low and made a false insertion to confuse the enemy, if he was watching. Then they bounced back into the dawn-thinning sky and surged toward the LZ. My heart pumped adrenaline as if through a fire hose. I tumbled out of the chopper, clutching my rifle in one hand and my aid bag in the other, fell flat, and wriggled for a low spot. I listened. Were we taking fire? I couldn't hear incoming. I lifted my head. Shouldn't somebody be doing something? Giving directions?

It was a cold LZ. Another dry hole. A whistle blew. Shadowy forms rose all around me like lumps of clay on resurrection day. I spotted Sergeant Richardson and identified Fullmer by the antenna growing out of his back and his sweet-talking into the mike, giving and receiving good radio check. I joined the command post element as First Platoon waded across a river to our right flank and swept south along the far bank while the Third Platoon and Svatek's Second Platoon followed the near bank.

"Where the hell *are* them little yellow bastards?" the farm boy fretted.

I didn't know which was worse—knowing they were out there somewhere and not being able to find them, or *finding them.*

Sunrise came and there was something almost mystical about it after the cold, damp night. For some odd reason, I felt wonderful. It was the beginning of a new day, a new adventure, the first day of the rest of my life. I exulted in watching American forms gradually emerge out of dawn's grayness to catch the first full rays of the sun's golden warmth. GIs moved quietly all around me, only their hel-meted heads and their shoulders visible above the grass. Only an hour earlier I had felt alone and vulnerable, unable to see anyone.

"White boy, what you grinnin' about?" L.J. demanded.

"Henderson," I replied, "it's going to be a good day."

"Doc, you are crazier than I thought you was."

Craziness in an individual was all right, sometimes. It was craziness in the world that bothered me. Like politicians arguing over the shape of peace negotiations tables mouth after month while soldiers kept killing each other.

That afternoon the platoon approached a stand of trees growing like an oasis out of the prairie. A rare breeze riffled the grasses and poked its silent nose into the trees and sniffed around the ruins of an abandoned enemy base camp that had been bombed by U.S. B-52s.

Huge, deep craters pockmarked the camp. It looked as if flaming meteors had streaked in from space to scorch, burn, pound, and rip apart. Even those few trees left standing were dead, their leaves hanging shriveled and brown from them, like dead bats.

Everything was dead. No crickets chirped, no birds sang, no mosquitoes hummed. Only silence, into which the platoon, strung out as though each soldier were alone in an alien world, entered with Marty Miles on point. Entered into a deep, fearful silence that none in the platoon dared disturb.

Our slow feet kicked up rust-colored dust that coated the dead forest. The low afternoon sunbeams turned the dust cloud a brilliant eerie red. GIs entered among the destroyed bunkers like kids into a Halloween spook house, prepared to bolt at the first sign of a ghost or goblin. I thought of Druids, of voodoo practices, of ancient cemeteries.

"I've heard of this stuff, but this is the first time I've seen it," Fullmer whispered, awed. "It's a defoliant. Agent Orange."

33

From *Facts On File,* September 19–25, 1968:

Defoliation Reports. U.S. officials asserted at a news conference in Saigon Sept. 20 that the American defoliation of selected areas of South Vietnam was "a complete success," had caused no harmful effect on human or animal life and had yielded no evidence of significant alteration to the country's ecology. In another report made public at the news conference, a U.S. Agriculture Department official, Dr. Fred H. Tschirley, said, however, defoliants had resulted in "undeniable ecologic change," that the change was not irreversible but that "recovery may take a long time."

According to the U.S. officials: The spraying of chemicals to destroy the forest and jungle cover used by Communist forces and to expose their supply routes to aerial observation had "unquestionably saved allied lives." About 3,500 square miles, or 5% of South Vietnam, had been defoliated during the war. The U.S. had spent $34 million on defoliation in 1967, and the 1968 campaign was being maintained on a similar level.

34

"Doc? Doc, wake up."

"Yeah, Fullmer. I'm awake. What is it?"

"Bravo Four-six needs to talk to you."

Sergeant Svatek, now of Second Platoon, was on the horn. "Doc, Hudson needs some help. Something has bit one of our guys. His eyes are swelling shut, his lips are as big as balloons, and he's having trouble breathing."

"I'm on my way." Bravo Company had set up interlocking ambush positions with its three platoons. Sergeant Richardson guided me to Second's perimeter, where another guide met me in the dark. I heard rasping, like the horn blaring on a deuce, while I was still fifty yards out. Sounded like the guy was in a bad way.

Svatek and several other GIs were crowded around a soldier lying on the ground, illuminating him with their redlensed flashlights while their medic, Rick Hudson, knelt working over the patient. Hudson's helmet lay nearby, and his aid bag was open. Sweat dripped from the dark cowlick that perpetually fell across his brow. His eyes met mine, pleading: What the hell can we do?

The guy couldn't have been tagged by a bamboo viper, the two-step snake—take two steps after being bitten and you fell over dead. That meant an insect. Spider or something. God only knew what kind of poisonous creepy-crawlies inhabited this shitbag country. One thing for sure, though: he was having an allergic anaphylactic reaction that could puff up his brain, close off his trachea, and suffocate him to death. Severe respiratory distress.

The guy was going to die unless we did something quickly.

Hudson had proved himself a good medic, both in the First Platoon when he replaced me and now in the Second

131

Platoon. Neither of us, however, was adequately equipped to handle a problem like this. We had neither epinephrine nor antihistamines, drugs of choice infused by I.V. for a severe attack like this. We had Benadryl capsules, but oral antihistamines were probably of little value at this stage.

Nevertheless, it was something. We had to do more than simply react to symptoms. I forced a capsule down the kid's throat with my finger. His throat was so swollen it was like trying to push a bean into a mouse's ass. Every muscle in the guy's body was strung as tight as drying rawhide. His body arched off the ground as he desperately tried to suck air into his starving lungs. Neck muscles stood out like cords. Veins popped out on his forehead, ready to explode. He sounded like a rooster trying to crow.

"A dust-off is on the way," someone advised. "ETA in ten minutes."

That might be too late.

"Better be prepared to do a trache," I warned Hudson. He paled.

I'm sure I turned just as pale as I tried to recall the procedure for performing an emergency tracheostomy. Instructors had written the steps on the blackboard at Fort Sam. We'd had to memorize them. There had been a test.

I rummaged in my aid bag for a blade. Death had crept up in the middle of the night, seeking another victim. I wouldn't let Death win—not without a fight.

Death. The end. Finality. In Vietnam it could come at any time and in any form. Slowly, stalking like a predator hiding in the shadows. Or swiftly, in a blinding flash of light or the shriek of a bullet. Bullets, shrapnel, concussion, and fire were the common harbingers of death in a combat zone. But death could come in many other forms. Even as an insect, a bug.

"Where *is* that goddamn dust-off?" Hudson chanted, echoing my own anxiety.

The soldier's high-pitched shrieking.

Then silence.

He stopped breathing. He relaxed.

I checked his pulse. I couldn't find anything. I felt for his heartbeat. Nothing.

Don't die on us!

I hammered the meaty side of my fist into the soldier's chest with such force that his arms and legs flopped off the ground. I took a deep breath, placed my mouth over his and blew against that oh-so-tiny opening in his throat. I willed the air to go through.

"I've got a pulse!" Hudson exclaimed.

The guy began crowing again. Oh, that sweet sound.

Tension sweat poured down our faces, dripping onto the suffering GI.

Don't die on us.

"No pulse!" Hudson snapped.

Again I hammered him. Hudson blew past the constriction into his lungs. We took turns performing one-man and two-man CPR. There! A beat . . . and another!

Twice more his heart ceased beating and respirations stopped. Both times we brought him back to life. It was as if we *willed* his life not to desert him and us. We hung on to that weak ghost of his spirit and massaged it and encouraged it and cursed death.

The company commander, Lieutenant Knapp, and the other soldiers crowded close with their red flashlight beams, then drew back and watched solemnly as the drama played itself out on the dark, dangerous banks of a canal on the Plain of Reeds in enemy territory.

"The chopper's landing!"

Hudson and I continued CPR as we loaded the GI into the belly of the Huey; then the dust-off medics took over. The guy was still breathing, his heart still beating, as the bird lifted and we watched it streak away into the night like a dragonfly.

Because Sergeant Richardson seldom said much, what he *did* say meant something. "You did what you could, Doc," he said. I felt his respect for me. I would never let him down.

"But was it enough?" I asked.

I waited up for the rest of the night to find out. I volunteered for radio watch. Approaching daylight found me huddled over Fullmer's PRC-25 at the platoon area's command post. I watched with little interest as the sky lightened. There was nothing mystical about the start of this day.

I had lost Forte on Widow Maker Alley. Now I thought I might have lost another patient.

The word came. Dong Tam had been too far.

I wilted.

So instead of going to Dong Tam, the dust-off took him to Moc Hoa, a nearby Special Forces camp where Doc Holley had set up a battalion aid station in response to Lieutenant Colonel Hackworth's demand that every swinging dick in his battalion go to the field.

The guy was okay and would be back with his unit before nightfall.

Sergeant Richardson lifted his eyes to the clear morning sky. Colonel Hackworth's command chopper was already flying. The man was always first up and last down.

"I wonder," Richardson drawled, "if that guy last night would have made it if the colonel hadn't insisted everybody go to the field, including doctors."

35

Operations on the Plain of Reeds continued to be grueling work while Lieutenant Colonel Hackworth's Hardcore Battalion remained a pitiful 40 percent below strength with only 383 men available for combat. Bravo Company had 99 soldiers. Morale remained low. Furtive whisperings about fragging Hackworth persisted. The sarcasm of the inventive GIs turned the saluting exchange of "Hardcore, sir" and "No fucking slack" into "Hardporn, sir" and "No slack fucking."

Few of the grunts had ever actually seen the colonel, except from a distance, but his orders and policies rode us hard and put us away wet. We felt the presence of an ethereal leader off somewhere in the sky above us, out of the reach of ordinary mortals. It was always, "Colonel Hackworth ordered this," or "Colonel Hackworth ordered that."

He cut the troops no slack, even on infrequent stand-downs at the Moc Hoa Special Forces camp. If we weren't on combat patrols, we were training for combat patrols.

Life in the 4/39th merged into a blur of hardships and uncertain activities. We hunted for the enemy but never seemed to find him in any numbers. We traveled so light that real food was only a distant memory. Letters from home provided a grunt's lifeline between reality and the Twilight Zone. Letters had a hard time catching up to us, though. I used some of mine for toilet paper; you had to have your priorities.

Henderson and Gass, the machine gunners, dropped in their tracks during a march break. Insects in vicious clouds swarmed their heads. Henderson looked around. Nothing out there except foul water, a sea of reeds, and distant clumps of trees.

"This looks just like the Florida Everglades," said Jim Sweeney, the FNG volunteer who had joined the platoon in my absence and been made a machine gunner. "Reckon it's possible we've somehow walked all the way to Florida?"

"Shee-it," L.J. scoffed. "We don't know where we are, where we goin', what we goin' to do when we get there, when we goin' to get there, how long we goin' to be there, nor when we goin' to be back."

KITDFBS.

Fullmer was fingering his PRC-25. "That about sums it up," he agreed. "If Charlie captures us and tortures us to make us talk, he is going to think the Recondos are some tough dudes, because we don't know anything to tell him even if we wanted to."

"Mushrooms," said the farm boy.

"Common boonie rats," Faulkenberg said.

"Hardcore Recondo," Ron Miller cut in.

"No fucking slack," said Mario Sotello, snickering. "No fucking slack is what the Hardcore Battalion gets. But at least we got new boots."

They were jungle boots with an innovative design. Canvas tops with drainage holes along the soles so the water could be pushed out as we walked. Pieces of steel had been inserted into the soles to deflect spikes and punji stakes. They were supposed to keep our feet drier. Only rubber waders could have kept us even semidry on the Plain of Reeds.

I initiated a new routine for staying awake during my shifts on radio watch at the platoon CP. I started it on an exceptionally lovely night when First set up adjacent to a wide river, in a large parklike area studded with graceful palms. The rising moon turned the river into a wonderful silver highway, which made it easy to see any enemy trying to cross it.

My routine consisted of eating at night instead of during the day. It never occurred to me that you couldn't hear as well as normal while chewing or that digestion dulled the senses. I started the watch by unlacing one boot and removing it and the wet sock. I massaged the foot carefully, dried it, put on a clean sock and then the boot, then repeated the procedure with the other foot.

After that, I received situation reports from the squads and passed on the platoon sitrep to Company. I had actually become comfortable using the radio. Then I began eating.

I packed each meal in a sock in the order I intended to eat it. I never knew which sock contained which meal, so it was always a pleasant little surprise. A little like Christmas every night. I usually began with a pecan roll, followed by a can of crackers and some plastic cheese, then a can of fruit topped off with a Charlie-rat main course and perhaps a Care package treat from home.

I opened each can slowly and carefully so as not to make any noise while I kept my eyes open for Charlie ghosting around. I forced myself to concentrate on eating and observing. I seldom permitted myself the luxury of thinking about home or my terminal marriage. Dianne could not divorce me as long as I was in a combat zone, according to the Soldiers and Sailors Relief Act. Nevertheless, she no longer even pretended to write me letters, and the army took my power of attorney away from her. We were at a stalemate. We weren't even arguing about the shape of the negotiating table.

It took me forty-five minutes to complete the routine, at the end of which I awoke either Lieutenant Keppel, Sergeant Richardson, or Fullmer for his watch. I repeated the procedure on my next guard duty. It provided some stability in otherwise shifting, uncertain conditions.

For breakfast I drank a canteen cup of cocoa warmed over a piece of C4 to knock off the chill of a damp night. I enjoyed watching dawn gradually light up the eastern sky to a warm glow of shell pink and then red as the sun came to the wet grass plains. Elephant grass, palms, river—they all coalesced into an oil painting by one of the Impressionists.

I held morning sick call. Doc Evans was in. Trench foot, insect bites, sore throats, coughs, hemorrhoids, minor scratches and cuts. Skin and gastrointestinal medications took up much of the room in my aid bag. Tinactin for superficial fungal infections and bacitracin for minor bacterial infections.

Field medics had all been issued a drug called griseofulvin in 500mg pills and instructed to *personally* dose each man in his platoon with 2000mg a day, four times the normal dosage. It was an antifungal chemical preparation that was supposed to incorporate itself gradually into the epidermis over a four- to six-week regime and reduce skin fungus diseases, but it made some of the men feel nauseated. Four times a day I went from man to man and stood over him to make sure he swallowed his pills, the same as I did once a week with malaria tabs.

"Doc, have mercy on us," Sotello begged.

"God gives mercy. I give pills."

Sometimes it seemed Vietnam was a war not so much against a seldom seen human enemy as against ubiquitous fungi and bacteria and parasites and rot. Plain old rot.

The beginning of the day was never complete until the tall Oklahoman, Sergeant Richardson, rode his long legs along the platoon perimeter, saying, "Saddle up, people."

Grumbling and bitching, we humped into our rucks and checked our weapons as we lined out for the day's mission. Battlefield pawns on a big chessboard, worn to nerves and rawhide by the grueling pace. Colonel Hackworth, we howled, was killing us.

A sea of thick black mud and water and grass as sharp as knife blades. Mud sucked at our boots until each step required superhuman strength to extract one foot and swing the other foot forward, where it completed one cycle and started another by being sucked into the mud. There was often nothing dry to sit on to rest. We took our breaks standing up in the mud and knee-deep sewage like newly planted rice shoots while the hot sun baked our brains. Had we taken hostile fire, we would have drowned trying to find cover.

U.S. Air Force fast movers dropped bombs on clumps of forest where Hackworth thought VC might be hiding. The explosions thundered in series to topple trees, start fires, belch volcanic flame and smoke into the sky, and ripple the water around our knees. When the platoons entered the lingering smoke, we found—nothing. Not even old bunkers or trenches. We lined out to cover more ground in a ceaseless search for ghosts.

The pace was getting to the men. They started snapping at each other. Even Henderson, normally even-tempered and joking, was heard to snarl at his little buddy Arles Brown: "Keep your white ass outta my way, man, or I'll knock your scrawny dick in the dirt. Hear what I'm sayin'?"

Tall, skinny soul brother Slim Holleman complained that Vietnam was a white man's conspiracy to get brothers killed off in a war.

The farm boy grabbed Holleman's black arm and thrust his sun-reddened one next to it. "Cut the shit, Holleman. What color am I, huh? My white cracker ass is right out here with yours."

Indefatigable Sergeant Richardson prowled up and down the ranks, soothing tempers, offering encouragement. Lieutenant Keppel was starting to catch on to Richardson's methods; First Platoon was fortunate to have two of the best combat leaders in the 4/39th.

No one in the platoon wanted to walk point. Patrolling out ahead of the element, acting as its advance eyes and ears, constantly on the lookout for booby traps, punji stakes, and possible VC ambushes, compounded the stress. Some men had nervous breakdowns on point. Everyone knew point was expendable. He would be the first to get it if we ran into trouble. Point could be a man's death warrant.

First Platoon rotated on point. Sergeant Richardson and Lieutenant Keppel were reluctant to order anyone to take the position. They listened to an endless variety of creative and colorful excuses.

"Sarge, I got a Dear John. My mind just ain't on things today."

"Sarge, I got blisters. I mean, I got *blisters.*"

"Sarge, I've lost my glasses and can't see shit."

"I'll take it," I finally volunteered. Medics weren't supposed to walk point.

Sergeant Richardson hesitated.

"I'll take it for a while, okay?" I insisted.

There had been no booby traps or enemy sign all morning. Richardson studied me. "God damn, Doc."

Then he fitted me with a heavy flak jacket lined with bulletproof steel plates.

"Keep it fastened," he said.

I stepped out ahead as the platoon penetrated a large wooded area. I flipped the selector switch on my M16 to full automatic. A slack man and two flank guards took up the patrol fifteen yards behind me. Fifteen yards behind them came the rest of the platoon spread out and staggered out at five-meter intervals. The green caterpillar.

Sotello could sweat off five pounds a day walking point. Now I understood why. I was drenched and stinking in my own sweat as I eased through the deep shade of the forest. Everything around me appeared threatening—the ominous shifting of shadows, the low vicious gossiping of a breeze hot out of hell's mouth, the menacing monologues of insects, even the rasping sound of my own breathing.

All my senses came alive. It was as if I could count the molecules that made up the earth. The veneer of thousands of years of human civilization was stripped away, and I was at the dawn of human existence, the first caveman venturing through a hostile world of man-eaters. Thirst, hunger, heat, humidity, pain, divorce—all ceased to exist, replaced by raw survival instincts and the telltale cotton mouth. Me against them.

Take one step. Scan the way ahead for trip wires, earth that appeared freshly turned, footprints, displaced foliage, movement, glint of metal.

Listen for footsteps, crawling, the snap of a twig, a smothered cough. Listen to my own instincts.

Sniff for the distinctive Vietnamese odor of *nuoc mam*, rice and fish.

Take another step. Look, listen, smell, consult my instincts.

By the end of the day I was so spent I craved nothing more than to lie down and sleep for the rest of the week.

Dr. Holley found out about my walking point and blew up on the next company stand-down at the Special Forces camp. I had tried to avoid him, knowing what his reaction would be, but I had to go to him to be sutured after I sliced my finger open to the bone while taking an outdoor shower: a VC spy had concealed a razor blade inside a bar of soap.

"Evans, you are assigned to the platoon to take care of the ill and the wounded," the surgeon lectured sternly as he sewed up my finger. "There'd be nobody to patch *you* up if you got wounded. You've become an outstanding field medic. Let the other men do their job; you do yours."

"I've learned my lesson," I admitted. "I've acquired a lot more respect for the point man."

Doc Holley caught my eyes hard and held them. "Dan," he said, "I want you to go home alive and in one piece when this is all over. Don't you dare go out there and commit suicide by being foolish. Most Medal of Honor winners receive their medals posthumously."

36

Little James "Billy" Scott was nineteen years old and weighed about 100 pounds after being soaked by a monsoon all night. His oversize helmet banged on his head like a loose hubcap. His big dark eyes were those of a young deer caught in the open away from its forest home. Billy was a conscientious objector, like Rick Hudson, but not the Browner type. He was a kid of deep religious convictions who simply could not carry a weapon. Conscientious objectors, when drafted into the military, were traditionally assigned to the medical corps. Billy was given to Charlie Company of Hackworth's Hardcore Battalion.

Whenever the 4-39th stood down at the Moc Hoa Special Forces camp to catch a breather from chasing Charlie out on the Plain of Reeds, company and platoon medics normally set up canvas cots in the aid station bunker tent and slept there. I first picked up the thread of Billy Scott's story late one night in the aid tent when shrill screaming jarred me awake: "Watch out! *Watch out!*"

I rolled out of my bunk and hit the ground before I realized Billy was having one of his nightmares. I jumped up. "It's okay, Billy. Nothing's happening."

"Watch out!"

"Billy! Wake up."

His eyes bounced around like a wild pool shot. After a moment he calmed down and apologized. In his dream, VC had crossed the Cambodian border, infiltrated the base camp, and were massacring us, medics and other soldiers alike, in our sleep. Billy had similar nightmares every time he closed his eyes.

"I keep trying to ward them off," he explained shyly. "It's gotten where I'm afraid to sleep. I'm not strong like you, Dan."

I believed it required more courage to overcome great fears than simple everyday fears. Billy Scott, in my opinion, might have been the bravest man among us. He lived with terror awake and asleep, but he continued to do his job.

The battalion surgeon, Doc Holley, took all his medics under his wing when they arrived in-country, but he had taken a special interest in Scott.

"Oh, Lord," he lamented. "Where are they getting these kids? He's such a sweet little kid, almost a mama's boy. Why isn't he back home teaching Sunday school?"

Scott was so frightened when he arrived in Dong Tam from Stateside that he hid out in the base chapel for two days. Doc Holley covered for him and went to the chapel and sat down with the kid in one of the pews where Billy had been praying.

"Billy, you have to come out. You can't stay here forever."

"Dr. Holley, I'm scared to death just *being* in Vietnam. I can't help it. I've prayed over it. I believe with all my heart that I will be killed if I go to the field."

Holley kept Scott in Dong Tam for as long as he could, then moved him out to a fire support base when his confidence improved. Soon battalion admin clerks shuffled a few papers and Scott found himself replacing platoon medic Ernest Osborne in Charlie Company. Osborne was big, macho, and a good combat aid man. He punctuated his rough speech with four-letter words and carried an M16 *and* a slingshot that propelled deadly steel balls. He found himself supplanted by a skinny wide-eyed conscientious objector who toted only an aid bag half his size. The platoon leader stared. Then he shook his head and walked away.

That was just like the army. I had wanted to go to the field and the army contrived to keep me in the rear; Billy needed to stay in the rear, and where did the army send him?

Scott's first mission was a night ambush, as my first had been. Shivering from dread, battling against the jitters scratching around like a live animal inside his bowels, the new doc with a squad of Hardcore boonie rats set up their ambush patrol alongside a peaceful river.

It was a quiet moonless night. Billy worked to keep his mind occupied. He couldn't sleep when it was his half-squad's turn. He sat hunched on perimeter, peering through a starlight scope that collected available light and permitted its user to see in the dark.

Suddenly he caught his breath. Movement in the greenish light of the scope picture. He kept watching, thinking it might have been his imagination, hoping it had been.

He saw a Vietnamese man squatting in the undergrowth. Black clothing. Black sweat rag tied around his head. Short, stubby AK-47 with the characteristic swept-forward banana clip.

The VC crept toward the American position.

Billy reported what he had detected to his squad leader. The squad went on full 100 percent alert. Everyone scanned the terrain out front bush by bush, tree by tree.

Nothing. The squad soon convinced itself that the FNG—the scared-shitless FNG—was probably seeing shadows. The squad relaxed. Even Scott himself was beginning to think he hadn't seen a VC.

Shortly afterward the night erupted in gunfire and terror.

Attacking VC caught the GIs by surprise and swarmed over the ambush position with the rapid-fire winking and blasting of their Chicom AKs. A Vietcong, the tree branches in his helmet silhouetted against the stars, charged at Scott, squeezing his weapon into full automatic.

Billy dropped to his knees and began praying. Flame blossomed point-blank. Lead slammed into the ground around the skinny medic.

He pitched forward, face down on the earth.

Bullets kicked dirt into his eyes.

He lost all control over his muscles. Horror melted him into the ground. He lay unmoving, as in death. He thought he might not be breathing.

Terror turned to something beyond even that as he felt the enemy soldier squat and quickly rifle his pockets. The sour-fish stench of *nuoc mam* almost made him retch.

He managed to control the trembling in his limbs until the VC melted away. Then his trembling let him know he was still alive. He lay there, playing dead, until the firing ceased and the enemy left. Tears streaming down his boyish face, brave little Doc Billy mustered some inner strength fed by the springs of his religion and, instead of fleeing or hiding or breaking down entirely, found his aid bag and went to work. Dead and wounded GIs lay scattered everywhere in the jungle.

When rescuers arrived, they found the little medic covered with blood and gore, treating the survivors and offering spiritual comfort to the dying. His patients lay bandaged around him. Doc Billy knelt, gave thanks to God for his deliverance, and prayed for the souls of those whom God had seen fit not to deliver. From that night on, the GIs in Billy Scott's platoon referred to him as *their* medic.

As for Billy, he would probably always have nightmares about that night.

37

Lieutenant Roger Keppel, the platoon leader, and Sergeant Richardson hauled us out of our bunks at Moc Hoa. Before we were fully awake and could even say "immediate reaction force" without stuttering, we were one. All we knew as we grabbed our gear and raced to the helicopter pickup zone was that some other battalion had stumbled into a shitpot full of NVA and was screaming for help. First Platoon was closer to the battle site than the other Bravo platoons, which were out in the bush on missions. Additional reinforcements would be inserted as they became available, but right now a single platoon would have to take up the slack.

It looked as if the enemy had finally made a stand.

Breathless from the mad rush across the darkened base camp and the prospect of a real battle instead of the cat-and-mouse games of the bush, boonie rats scrambled into four slicks and were yanked into the night sky. The platoon went hurtling through the night. Grunts inside the choppers stared out the open doors. The darkness hid wide scared eyes and grim pale faces.

The battleground came dramatically into view. Henderson pointed at luminous jade and vermilion tracers crisscrossing the black landscape in spectacular streams of death. Balls of white flame—grenade and rocket explosions—burst singly and in clumps, making the air vibrate and coming to us as distant thunder. I felt an involuntary shudder from Fullmer, crowded in on one side of me. Sergeant Richardson, on the other side, checked his weapon.

"Lock and load, people," he shouted. "Hot LZ!"

The platoon had been joking about the war while on

stand-down during the day at Moc Hoa. Fentress and Faulkenberg had started it. Some of the others soon joined in.

"Okay, sports fans," went the chatter, "we're now at Moc Hoa U., and it looks like it's going to be a great evening to resume the Army–Gook U. duel. Both sides have suffered from injuries during the season, but they appear to be recovering. I can safely say we're going to have some real fireworks. . . . I'm Recondo Fentress, and I have with me here tonight someone all you Army fans will remember. Battling Mario Sotello, how do the opposing sides look to you?"

"Well, Recondo, let us look at it this way. Gook U. doesn't have the size of Army, and they appear hesitant to meet on the open field. But they do have an excellent ground attack at times, and these little guys just don't seem to know when they're licked."

It wasn't a joking matter anymore. Now the jokes seemed to have been prophetic.

Night wind howled past the open doors of the Huey slicks. The helicopters hung momentarily at altitude, then suddenly darted down to just above the ground. I felt the exhilarating rush of speed and danger as the choppers charged toward the battlefield. Rockets and grenades exploded like strings of fireworks. Forest and underbrush flashed into momentary relief at the center of the detonations.

I thought we were going to land directly in the colored river of red and green tracers.

"Let's go in like Recondos and save their asses!" Sergeant Richardson yelled.

"It has done hit the fan down there," Henderson shouted back.

The choppers landed to the rear of the action. A soldier using his helmet to shield his light and make it directional guided us into a clearing overgrown with elephant grass. A number of shadowy figures appeared, some supported or carried by others, and tried to clamber aboard the Hueys even as First Platoon offloaded, spilling into the grass and spreading out. I was aware of stray tracer rounds zipping overhead like angry supersonic fireflies and the overpowering background chatter of automatic weapons and exploding grenades.

"We need a medic," pleaded a sergeant who had his arm around another soldier, supporting him.

The wounded soldier was a medic. Blood-soaked bandages girdled his torso.

"Morphine?" he begged.

I sacked his pockets for the five morphine Syrettes every medic carried. I injected one into his leg and kept the other four. He wouldn't be needing them.

The choppers were in a hurry to lift off. I helped the sergeant load the wounded medic into the nearest chopper. The Hueys jumped back into the air and skimmed the trees as they darted away from the battle.

"Can you come with me?" the sergeant requested. "I've got guys wounded in the woods on the other side of the canal. My company's pinned down."

Sergeant Richardson and the lieutenant were holding a quick conference with an officer from the on-ground battalion, preparatory to feeding First Platoon into the defensive perimeter.

"Get back to the platoon as soon as you can, Doc," Richardson urged. "We may be needing you."

After a quick check on the Saint Christopher medal around my neck and the briefest of silent prayers to my guardian angel, I fell in behind the other sergeant and two infantrymen. We headed across the clearing and entered a wood line. Soon we came to a canal. We dropped to our bellies. There was fighting on the other side of the canal. I also heard heavier fighting out of sight on our left flank. There seemed to be nothing much happening on our side of the canal at the moment.

"Wait here," the sergeant instructed. "I'll wade across and bring the WIAs back to you here."

The two jittery grunts and I burrowed into ferns and rotted downed trees. I heard more helicopters to the rear buzzing into the landing zone to offload troops. The fierce firefight to our left seemed to have dropped back farther behind us. A steady stream of red tracers poured from the reinforced American perimeter while green enemy tracers answered.

The battle was moving up the canal toward us. Bullets

whined and cracked and chipped at the foliage, seeking flesh.

"Jesus, protect us," one of my companions whispered in soft prayer as we flattened ourselves and tried to become a part of the earth.

Green tracers began flying across the canal from out of the woods into which the sergeant had entered to bring back his WIAs. I guessed that meant he wouldn't be coming back.

We found ourselves trapped in no-man's-land, between the enemy fire across the canal and from our right and the GI perimeter to our left and behind us. The colored tracers flitting and caroming and ricocheting through the trees were actually quite beautiful, though deadly. My heart raced.

"We can't stay here. We'll be killed," my infantry escort shouted. "What are we going to do?"

"You can pray," I snapped. I didn't know what to do either.

I understood now what it meant to be caught between a rock and a hard place. It would have been suicide to try to rejoin our own lines. We had no radio with which to contact our side. Without some way of announcing our approach, we were only shadows easily mistaken for the enemy. If the VC didn't cut us down, our own guys would.

Trapped in no-man's-land, we hugged the earth like jealous lovers while the battle intensified. I wondered if I could treat my own sucking chest wound. Once—an eternity ago, it seemed—I would have felt faint at even the thought.

As if being trapped between opposing ground forces wasn't menacing enough, a fierce little U.S. Cobra gunship suddenly appeared like a giant mosquito. It fired a pair of rockets whose irregular contrails flew so close to our heads they seemed to suck our lungs into a vacuum. The rockets exploded, shaking the earth and raining forest debris onto our helmets.

The Cobra darted around above the crisscrossing tracers, making itself an elusive target. It made a wide chandelle over the firefight, throwing its shadow against the night sky. Then the wicked little bird dropped and followed the narrow canal back in, all its armaments blazing and smoking. Flashbangs in strings detonated along both banks of the canal. A geyser of water erupted from the canal, soaking us.

Green tracers searched for the little airborne fighter with the big kick as it rose into the stars and circled high for another run. It was working over no-man's-land between the Americans and the VC to prevent an enemy attack. It just so happened that three terrified troops were hiding in the bushes of the chopper's target area.

"Oh, Lord!" one of the grunts next to me wailed. "It's coming again."

The Cobra was a vicious-looking machine, even in the dark and even when its thin fuselage bristling with rockets wasn't pointed at *you*. It dropped at blinding speed and pulled up short about fifty yards away. It hovered momentarily, but in that brief pause I found myself staring directly into its wicked maw.

All kinds of thoughts flashed simultaneously through my brain. I now knew how awed the VC felt when this happened to them, and for the first time since arriving in Vietnam I actually thought I was going to die. That thought left me humbled. I also recognized two options, neither of which was ideal: we could lie here and get blown to little pieces by our own airpower, or we could jump up and get blown to bigger bits by ground fire.

We were dead, as in dead meat.

No time for hesitation.

"Di-di!" I yelled, using a Vietnamese term that GIs had appropriated, which meant, more or less, "Get the hell out of Dodge. Fast."

I sprang to my feet to lead the wildest retreat of the night as the Cobra let go its fiery meteors. I had taken only about two steps, the infantrymen on my heels, before concussions from the exploding rockets picked us off the ground and deposited us into a pile of legs and arms.

Stunned but miraculously unscathed, we unscrambled ourselves and took off like Wile E. Coyote chasing the Road Runner.

I led the retreat back through the trees the way we had come minutes earlier with the sergeant. When we reached the clearing again, on the other side of which our troops had set up their defensive perimeter, we flopped onto our bellies and started low-crawling through the grass like snakes, with scarcely less speed than when we were on our feet. Aerial flares illuminated the clearing in eerie green shifting light.

Once we drew near our own lines, we lifted strident voices from the weeds in a cacophony of desperation. It must have startled the hell out of the GIs.

"We're Americans! We're American GIs out here!"

"Americans?" a hesitant voice responded.

"We're coming in. Let us in."

"Wait one. What's the password?"

"How the hell should I know?" I demanded, irritation replacing fright. "We flew in on the choppers to save your asses."

"Then what are you doing out there? Our asses aren't out there."

"Making house calls. What the hell you think we're doing—going for a stroll?"

"They might be fucking gooks pretending to be GIs," said another voice.

"Can't you tell the difference?" I shouted back. "Listen. Dodgers, White Sox, President Nixon. What does that sound like?"

"What's your outfit?"

"The 4/39th. Bravo Company," I said, answering for the three of us, to make things simple.

"Who's your commander?"

"Colonel Hackworth."

A pause. "Oh, *him*," A laugh. "Maybe you guys'd be better off staying with the VC. Come on in."

Once back into the perimeter, I straggled from position to position until I located First Platoon. Sergeant Richardson and Lieutenant Keppel had the outfit in a defensive posture, but it was not in direct contact.

"Didn't you pass on the word that we were in the wood line and would be returning?" I asked Lieutenant Keppel with an accusing edge to my voice.

"Oh, Jesus, Doc," he exclaimed. "In all the confusion I forgot you were out there."

"*Xin loi. Xin loi,*" quipped Dale Gass, the pig farmer. "So solly about that, troop. So solly."

"Don't mean nothing," I said.

38

By dawn the attacking VC had disappeared into the forest mists like ghosts, dragging most of their casualties with them. Most battles in Vietnam ended like that, at daybreak with the North Vietnamese forces pulling back and both sides licking their wounds. First Platoon had remained in reserve during the night and not participated in the fight to any great extent. Morale was high in the cool dawn as a few of the men heated up some Ranger coffee and we waited for choppers to take us back to Moc Hoa.

The battalion we had reinforced sent out scouting patrols to follow blood trails. Loaches and Hueys buzzed around trying to find the withdrawing enemy forces. Find 'em, fix 'em, and fuck 'em over. I didn't expect them to have much luck. The VC knew how to disappear. As Mao Tse-tung—"Mousey Hung"—said, they were like fishes in the sea.

I never learned what happened to the sergeant and the wounded men he wanted me to treat. I assumed he had rejoined his company and evacuated his WIAs. GI casualties in the skirmish were listed as "light," whatever that meant. They were always listed as "light." First Platoon suffered no casualties, although I had come close to getting my name listed on the board. I tried not to think about how, last night, I had almost been able to smell the corrupt one's fetid breath of death. It left me shaken, so that upon our return to Moc Hoa I slept most of the day before getting up in time for afternoon chow.

Morale was higher than I had ever seen it. I had noticed a subtle change coming over First Platoon and, by extension, over the 4/39th during the past few weeks under Colonel Hackworth's command. The men still bitched about the colonel, but talk about fragging him had all but died out.

The week before, in fact, fractious Bravo Company with its supposed bounty on the colonel's head, had fallen into a little firefight with a contingent of VC. First Platoon brought up the company's left flank as Lieutenant Knapp, the company commander, placed the outfit on skirmish line for an assault against the enemy concealed in a clump of the delta's ubiquitous nipa palms. First Platoon had therefore remained out of the mini-battle, which started with the mad clatter of M16 rifle fire and replying AK-47 chatter. Someone noticed that the battalion commander's command-and-control helicopter had landed and that Colonel Hackworth himself was leading the charge.

"Man, that mother has got some balls," L.J. conceded, "turnin' his back on *this* outfit with everybody shootin'."

Hackworth seemed to be saying to Bravo: "Shit or get off the pot. Here's my back to you. Is this the way you do it?"

As far as anyone in Bravo could remember, a battalion commander had never gotten on the ground and personally led a company in a fight. Bravo swept through the VC, killing two or three of them and suffering no casualties of our own, not even a sprained ankle. Afterward, the colonel mingled with the men. He praised Lieutenant Knapp for his professionalism and observed that the Recondos had come a long way. Everybody was on a high, like after winning a football game or something. And there in the middle of the celebration was Colonel Hackworth, a rather short, squarely built man in his late thirties with a jaw that might have been drawn with a carpenter's square, laughing and chatting with men who had sworn to kill him. The men were laughing and joking back with him.

"You know," Slim Holleman pointed out, "the man be right up there gettin' shot at with the rest of the grunts."

"Maybe he ain't so bad after all," said Faulkenberg.

At Moc Hoa, Lieutenant Knapp assembled Bravo Company in a loose formation while it was still on a high from the night's fight. The lieutenant was one of those rare officers who possessed a certain leadership charisma that compelled men to follow him. He and Doc Holley were among the few officers I respected. Bravo would have followed Knapp into hell with empty canteens. His return as commander of the Battlin' B after Lieutenant Neumann was wounded had been the best news the company had received in weeks.

While away from the company, Lieutenant Knapp had served as Colonel Hackworth's assistant battalion operations officer. Working with Colonel Hackworth, Lieutenant Knapp said now, addressing the company, he had come to know the man well. The angry grumbling against the battalion CO emanating from Bravo Company disturbed him. He wanted to set us straight about Colonel David Hackworth.

He proceeded to supply the colonel's bona fides, some of which we already knew. Colonel Hackworth, he said, had served three tours in Korea and was on his fourth tour in Vietnam. He was the most highly decorated soldier in the U.S. Army; he had won almost as many medals as Audie Murphy. Experienced officers at all levels were at a premium in Vietnam, there being so few of them. Experienced officers saved GIs' lives. Hackworth had written a book, *The Vietnam Primer*, that was the training bible for new infantry officers at West Point.

"During the short time I was Colonel Hackworth's assistant ops officer," Lieutenant Knapp continued, "I learned to respect his intensity and judgment. This battalion suffered more than five hundred casualties during the six months before he arrived. Since his arrival, the battalion's casualties have been minimal. He also got us out of security duty in the booby trap–infested area around Dong Tam."

The men listened in total silence.

"Everything Colonel Hackworth has made us do in the battalion is meant to save lives and cut down on casualties. Cleaning our weapons prevents them from misfiring in combat. Foxholes and sandbags protect us from incoming mortar rounds. Not getting fresh water at times and not always having three squares a day forces us to live off the land like the VC."

Out *G*-ing the *G*. Out guerrilla-ing the guerrilla.

The lieutenant's voice rose dramatically. "Men, Colonel Hackworth is the way for all of us to go home alive. His way is for us to become the most effective combat outfit in the entire 9th Infantry Division. We are becoming lean, mean fighting machines. By becoming the best at what we do, by striking at the VC first before he can do it to us, we minimize our losses and get the job done. Bravo Company is going to be the best damn company in the division. Bravo is going to cut a swath through Charlie that will help end this war so we can all go home."

L. J. Henderson, Fullmer, the farm boy, and I left the formation together, carrying our rifles. Carrying weapons at all times, even while in base camp, was another Hackworth order.

Henderson was almost swaggering. "Doc, what you think?" he asked, flashing his good-natured grin. "Am I lookin' lean an' mean, or what?"

"L.J., you be one bad motherfucker."

"That is us, man. We be *bad*. The Bad Battlin' B."

He paused to light a cigar.

"We *can* kick some gook ass," he said. "Hear what I'm sayin', troop?"

39

The Communist spring offensive continued with H&I—harassing and interdicting—mortar fire on American fire support bases and installations and even on Dong Tam. Bravo Company was jerked out of the grass and filthy-water hell that was the Plain of Reeds and returned to the Dong Tam area of operations to help relieve some of the pressure. We loaded into a convoy of armored personnel carriers for a sweat-producing safari to a place called Ban Long. Just another easily forgotten name of an easily forgotten shithole.

"Another place where the little yellow assholes get another chance to shoot my black ass," Henderson declared. "Hear what I'm sayin'?"

The Recondos slogged here, we slogged there. VC sneaked around in the night and mortared Dong Tam and the FSB at Vinh Kim while avoiding us. The mortaring made distant flashes on the horizon, like heat lightning, while the sounds of the explosions traveled slower across the terrain, like claps of faraway thunder.

It was a frustrating business, chasing ghosts. We searched hamlets whose inhabitants had abandoned them to hide out until activity settled back to normal chaos. We set up night observation with starlight scopes on villages whose inhabitants were believed to be sympathetic to the enemy. We patrolled deep in enemy territory, following trails along which Commies had strung red, blue, and yellow–starred Communist North Vietnamese flags and placed signs reading "Tu Dia"—"Kill Zone." We ripped down the flags, and Fentress pretended to wipe his ass with one. Bravo joined with other companies in broad sweeps and hammer-and-anvil ops.

Hardcore drove mortar attackers off Dong Tam's perimeter without seeing one verifiable enemy soldier—just three unarmed Vietnamese who shrugged and claimed they were rice farmers.

"Yeah?" Sergeant Richardson said. "Then my great-aunt is Ho Chi Minh."

We captured exactly one old betel nut–chewing mama-san.

"No fuckin' slack," Henderson quipped sarcastically. "Catchin' that old broad is goin' to turn the course of the whole war."

Rice paddy mud and frustration sent morale into another decline. Slim Holleman led the bitching. A homeboy with attitude, he thought everything in life boiled down to one thing—race. Henderson ragged him that he should transfer to Third Platoon and join the jive-assing, dope-smoking Soul Patrol.

"Vietnam ain't no war, man," Holleman erupted. "It's generalcide, it's—"

"It's *what?*" Gass whooped. *"Generalcide?"*

"Yeah, man. They killin' us off."

"You mean *genocide.*"

Holleman's thick lips went out, sensing an offense. "Generalcide," he insisted. "The generals is sendin' the black man over here to get us all killed off so we can't reproduce."

Henderson was opening a can of C-rat peaches and smoking a cigar. He laughed. He was always quick to point out absurdities. "Kind of a nigger control program," he said.

"Man, listen to your shit. You a bro', man. Don't talk like that in front of these white boys."

"The white boys are gettin' fucked up, same as we are," Henderson said.

"They is more brothers sent to Vietnam than they is white boys."

Sergeant Richardson had heard enough. "Bullshit," he interjected sharply. "That's just not true." He got up, disgusted, and walked away.

"They *is* more brothers," Holleman said, pouting.

Richardson's "Saddle up!" ended further conversation. Holleman snatched up his M16.

More patrolling. Henderson had been predicting heavy shit for weeks now, but so far not even the chopper mission to reinforce the trapped in-contact battalion qualified for his definition of "heavy shit." Dread something long enough and you almost *wanted* it to happen to get it over with and relieve the anxiety.

"It's comin'," Henderson insisted.

The platoon was strung out along the My Tho River. Word passed swiftly down the file—an open-handed knife-cut motion across the throat. *Danger.* Boonie rats dropped into hiding.

A sampan skimmed around a bend in the muddy river, the sun bright on two men paddling furiously. The dugout rode low in the water from the weight of a cargo of bananas and other produce bound either for market or to supply a VC camp. One of the Vietnamese, in black and cone-shaped hat, looked to be in his thirties or early forties; the other was a kid. We were suspicious of them, if for no other reason than that most males between the ages of seventeen and sixty had been conscripted by either the VC or the ARVN.

"Waste them if they try to *di-di*," Sergeant Richardson instructed. He stepped into the open and hailed the sampan. *"Lai dâi!* Hold up."

The men had civilian IDs. Higher-higher ordered they be brought in for questioning. Richardson tied their hands behind them, secured them together with a short line, and made them walk a few feet ahead of our point man. Better they should be blown to pieces by a booby trap than Sotello or Ron Miller or someone else in the platoon.

The elder Vietnamese was an ingratiating little character with a perpetual smile who bummed cigarettes and C-rats at every rest break. He gobbled C-rations the way the farm boy might have gone after pork chops. "Numbah one! Numbah one!" he cheered. The kid, sullen and blank-faced to begin with, grew even surlier as we passed small farm settlements that looked recently abandoned. He seemed to blame us for it; he looked as if he would cut our throats if we gave him the opportunity.

Attached to each abandoned hooch was a built-in bunker to shield the family in the event of a firefight or mortar attack. What a hell of a way to have to live, I thought. Next to the huts sat enormous clay jars used for capturing monsoon rainwater for use during the dry season. I brushed aside water bugs, filled my canteen from one of the jars, and hoped two iodine tabs would be sufficient. Better than drinking sewage water from the canals and streams.

Shortly after sundown, the platoon slipped into its night ambush position. Somebody had to guard the prisoners. Lieutenant Keppel assigned the older man to me. He grinned continuously, chanting, "Numbah one! Numbah one!" as I retied his hands in front of him and then tethered him to my own wrist with a second rope. Fullmer took my weapon to prevent the prisoner's trying to grab it to make his escape.

The arrangement brought with it a problem: either I stayed up all night and watched the little man sleep or we bedded down together. The top of his head barely reached my shoulder; he weighed about as much as a medium-size German shepherd. His unimposing size and inoffensive manner decided for me.

It was another odd episode—a suspected Vietcong and an American GI lying down together to sleep like the lion and the lamb. Which one of us, I wondered, was really the lamb and which the lion?

I blew up my air mattress while my captive watched, still grinning every time I cast a glance in his direction. I pulled the Vietnamese to the ground next to me while I stretched out on the mattress and drew my poncho liner up to my chin. The prisoner wore only thin black cotton pajamas. He curled himself into a ball on the ground next to me, like a leashed dog sleeping at the foot of its master.

The cold tropical night settled over both of us like a damp blanket. I felt him shivering like a wet dog. I tried to ignore him. But then I couldn't sleep.

"Oh, what the hell."

I shared my poncho liner with him.

"You two married or what?" Fullmer joked.

Sometime in the middle of the night, I woke myself up shivering. The prisoner had all the cover. I wondered if it was some kind of omen.

40

The word said something big was coming down. Bravo Company received orders to return to Fire Support Base Moore. First Platoon humped four klicks across swamp and jungle to reach Highway 4, where trucks were supposed to pick us up. Instead, a ratty old Vietnamese bus loaded with pigs, chickens, and people who had infinite patience for this kind of warfare hit a mine that lifted it into the air and blasted a crater in the road big enough in which to hide a cyclo and its passengers and driver. Body parts and pieces of bus blew everywhere.

The trucks couldn't pick us up because of the blocked road. We had to hoof eight more klicks to reach the FSB.

"Gooks'll do any damned thing, even get themselves blown up, to fuck up our day," Farm Boy complained.

Lieutenant Knapp assembled the Bravos for warning orders from Battalion.

"We've been tasked with a special mission for the next three days," Knapp explained. "You'll be issued LRRPs instead of C's." LRRPs—long-range reconnaissance-patrol rations, pronounced "lurps"—were freeze-dried cooked meals weighing only a fraction of equivalent C-ration meals. "We'll be traveling light. You'll share one LRRP for every two men per meal."

Now Hackworth was going to starve us to death.

"We'll be out in Indian country for three days," the lieutenant continued. "Radio transmissions will be kept to a minimum. All the civilians in the AO have been ordered out. We'll be in a free fire zone. Any asshole you see is fair game."

Whatever else Hackworth might be, he knew how to mold warriors. I'd never seen Bravo Company so fired up as it prepared for sweep-and-destroy into the heart of enemy territory. A three-day marathon during which Hackworth apparently hoped to drive the VC and NVA operating in the area to bay and *make* them fight. Even Slim Holleman camouflage-painted his face with the rest of us; I hadn't camouflaged since basic training. I also strapped a knife to the calf of my leg, wore a drive-on rag around my head beneath my helmet and tied strips of cloth around my calves to help keep the leeches from crawling up my legs. Horror stories about leeches crawling into GIs' anuses and urinary tracts gave me the creeps.

Fullmer made love to his radio, cleaning it, replacing the batteries and headset, and calling for radio checks, while the rest of the platoon counted grenades and ammo, cleaned weapons, and wrote quick letters home. I posted a letter to my folks and received a last letter from Dianne in response to the army's having stripped her of my power of attorney:

Dan,
   . . . I've talked several times to my lawyer and I can get a divorce in three months.

No, she couldn't. She couldn't divorce me until I returned from Vietnam.

The only thing is, my parents have asked me to wait until you come here in the States and then for me to file. In the meantime, you can do what you want. As far as I'm concerned, you're not my husband and I'm not your wife—only by a minor legal rule.

Dianne

"They over there sleepin' in soft warm beds with Jody the draft dodger," said L.J. Henderson, "an' they ain't never thinkin' that maybe we won't *never* come home."

"Don't mean nothing," I said.

I thought she could have waited until I returned stateside to slip me the shaft. I wadded up the letter and shoved it into my ruck. I read it later and felt sad, but for the moment I had to concentrate on the mission, keep things together. My primary purpose as platoon doc was to get my men and myself out of this war in the condition in which we arrived. I simply had to dismiss Dianne and the rest of the real world from my mind. Plenty of time for them later.

First Platoon with blackened faces, LRRPs, and a license to kill looked like a bunch of bloodthirsty savages as we piled onto and into armored personnel carriers. I thought I could hear the score from *The Sands of Iwo Jima* playing in the background. The APCs resembled steel prehistoric monsters lumbering in the hot sun, all in a staggered row.

Bravo Company unassed the APCs off the side of some highway. I figured Lieutenant Keppel knew where we were. We grunts had no reason to know. We were in Vietnam; that was enough. Boonie rats thrived on KITDFBS.

At first we followed well-worn trails. They soon gave way, however, to marshy jungle populated by nipa palms, mangrove thickets, and fig strangler vines. Firmer ground here and there, like islands covered with waist-high grass and low scrub brush, parted the noxious mists rising from the swamps. Bog sounds filtered through the high-pitched hum of each man's personal swarm of mosquitoes.

Point men armed with machetes blazed trail. We could have passed right by a battalion of NVA without seeing anything other than the emerald hell that enveloped us. Each soldier's view was limited to the man directly ahead of him and the one directly behind him. The world seemed hushed, expectant, dangerous. I thought of Joseph Conrad's *Heart of Darkness*.

Crossing the rivers was a fight. One man at a time went over. The mud on the shallow river bottoms almost sucked off our boots and trousers. We had to use bamboo poles to lift grunts out of the bogs.

The deeper, wider rivers required more time and effort. One man stripped and swam across with the end of a rope, which he attached to a tree on the far side. The rope was then stretched tight. We crossed hand over hand, dangling on the rope. The last man across untied the rope, wrapped it around his waist and was pulled across.

Sergeant Richardson halted the platoon periodically for "leech breaks." The men burned the leeches off their skin with matches or cut them off with knives, then stomped them and their own blood into the mud.

"Everything that is nasty and not wanted anywhere else in the world is shipped to Vietnam," Fullmer decided. "This country is the garbage dump of civilization."

"The asshole of the world," added Charlie Reese from Zanesville, Ohio.

"The outhouse of Asia," said Sotello.

"Can the bullshit, people," Sergeant Richardson hissed. "You want to tell every gook within ten klicks that we're out here?"

Henderson went mock wide-eyed and said around a cold cigar he was chewing on, "You mean they don't already know?"

In the afternoon the platoon approached a hooch in a jungle clearing that had been converted to a rice paddy. The hooch sat about one football field away. Point had spotted movement near it. Although our tongues were slapping our ankles, the prospect of action shot fresh adrenaline into our weary bodies. We hid in the deep shadows at the edge of the clearing and waited.

Soon we spotted him: a VC wearing back pajamas. A small man scooping rice or something into a grain sack from a large clay bowl. The soil felt wet and warm on my belly as I lay squinting through the rising heat devils, trying to make out the dink's features. The distance was too great and I couldn't quite make him into something human.

Lieutenant Keppel nodded thoughtfully and passed the word along to Frampton, one of the platoon's best marksmen: "Waste the gook."

The Vietnamese continued what he was doing, unaware that one of Colonel Hackworth's killers was drawing a bead on his heart. That living man out there, a stranger to us, was about to pass from existence. I waited with bated breath for what seemed an eternity.

Crack!

Like a green branch splintering in my spine and thrusting into my guts. The VC dropped as though the invisible fist of God had come down and smashed the base of his skull. He was dead, wasted, flies already crawling on his glazed eyes, by the time the platoon fanned out and reached the hooch. Blood oozed from his skinny abdomen and was sucked up by earth that had been feeding on human blood for decades. He looked so small and so vulnerable. What an appropriate word—"wasted."

First Platoon stared. Death made men silent. Frampton, the marksman who had shot him, took a quick glance and then walked away.

Finally Fullmer said, "Payback for Forte and Teddy Creech and Gene Harvill."

I was glad the gook was dead, if his dying meant one of us had a better chance of living. After all, he would have killed us the same way, given the chance.

The hooch was full of rice in bags ready for transport, enough to feed a VC company. Fullmer coaxed a sitrep into his PRC-25, giving our body count and describing the cache.

Sergeant Richardson turned to the platoon. "Give it a Zippo," he said.

Someone lighted a chunk of C4 and tossed it blazing onto the grass roof. Flames enveloped the tinder structure. We stared, mesmerized. It was the first time we had torched one of the little houses. I saw a strange transformation in the faces of the Recondos staring into the heat of the fired hooch and at the dead man who seemed to be settling back into the earth underneath the sun and our gaze. I felt vaguely criminal and at the same time strangely satisfied.

Something had changed in the platoon. Before Hackworth, we had fought merely for survival. Now Hardcore warriors were on the prowl, ready to release blood for God, country, and mom's apple pie. "Blood ran knee deep in the glory of God!" trumpeted crusaders at the Battle of Hagia Sophia.

We came upon other huts, abandoned now as we swept through. The dangerous green caterpillar crawled across the land seeking someone to kill, something to burn. Tendrils of black smoke rose above the jungle in the wake of Hardcore's badass Recondos. I thought of Sherman's scorched-earth march through Georgia during the Civil War.

I turned back once for a look at the smoke, half expecting to be transformed into a pillar of salt. Flames reflected in Henderson's eyes as he also turned back.

"We oughta burn this entire stinkin' country back three generations," someone said in a unrelenting tone. "Kill 'em all, let God sort 'em out."

41

Colonel Hackworth's Hardcore Battalion moved up another notch in competition. He called it "out *G*-ing the *G*"— out-guerrilla-ing the guerrilla. Under his command, the 4/39th began taking the fight directly to the enemy.

"The only way to defeat the present enemy in the present war at a low cost in friendly casualties is through adopting the enemy's own tactics," he announced.

He was into unit- and warrior-building. He gave the companies new call signs and designations to reflect the battalion's beefed-up combat commitment. Alpha Company became Alert Company; Bravo was Battle Company; Charlie became Claymore; and Delta became Dagger. Each company was assigned a speciality.

Alert and Claymore became, respectively, long-range and

short-range ambush elements. Hackworth assigned Battle and Dagger to rangerlike guerrilla operations. Battle was given airmobile capabilities—choppers to lift us swiftly all over the fifty square kilometers of our area of operations while Dagger ranged about on foot. Alert and Claymore set up moving ambushes.

Such changes improved the overall success of the battalion and did wonders for morale. I noticed marked changes in the outfit's temperament and character. I was in the best physical and mental shape of my life. Thirst and hunger were no longer my constant companions; I had learned to eat and drink less. Stupid things like sending out Meals on Wheels were in the past. While contact with the enemy picked up, friendly casualties actually declined. We were becoming gung-ho, give-no-slack Recondos. The meanest motherfuckers in the valley and proud of it.

Brown helmet covers marked us as something special. After "Hi-Ho Silver" Silva, the battalion clerk, was transferred to a combat unit for having "FTA" inscribed on his helmet, the rest of the men turned their green helmet covers inside out to hide all the graffiti and display the brown camouflaged side. The phrases on my helmet—"Kill a Commie for Christ" and "War Is Good Business; Invest a Son"— were now hidden from sight. Brown helmets became a mark of distinction, setting the Recondos apart from the average garden-variety infantry battalions.

Guys seemed to walk a little taller. Very little talk of fragging was heard. Any stand-downs at Dong Tam resulted in Recondos gathering at the Enlisted Men's Club to boast to other units of our prowess. Salutes were rendered with a resounding "Recondo!" and returned with an equally resounding "No fuckin' slack. Hardcore, sir!" Hackworth was now *our* "old man," the best damned commander in Vietnam. No fuckin' slack, sir.

A tight outfit made it easy for young men to get into war, melded together as they were by danger and need into a single functioning oneness.

"I *love* you guys," Dale Gass blubbered one night after too many stand-down beers.

Eusebio Fernandez jumped up. "Keep away from me, troop. I've heard about the sex habits of you farm boys."

Most of the guys might not have said it the way Gass did, but we all felt it. We were brothers, closer than brothers. Black and white and brown, it made no difference. Brothers. Even the black half-radical Slim Holleman felt it.

"It's them *other* white boys I don't like," he said.

Hackworth uprooted the 4-39th, loaded us into deuces, and we departed for new digs in western Dinh Tuong Province. The trucks rumbled twenty-six miles southwest on Highway 4 and offloaded the troops onto a flat, muddy rice field on an otherwise characterless plain near the hamlet of Giao Duc. The price of a prostitute in the village was a sure sign that Americans had not operated in this AO before. A C-ration candy bar was good for a quickie. Some girls would throw themselves on their backs in exchange for a wooden ammo box, which they probably passed on to the VC. The mortar platoon was to become the happiest platoon in the division, hanging around base camp after it was constructed, patronizing all the fresh girls. It wouldn't be long before the medics' old nemesis—VD—reared its head. Battalion medics started lining up all the hookers every Tuesday to fill them with penicillin. It made more sense to treat the whores every Tuesday than to treat thirty or more GIs every day.

The Hardcore Battalion had penetrated deeper into enemy territory than any other outfit before us. No American unit had ever operated in the area. Because of its inaccessibility, the Mekong Delta had long been considered a VC sanctuary—home turf, a safe haven. Regular infiltration routes dotted with way stations and permanent VC base camps bisected the AO. It was an undisputed VC stronghold.

The platoon seemed a little jumpy, uncertain, from the time we offloaded. While we were nervous at the prospect of operating, as L. J. Henderson put it, "in a place where no white man has gone before—and taken his niggers," we also felt a certain pride that *we* had been called upon.

Henderson wiped sweat from his brow and chewed on his unlit cigar stub. "I been tellin' you," he said. "I been *tellin'* you. Hear what I'm sayin'?"

"Reckon Charles has already heard about the Recondos and already *di-di mau*ed?" the farm boy asked.

"They're probably sighting in on us right this moment, even as we speak," Fullmer predicted.

Everyone looked around.

Division had assigned the name Dickey to the new fire support base camp: FSB Dickey. But Hackworth blew up when he heard the name. "No way are my Hardcore troops gonna operate out of a base called Dickey!" he roared. The name was changed to FSB Danger.

While the base camp was under construction, the companies occupied a religious shrine and an old schoolhouse. Half of the men worked on building the base camp while the other half patrolled and pulled base security.

FSB Danger began to take shape with the help of a couple of bulldozers from Division engineers. It was a four-sided mud fort with fighting bunkers cut into the berm walls all the way around. Cyclone wire covered the bunker openings to catch and detonate incoming RPG rounds. Perforated steel plates were laid over the tops of the bunkers, then covered with a three-tiered layer of sandbags that could withstand a direct mortar blast. Concertina wire laced with booby traps and flares ringed the entire encampment. An artillery battery of six 105mm howitzers set up station in the middle of the base; infantry moved in around them in the best French tradition. Everyone received an assigned battle position that linked defenders into manned observation posts at each corner of the FSB. Hardcore was locked and loaded, ready to go.

Operations began on delta terrain, with which the battalion had become familiar within recent weeks. No American soldier in any war, including the Revolutionary War, ever suffered more than infantrymen fighting in Vietnam's Mekong Delta. Soldiers were always in water, since even at low tide a foot of brackish water covered the rice paddies and most of the dry land had been booby-trapped. The myriad crisscrossing canals meant neck-deep mud at low tide—and water and mud over the head at high tide.

There were leeches, mosquitoes, snakes, and red ants with a bite so painful they'd make a soldier jump up and shout "hallelujah" right in the middle of a firefight. Immersion foot again became the soldiers' constant enemy. Feet rubbing against the insides of boots produced infected ulcers. Whole chunks of flesh peeled off the men's feet.

"Doc, look at my poor wrinkled, bleached-out feet," Henderson pleaded. "You think I'm turning *white?*"

Shortly after ops began, First Platoon was assigned a Tiger Scout named Doi. Tiger Scouts were Vietnamese who had been hard-core VC or NVA before they surrendered under the *chieu hoi* program. Their job included guiding U.S. troops to enemy units; leading them to hidden caches of weapons, ammunition, and supplies; and identifying known VC on sight. Since Doi spoke no English, the only man in the platoon who could talk to him was Lieutenant Keppel, who had taken a three-month course in Vietnamese at Fort Bliss, Texas, before coming over. Back then, he still had illusions of a safe job with Intelligence in the rear.

Eusebio Fernandez sidled up to Doi, eyeing him. "I don't trust this hombre's yellow ass," he declared.

Sergeant Richardson shrugged and laconically explained Doi's responsibilities in terms that prompted even Slim Holleman to grin his approval: "We'll let him walk point. He can be a minesweeper, if nothing else. If he's good, he'll cut down on our booby-trap casualties. If he's not so good, all we've lost is another gook."

For the enemy, FSB Danger was like a flea in a dog's ear: the VC weren't about to let it stand. Our patrols immediately contacted enemy sent against us to throw us out. Division was thrilled with all the contact. Battalion commanders were required to carry around three-by-five cards on which to maintain up-to-date data on body counts. Woe to the commander who failed to keep a consistently high body count.

Hardcore Battalion changed the old army axiom from "If it moves, shoot it; if it doesn't, paint it" to "If it moves, shoot it; if it doesn't, count it."

Recondo companies and platoons began a contest to see who could rack up the highest body count for ol' Hardcore Hackworth.

42

From *A Distant Challenge: The U.S. Infantryman in Vietnam 1967–1972* (Chapter by Colonel David H. Hackworth):

GUERRILLA BATTALION, U.S. STYLE

By mid-1969 the 4th Battalion, 39th Infantry, had set Vietnam's guerrilla-dominated Delta on fire. This battalion's achievements weren't accomplished with conventionally trained soldiers, led by conventionally oriented leaders, but by American soldiers who fought and thought like their guerrilla foes and by leaders who followed Mao's handbook on guerrilla warfare.

Since early January 1969, the battalion, known as the "Hardcore Battalion" throughout the 9th Infantry Division, had lived and fought under virtually the same harsh and demanding conditions as the Vietcong. The troopers had become lean and hard and had the sort of pride that comes only from sacrifice. There were no suburban luxuries like cold beer and tape recorders, for example. According to one expert on guerrilla warfare, the Hardcore Battalion had become more proficient at this form of warfare than the elite guerrilla units that they challenged daily in western Dinh Tuong Province. The helicopters and air strikes helped, but the attitude of the men was the determining factor.

Surprise, deception, mobility, imagination, cunning, and familiarity with every stream, trail, hamlet, and village within the area of operations (AO) were the characteristics of Hardcore's tactics. The battalion acquired an ability to move at night with stealth and ease, and when it struck, it struck hard.

43

Recent intel revealed that in addition to the 502nd VC Heavy Weapons Battalion and the 261st VC Alpha Battalion operating in our AO—or to us operating in theirs—hardcore NVA units were moving in, either to run us out or to kill us. The National Liberation Front broadcast a special message urging its troops to inflict heavy casualties in a final "all-out war effort." There was no shortage of targets in such virgin hunting territory. All companies in our battalion were fast logging up an impressive body count record.

L. J. Henderson went around sniffing. "I can smell it," he said.

"L.J., you been smelling trouble ever since the colonel took over."

"I *can* smell it."

Out *G*-ing the *G* was working. Time and again Hardcore elements jitterbugging or eagle-flighting or simply slogging through the boonies caught Charles with his pants down.

Battle Company was airlifted into a hamlet thought to be a base camp for the 502nd VC. Cobras worked it over as the slicks came in fast. VC in black PJs scurried for the jungle like surprised roaches. The door gunner on my lift swung out on his mounted M60 machine gun and let fly. Tracers blasted feathers and blood from a flock of chickens in front of a hooch. The gunner's laughter trailed back into the Huey's belly.

Surletta from Second Platoon opened fire on a man running from a hooch as Battle unassed the choppers. The range was about 200 meters—but the enemy dropped. When he got up again, more gunfire brought him down to stay.

"Hardcore Recondo!" rang out a war cry.

Battle Company moved swiftly and violently through the ville, shooting those who fled and dragging everybody else into a cowering group in the center of the village. GIs were yelling and screaming and kicking the villagers. Babies wailed; fearful mothers suckled them to keep them quiet.

One VC jumped into a canal and dived underwater. A Huey hog circled and dropped a grenade. The VC's body floated to the top, its wide-eyed face undulating among a tangle of water bamboo.

Battle Company toted up eighteen dead VC and captured seventeen more. Sergeant Richardson thought they might be NVA soldiers, since they were taller and stockier than the local VC. We dragged the dead ones into piles and pounded Hardcore Recondo battle pins into their bare chests to let everyone in the AO know who had done this. I found a wad of money on one of the cadavers, which I kept. He didn't need it anymore.

The prisoners stared sullenly when Lieutenant Keppel interrogated them in their own language. They steadfastly refused to talk until a chopper landed and picked up one batch and left another behind.

"They're going to have a flying lesson," Lieutenant Keppel explained and flapped his arms like wings in demonstration.

That did it. The VC were terrified of aircraft. Most of them had never been inside a chopper. They stared wide-eyed at the helicopter as it took off open-doored with their comrades huddled inside. They fully expected to see their friends come hurtling out in a first, last, and only flying lesson. They began chattering like magpies. Vietnamese myths stressed cleverness and cunning, not self-sacrifice.

Battle Company logged another body count after trackers picked up our trail. Pushing ahead of them, we crossed a river that nearly swept Sergeant Joye downstream. Eusebio Fernandez and I jumped in and pulled him to shore.

"Doc," William Joye said after expelling water from his lungs, "I'm going to give you my next pair of dry socks."

Lieutenant Knapp dropped off four men to set up an ambush as the green caterpillar crawled on. The trackers ran into it. A whump of grenade, a spatter of M16 fire, and Lieutenant Knapp called in a body count of three.

First Platoon scored during an eagle-flight insertion in which word was passed that there was game in the area: "Bandits have been spotted. All stations copy: Bandits in the area."

"Roger that," acknowledged Fullmer, stroking his PRC-25. "Battle Red Fiver-Six. Acknowledge: Gooks in the woods."

"Kill a Commie for God and Colonel Hackworth" came up on the air as one gunship spotted a sampan full of VC and another pinpointed five scrambling into the woods.

Doi the Tiger Scout and Lieutenant Keppel interrogated two prisoners who, less than committed to the cause, led the platoon to where four unsuspecting VC loitered at the entrance to a bunker constructed into a high rice-paddy dike. I participated in a mad minute of M16 fire. The VC did the chicken in the sunlight. Their skinny little bodies jerked and leaped as hot lead punched holes through them.

Two were killed instantly. The third lay gaping like a dying fish for a few minutes before he expired with a rattling gasp. I patched up the fourth; he had a sucking chest wound. A chopper evacuated him, but he wasn't going to make it. *Xin loi.* Sorry about that, Charlie.

Lieutenant Keppel called in a body count of four.

First Platoon scored again a few nights later when we killed three Vietnamese in a sampan. Then we killed another hiding in a hooch. That gave the platoon a body count of eleven during the past forty-eight hours. Everyone was on a high. *Eleven,* and not even a scratch on a GI. Slim Holleman went down the line giving everyone high fives. It was like a football game. Who scores the most wins.

"We can do even better than this," Lieutenant Keppel told us.

First Platoon led the body count competition in Battle Company, but Second and Third weren't far behind. Second Platoon's blooper gunner nailed a VC crossing a stream. The M79 round blew his head completely off. He was in midstride when it hit him. He took one more step without his head before his body plummeted to earth.

Third Platoon engaged fifteen or sixteen VC in a skirmish

across a stream. The VC were armed with automatic weapons and light machine guns. Someone in Third fired an anti-tank LAWs rocket, killing three VC before they broke and ran.

Third then nailed five more in a sampan ambush. They wore khaki trousers, blue-and-white shirts, and straw hats. Hard-core NVA. The enemy was also moving up a notch in competition.

Battle Company's casualties during the action were listed as light. Second Platoon lost two men to booby trap wounds. Sergeant Joye, whose glasses had been swept away when he almost drowned, stepped on a mine. It riddled his left thigh. I hated the booby traps; they were so impersonal.

"Doc . . . Doc?" Joye groaned. "How bad . . . ? I-I can't see it."

"A million-dollar wound," I assured him. Enough not to leave him permanently disabled but enough to get him sent back to the land of the big PX. "You still owe me a pair of dry socks," I reminded him.

After more than thirty hours without food or sleep, Hackworth's Battle Company flew to Dong Tam for refitting and rest. The colonel said he also wanted the REMFs to see what real combat soldiers looked like. Sergeant Wallace, back from his dad's funeral, was waiting for us. Big ears, big smile. The platoon was so happy to have him back that boonie rats pounced on him and pummeled him good-naturedly all over the barracks.

"I've been hearing *ba-a-a-d* things about First Platoon," Sergeant Wallace said. "You guys have been kicking the slopes in the ass."

We showered and headed for a food-and-booze party at the company assemble area with the local Red Cross girls, the Heavy Blues as they were called. We were lean, mean, and dangerous. Some thirty-eight enemy KIAs to our credit against no friendly KIAs. What a score. Wipeout.

"Let's hear it for Colonel Hackworth!" shouted Earl Marshall Hayes, a newbie from North Carolina with a thick southern accent.

Sergeant Richardson thrust his beer aloft. "I'll drink to that."

We all drank to that.

Incoming mortar rounds peppered Dong Tam that night. First Platoon slept soundly through the attack. REMFs ran into the barracks to warn us.

"Go away," Sergeant Wallace protested. "The Hardcore can't be killed in base camp. It's a rule."

44

On our next patrol, First Platoon captured two suspected VC in a sampan. They stood wearing their inscrutable Asian faces while First Platoon argued their fate. Although they possessed proper identification, probably forged, and had responded immediately to being hailed off the river, their ages and the prevalence of enemy in the area of operations suggested they were probably VC. Some of the men suggested shooting them on the spot and counting two more bodies for the colonel. Lieutenant Keppel and Sergeant Richardson kept a lid on the steam; we couldn't commit murder.

"If we let 'em go an' they *are* VC," Slim Holleman protested, "they gonna sneak back up an' bite us on the butt."

"*You* going to be the one to shoot 'em while they're standing there looking at you?" Sergeant Richardson snapped.

"Not *me*. We *all* shoot 'em."

I had already decided. "You can count me out. I'm not shooting down anyone like this."

Sergeant Wallace sided with me. So did Fullmer, Henderson, and most of the others. Holleman came around. Lieutenant Keppel released the dinks; there was no official reason to detain them.

"If we start back now, we can get back to Danger in time for a hot dinner meal," he said.

"Hey, hey, hey!" Henderson exclaimed, his bright grin breaking the tension. "This nigger is on the way."

The mere mention of hot chow was enough to raise spirits instantly after a couple of lean days in the bush. The green caterpillar stretched out, moving fast. Point might have become a bit careless in his haste. Scarcely a half hour after we released the sampan dinks, the platoon was crossing an abandoned rice paddy between two wood lines when the point man stepped on a mine.

A sharp bang. A piercing scream. A combat boot—with the foot still in it, I thought—flew through the air. By the time I reached the guy, he lay writhing on the ground in agony, bellowing. I was surprised to find his foot still attached to his leg. The concussion grenade had blown off his boot. His foot wasn't so much as scratched, although the blast had probably shattered every bone in his foot, ankle, and lower leg.

"There goes hot chow," someone groaned.

"Maybe not," Lieutenant Keppel said. A hog prowling the skies overhead fell victim to Fullmer's silver tongue over the radio. Although the bird was not a medevac, it agreed to pick up the wounded point man and deliver him to Dong Tam. It had been a slow day, and the gunship pilot was about to call off his search anyhow.

We might still make it back in time for a hot meal. A couple of guys lifted the wounded man and jogged with him back into the clearing of the old rice field where the chopper could land. Richardson busted green smoke; there was almost no wind. The Huey came in low, flared.

Just as the chopper's skids kissed the earth, the surrounding wood line erupted in a furious rattle of rifle and light machine-gun fire. We had walked into an L-shaped ambush.

"I *tol'* you not to let them gooks go!" Holleman bawled.

They had set us up all right. The Huey bounced immediately back into the air, its door gunner raking the woods with his M60. The only cover the field offered was a low weed-covered dike that crisscrossed the clearing at right angles to the main ambush. Grunts scurried for it like roaches while bullets chewed up the ground through and among us.

Jones, the wounded point man, lay on top of the dike, screaming from terror now as well as from pain. I low-crawled to him, grabbed him by the collar and rolled with him behind the dike. Bullets shrieked overhead, so near I felt as if they were stealing my breath.

"Fire! Fire! Fire!" Sergeant Richardson shouted.

The platoon opened up with everything we had. I emptied one magazine, rolled over to eject the empty and slap in a fresh. Jones screamed in counterpoint to the fury of the skirmish. Farther down the dike, Eusebio Fernandez lay on his back launching grenades from his shotgunlike M79 without exposing himself to enemy fire, going through a rapid cycle of firing, breaking the weapon open, loading, firing again.

Amazingly enough, there were no wounded, no cries of "Medic!" Jones's stepping on the mine had in fact been a lucky break for the platoon. It had prevented us from walking blindly into the ambush kill zone; the lurking VC had been forced to trigger the ambush at long distance. The incident blamed for almost costing us a hot meal had in fact probably saved lives.

Fullmer and Lieutenant Keppel lay with the PRC-25 cradled between them. Fullmer crooned something into the mike and the lieutenant reached for it. His boyish face looked drained of blood.

More sight pictures: Sergeant Richardson's lanky form crawling up and down the dike, tapping helmets, directing fire, letting the troops know he was there with them.

Dale Gass cursing because he had ripped the belt from the feed of his M60 as he dived for cover and was having difficulty getting the gun into action. His hands were shaking. The ambush on Widow Maker Alley that had claimed Forte's life was probably all too fresh in his mind.

Sergeant Wallace flat on his belly, crawling to add his firepower to the platoon's flank.

Jones's screaming was getting under the other troopers' skin. Someone shouted, "Shut that motherfucker's mouth before I give him something to *really* scream about!"

I broke out a morphine Syrette and within a minute or so Jones was tripping to Disneyland. I thought he was going to start plucking bullets out of the air. He grinned. "Doc, this one's sending me home," he predicted. "Oh, Lord. Lucky, lucky me."

Only in the Nam would a guy with crushed bones consider himself lucky.

Lieutenant Keppel had his map out and was shouting into Fullmer's radio mike. (Question: Know what the most dangerous thing in the world is? Answer: A green lieutenant with a map in Vietnam.) He called in grid coordinates to the 105mm howitzer redlegs at FSB Danger: "Fire mission! Fire mission, over! Danger close." God, I hoped he got it right. I hoped he wasn't at the bottom of his class when it came to calling for fire. The radio was the biggest killer gun of all, but you had to know how to point it.

God's wrath came howling across the late afternoon sky. Closer. *Closer.*

Up and down the dike, men stopped firing and either buried their heads underneath their arms or turned drained faces to the sky in supplication.

Cracking electriclike detonations lawn-mowered through the enemy's ambush site, uprooting trees and shredding vegetation. Throaty cheers of relief and approval rippled from behind the dike as howitzer rounds stomped all over the woods and a pall of acrid blue smoke rose in clouds.

The lieutenant had done okay. This had been his first major test in First Platoon leadership. He had broken the ambush.

The VC were rarely bold enough to make contact and then sustain that contact unless they had a far superior force and could operate under cover of darkness to somewhat neutralize our air and artillery supremacy. But in this AO, the enemy was as thick as lice and full of surprises.

Unknown to us and completely unexpectedly, the ambushers reorganized and reconsolidated while we summoned a dust-off to medevac Jones. Miraculously, no one else had been wounded in the skirmish. At least not on our side. No one suggested we scout the woods for a body count. Not with the sky starting to purple out from approaching nightfall—and not when a force estimated to be easily twice our size lurked out there somewhere waiting for us.

I could almost hear John Wayne saying, "Quiet out there. Yeah, *too* quiet!" as the farm boy helped me load Jones into the dust-off. I kept glancing back over my shoulder toward the distant darkening woods where clouds of smoke, like evening fog, seeped out of the foliage.

Then Jones was gone with the throbbing of the chopper, and everything went dead silent. No longer were we thinking about reaching Danger in time for a hot meal; we simply wanted out of there before the start of the Vietcong night.

"Saddle up, people," Sergeant Richardson called out softly.

But even as his voice carried through the cooling air, firing erupted once more. This time from the wood line behind us and on the opposite side of the clearing from the first ambush and the smoking forest.

Recondos flattened themselves on the other side of the dike.

"I *tol'* you we should have shot them dinks," Holleman raged.

He wouldn't get an argument about that. Not now.

Sergeant Richardson shouted for the platoon to conserve ammo. He and the lieutenant huddled on the ground in earnest conference while I crawled along the dike, checking the men. The firefight was too much for one FNG replacement. I thought he had taken one in the gut, the way he curled around himself. His entire body trembled violently, and he was whimpering.

"Man, are you hit?"

Eusebio Fernandez laughed harshly. "Doc, he ain't hit. But you might want to change his diapers. He's shit on himself. Can't you smell it?"

VC firing had picked up to a full crescendo that sounded something like a troop of monkeys pounding on a few hundred empty trash cans. We returned lead at a more measured pace, trying not to expose ourselves to the murderous wall of death pouring from the jungle. We were bound to sustain casualties at this rate. I was always amazed at how difficult it was at times to kill a man. How easy it was at other times. I stuffed bandages into my pockets just in case I lost my aid bag.

The strain of leadership showed deep in Lieutenant Keppel's face; his features had edged and sharpened. Sergeant Richardson's face was a matching blade. They didn't have to say anything for us to know that we were in a bad position. The clear blue of day was rapidly being eaten alive by the purple of approaching evening. Darkness belonged to the enemy. Rightly or not, we ascribed almost magical powers to the VC when it came to them in the night. They were the princes of darkness, the evil phantoms who rose from the swamps and forests like mist to kill and plunder.

I imagined them maneuvering now to surround us and prevent our escape. They would start to move in on us after dark for the kill. It would all be over by the time the stand-down platoon at Danger could organize a rescue effort from the air. Artillery would only delay the inevitable; the firing from the jungle was more dispersed now to minimize damage from artillery.

The enemy was obviously intent on eliminating First Platoon to a man. ("General Custer, how many goddamn Indians did you say are out there?") Strain on the faces of the men prone and fighting behind the dike reflected the predicament in which we found ourselves.

"I'd like to get a body count on the little cocksuckers," Lieutenant Keppel hissed.

"Lieutenant, listen," Sergeant Richardson reasoned. "The little cocksuckers would like to get a body count on *us*. And that's what they're gonna do—*soon*—unless we *di-di* our asses out of Dodge. This ain't good ground, L.T."

Fullmer was chatting up his radio. It was his security blanket. It was our one line to reality when everything went to shit.

"Battle Red is ordering us to break contact—if we can," Fullmer called out. "He wants to know if we want more arty."

Sergeant Richardson frowned. One short round could wipe out half the platoon and make Charlie's job easier. Do the job for him.

"Tell him to stand by," Richardson decided. "Lieutenant," he said, "we have to get out of here now, before we're surrounded."

Keppel made up his mind. "Let's do it."

The grassy dike provided some cover by meandering across the clearing of the old rice field to where it abutted the forest about 100 meters away. I lay on my belly drawing in deep breaths tasting of cordite and fear. Heart, please slow down. I had made runs the full length of a football field back when I still had illusions of being a football star. I had never made a 100-yard touchdown, however, with all the fans in the stands armed and shooting at me.

Sergeant Richardson organized the retreat. The rout. The stampede. L. J. Henderson and his M60 machine gun, along with a small fire team, would stay behind to provide cover fire while the rest of the platoon scrambled along the lee side of the dike to the woods. The platoon and the other machine gun, with Gass on the trigger, would then cover the withdrawal of Henderson's element.

"What if there are dinks in the woods too?" worried Marshall Hayes and little Arles Brown.

"Then we'll walk right through them," Sergeant Richardson growled. "Ready? *Go! Go! Go!*"

Henderson lay down on the trigger and sprayed the woods. I heard him shouting at the VC, cursing them and their ancestors, as my muscles bunched, propelling me to my feet and catapulting me forward into what was surely a record-breaking 100-yard dash to the goal line. The air around us came alive with the explosive energy of hot, shrieking lead seeking flesh. Guardian angel, are you watching this?

I could scarcely believe our luck. The enemy couldn't shoot for shit. All of us reached the wood line without sustaining a single wound. It was like running through raindrops, not a single one of which struck us.

We lay down heavy covering fire for Henderson. I fired another full magazine into the distant thin blue haze of gun smoke that masked the enemy position. I saw no targets, but I imagined VC falling everywhere. Too many John Wayne movies as a kid. I slapped in a fresh mag of 5.56. Doc Evans, the fighting medic.

"Dirty little bastards!" Dale Gass the pig farmer exploded. "Did you know they were having steaks tonight at Danger?"

The miracle held. Henderson and his element joined us, also without sustaining a scratch. Darkness was already settling in the jungle. Shadows lay thick and purple, and they were growing denser by the moment. Between us and FSB

Danger lay the enemy blocking force. We would have to circle wide, moving fast, to get around the VC and come onto the home stretch.

"Feets, grow wings!" Henderson quipped as the green caterpillar shifted into high gear.

Flying through the darkening forest in a strung-out file. Breath caught, painful in burning lungs. Fear sweat showering from straining bodies. Sounding like peddlers of pots and pans as canteens and rucks and knives and ammo and weapons and helmets rattled and clanged and added to the sense of urgency. Each GI a full sporting goods store in comparison to each VC with his sandals or sneakers and his one pocketful of rice and one pocketful of bullets. Heedless of booby traps and possible new ambushes. One thought in our collective mind: escape death's scythe.

VC were running off to our flanks, keeping pace with us through the jungle, trying to cut us off and bring us to bay, like hounds after hares. Wild rifle shots rang out.

First Platoon ran. First Platoon *ran*. It was encouraging to know that while the lion merely runs for his supper, the gazelle runs for his *life*.

River ahead. Barely slacking stride. Plunging into it neck deep. Wild glances toward the backtrail. Getting darker. Crawling out of the river. Charging back into the woods. Wild in flight. More gunfire, farther away now, behind us.

Lieutenant Keppel called a listening halt. The trail led past a grass hooch; the hut was dark, with not even a cook fire burning. I knelt alongside the trail, facing back, taking a few hasty breaths and then holding them in order to listen. My finger remained frozen to the reassuring hard curve of the M16's trigger. My eyes saw things that my brain knew— or at least *hoped*—weren't there. Threatening shadows darted and skulked and loomed among the palms, ferns, and strangler vines.

It was suicide to keep up our wild flight through the darkness. The VC knew the area a hell of a lot better than we did, plus they could see in the dark like cats. The lieutenant—Battle Red 56—checked in with Company. The dreaded word passed from man to man: not much could be done until morning; First Platoon had to make it through the night.

A hoarse whisper: "Oh, God. We're trapped out here with *them.*"

"The fortunes of war," Sotello murmured. "And so it goes."

"Can the talk," Sergeant Richardson ordered. "Not so much as another word."

Voices carried long distances in the night. It was going to be a long night. I wondered if we would ever see another sunrise. For one of the first times since I left the relative safety of the 9th Med, I acknowledged what a fool I must have been to volunteer for this. Surely Colonel Arnold's chickenshit was preferable to this. At least I would have remained alive to face the mad colonel's Article 15s had I stayed at Dong Tam to begin with.

We formed a circle, like defensive buffalo with all horns facing out, and waited for full darkness. The hour dragged through twenty-one years of my life. I had volunteered for Vietnam, volunteered again for combat duty in order to prove—*something*. I didn't even know what I was trying to prove. That I was a man? That I might be a war hero? Something to my father who had fought in World War II?

What did it matter now what I thought I was trying to prove? What I had learned so far was how to hit the ground every time I heard a loud noise, how to call in artillery fire missions on the radio and scare other men shitless, how to heat C-rats over a burning chunk of deadly explosives, how to field-strip an M16 in the dark and then shoot somebody with it, how to lie on the ground with bullets screaming overhead while I patched up some maimed and frightened young comrade.

All of which were valuable skills in the real world outside, right?

At least I was no longer squeamish at the sight of blood.

After full nightfall, we backtracked and crawled into the thickest patch of brush and thorns we could find. We built the perimeter so tight we lay almost shoulder to shoulder facing out toward the danger-ripe darkness. And there we lay at full alert, peering apprehensively into the Vietcong night, hoping that if we had to see the enemy at all we would see him before he saw us. Some of us prayed silently.

After a few hours the signal passed from man to man with

jarring presence: *Danger near!* One of the men with a star-light scope spotted three enemy soldiers creeping about in a wood line opposite our position, obviously searching for the trapped American platoon. Sergeant Richardson had already preplotted and registered fixed targets for the 105s at Danger. Lieutenant Keppel requested a fire mission, lying close to the ground and whispering into Fullmer's radio mike. We scarcely dared breathe, out of fear of betraying our hiding place.

High-explosive 105 rounds crashed and flashed and started small fires in the enemy's wood line. A single scream of panic and pain from the enemy slashed the night's mantle of darkness—and then all was quiet again in the forest while we waited and prayed for dawn. Eyes burned for want of sleep, but none dared close his lids for fear it would be his last time.

The hours dragged.

Finally I made out the leaves of the tree above me against a sky growing lighter by the minute. Then I saw an insect on the leaf, a beetle of some sort who gave not a whit for the human drama being played out around it. It was all a matter of perspective, I thought; perspective determined what mattered. For the beetle, perspective involved a succulent leaf and avoiding a larger predatory insect or a bird. For the GI, perspective centered on hot chow safely behind wire and evading little yellow guys armed with AK-47s. All perspective. What bothered the beetle appeared ridiculous to a soldier, while the beetle surely would have considered a soldier's fears equally ridiculous or insignificant.

Dawn drove the VC back into hiding. GIs owned the daylight. We stirred one by one when the sun was well up. Hungry and exhausted as we were, we still found the energy to smile at each other, as though awakening out of a nightmare. The realization that we had *all* survived the night left me a little stunned, a little groggy, a little disbelieving.

The tired green caterpillar tramped across rice paddies and through wood lines and arrived at FSB Danger in time to help fill sandbags to reinforce defensive bunkers. No one in the platoon complained about manual labor on this day. We were still reliving the miracle of having survived a Vietcong night.

<u>45</u>

My guardian angel, it seemed, had spread her wings to protect not only me but also the entire platoon. Our escape from the ambush at the abandoned rice field gave us a feeling that maybe we lived a charmed existence, that nothing was capable of harming the protected First Platoon. We merely laughed, with some pride, over a rumor that the VC infrastructure had placed bounties on the heads of Hackworth's Hardcore Recondos. Let the little yellow bastards try to collect. The mean green machine with its new spirit of aggressiveness would clean their clocks for them.

Tension in the AO, the excitement of the deadly contest between the 4/39th and the North Vietnamese elements trying to destroy the Hardcore or run it out of the delta, was almost palpable. Each passing day saw the stakes raised in the competition. The enemy seemed always on the go, moving equipment, troops, and supplies. VC who customarily operated in squad-size or, at most, platoon-size elements now fielded companies. While the GI boonie rats at the bottom of the chain of command had little need to see the big picture, word had it that somewhere out there in the vast wasteland of the Mekong Delta in the Recondos' own backyard was a major NVA command and training post. If we could find and destroy it, we would cripple the opposition and claim the ball game.

The Hardcore was running up a high body count and winning the war. First Platoon was on a roll, charmed that we were and continued to be, running through the raindrops, untouched. Even Henderson's pessimism seemed to be mellowing.

Battle Company eased into a banana grove at dawn to place surveillance upon a village suspected of providing

Charlie locally with many of his food supplies. The ville appeared much richer than its neighbors; most of the hamlets were accustomed to being regularly sacked and then kept poor by maruading VC tax collectors. Evenly spaced hooches, well-beaten paths, canals, and irrigation ditches marked the settlement, as did large flocks of chickens and fat geese, potbellied pigs running loose among plentiful herds of water buffalo, large stacks of hay, and well-kept banana trees and citrus groves. For some reason, Charles wasn't taking everything this hamlet produced—probably, we suspected, because the village itself was made up of Vietcong cadre.

Inseparable buddies Fentress and Faulkenberg, who were watching the river adjacent to the hamlet, spotted four armed VC coming out of the jungle and wading into the water to cross to our side. Faulkenberg's excited voice burst whispering from Fullmer's PRC-25 at the platoon command post: "Battle Red 55, four Victor Charlies passing in front of our Oscar. Request permission to interdict. Over."

The platoon dug deeper into silent cover. Rarely did we obtain the upper hand like this. Four easy kills for the platoon's body count.

However, there was always the 1 percent who never seemed to get the word. One platoon grunt, who had been taking it easy sprawled back against a banana tree on the far flank, was about to toss a wrench into the crankshaft. Not knowing about the four VC on the platoon's other flank, he blinked in astonishment as a VC soldier armed with a bow and arrow ventured out of the woods in front of him. The GI snapped off a shot—and everything went to shit.

First of all, he missed his target and the guy bolted like a startled deer. So did the four others who were about to enter Fentress and Faulkenberg's kill zone. Lieutenant Keppel leaped up and jumped on the GI who had fired the shot; Lieutenant Sterling, an artillery forward observer assigned to the platoon for certain missions, got on his radio and ordered a fire mission on the four fleeing VC; and Faulkenberg's frustration came out in an angry stream over radio air: "They got away from us! Who was the silly turd that fired that shot? We had the squint-eyed little bastards dead to rights."

A howitzer round was on its way. I heard it shredding the air coming toward us. For some reason, I knew it was going to fall short, that it wasn't going to reach the patch of woods into which the four VC had fled. It was going to land . . . Jesus, it was going to drop right on top of Lieutenant Sterling!

I sprang up and darted through the banana grove.

"What the hell, Doc . . . ?" Sergeant Richardson shouted.

"It's a short!" I answered without stopping. "Gonna be casualties."

The top of a banana palm disappeared in a hailstorm of shredded fronds. The big shell exploded an instant later with a crumping flash of light and a tremendous eruption of earth and debris—right where the redleg lieutenant had been.

I leaped into an open ditch and landed almost on top of Sterling and another soldier. I threw myself at them, already checking for injuries. Dirt and leaves still sifted from the sky. Smoke oozed from the shell crater not three steps away. I was stunned to find everyone still had all his pieces intact.

"Back off, Doc. We ain't hit. Unless you want to clean the shit out of our drawers."

The platoon's incredible luck still held. The howitzer round had been equipped with a delayed fuse that provided just enough time after impact for the two soldiers to dive for cover behind the raised dike lip of the ditch. They wouldn't hear well for a few days and their eyes resembled goggles, but otherwise they had benefited from First Platoon's charm.

What an insane war it was. American politicians threatening to bomb the North Vietnamese back to the Stone Age, warriors coming at us with bows and arrows, peace negotiation arguments over the shape of tables, and First Platoon's grunts surviving it all.

My God. Last two men on the field please turn out the lights.

46

From *Facts On File*, April 3–9, 1969:

U.S. DEATHS TOP KOREA TOLL

American combat deaths in the Vietnamese War exceeded U.S. fatalities suffered in the Korean conflict, according to casualty figures issued April 3 by the U.S. command in Saigon.

The death of 312 U.S. troops March 23–29, the sixth week of the Communist post-Tet offensive, raised the total of American fatalities in Vietnam since Jan. 1, 1961, to 33,641, compared with 33,629 U.S. soldiers killed during the Korean War (1950–53). Communist and South Vietnamese fatalities in the March 23–29 period were 4,314 and 357, respectively. U.S. deaths since the start of the Communist drive Feb. 22: 1,178.

The heaviest engagement of the war continued to be fought around Saigon and in the vicinity of the demilitarized zone, between North and South Vietnam. Communist rocket attacks, however, appeared to have slackened. The launching of three new allied drives aimed at stemming the Communist offensive were disclosed. . . .

Among the major actions between March 25 and April 7:

A U.S. Army unit 50 miles northwest of Saigon came under heavy Communist mortar and ground assault March 25. The attack left eight Americans dead and 17 wounded, but the defenders held their positions. Two Communist bodies were found after the incident.

North Vietnamese forces suffered heavy losses in two ambushes of U.S. military convoys near Godauha, 45 miles northwest of Saigon, March 25 and 28. In the first incident, March 25, the Communists were thrown back with 85 men killed. U.S. losses totaled two dead and four wounded. In the second engagement, an American supply convoy of more than 100 vehicles came under attack by North Vietnamese troops positioned on both sides of the road. About 20 tanks and armored troop carriers leading the convoy were fired on. The forward armored column turned off the road and drove into the enemy fire, while the remainder of the convoy sped through the gap. In the day-long battle that ensued, 46 North Vietnamese were reported killed.

The launching of an allied counteroffensive near the DMZ March 15 was disclosed March 24. A force of about 3,000 U.S. Marines and South Vietnamese took part in the operations, called Maine Crag. The purpose of the drive was to block a North Vietnamese threat to allied bases along the northern frontier and to cut North Vietnamese supply lines from Laos into South Vietnam. Thus far the Marines were said to have killed 43 Communist troops and to have captured two prisoners and 129 rifles.

Heavy fighting raged in the northern provinces March 27–30. About 120 Communist soldiers and 14 Americans were killed in a clash near the DMZ March 27. In the March 29–30 clashes, government forces were said to have slain 50 enemy soldiers about 20 miles south of Quang Ngai, while U.S. troops killed about 70 Communists in the area of the March 27 skirmish.

47

With a pulse of rotor blades, four slicks jerked First Platoon into the air and hurtled across the sky with us. The platoon's strength had reached an all-time high of twenty-three soldiers. I occupied the second chopper with Lieutenant Keppel; Doi, the Tiger Scout; Sergeant Wallace; Wallace's RTO, Ron Miller; and two door gunners. Sergeant Richardson; his RTO, Harry Fullmer; the farm boy; and four other boonie rats scrambled into the third bird, while the rest of the platoon divided itself between the lead Huey and the tail chopper.

The only thing we knew about this emergency mission was that the airlift would insert us on a target near the Cambodian border. Presumably, Sergeant Richardson or the lieutenant would brief us when we landed.

For some reason, I had marked the date: March 19, 1969. I had arrived in-country on October 7, 1968, over five months and an entire lifetime ago. Almost to "hump day," halfway back home from the one-year tour. The closer I got to hump day, the more anxious I became.

Some guys, during their last few weeks in-country, fought against going on any missions for fear of getting it now that they were almost home free. I hadn't reached that point, but I understood how the anxiety built and built the closer you got to DEROS. Sometimes I awoke suddenly in base camp and *knew* that the charm enjoyed by First Platoon couldn't last forever. At such times I reached for the Saint Christopher medal the girl at the bridge had given me. She had said it would keep me safe from the Vietcong—and it had. So far.

The only other thing I could ask of it was that it also keep my platoon buds safe. I wanted to send no more comrades home in body bags; they were under my care. Forte was enough.

March 19. The choppers in formation sped across the sky—into the beginning of a week-long nightmare.

The choppers rose to an altitude of 1,800 feet, out of small arms range, and flew in staggered single-file formation. I expected a long, peaceful flight. I had learned to enjoy flying since during my few days with the 247th Medevac. I rode the right jump seat next to the open door and watched the patched green of Vietnam pass below. A sense of calm overcame me, like watching fish in an aquarium.

A jolt suddenly disturbed the aquarium. Before it fully registered in my startled brain, the Huey dolphined in the air and literally dropped out from underneath me. Incredibly, I floated from my seat, weightless. The featherweight Doi rose past me and bounced off the top of the cabin. Sergeant Wallace grabbed the aluminum leg of his seat and reached for Doi with his free hand to keep the little scout from flying out the open door.

I floundered in midair, clawing at everything around me for a handhold. My legs were already drifting out the door. I latched on to a seat support bar at the last moment and pulled myself back inside the cabin. What the hell was going on? My heart raced like after the retreat from the rice field with the VC chasing us.

The door gunner appeared the calmest among us. He hung on to his M60 and jabbed a thumb toward earth. "We're going down," he shouted. "Hang on!"

We were *crashing*?

The main rotor, dragging, dipped, and the tail swung violently around, hurling the passengers against each other. The heavily laden chopper slowly began rotating like a falling leaf as it plummeted toward earth. We hadn't been shot down; the engine merely died. Helicopters were like bumblebees—nonaerodynamic. They weren't supposed to fly in any logical sense in the first place. Ours had now turned into a rock. The pit of my stomach rode up into my throat, with the sensation of riding the steepest roller coaster.

Mom would have to answer the door sometime soon to let the officer in to tell her about her son. Dianne would receive survivor's benefits instead of a divorce.

Surprisingly, after the initial shock, I felt the same aquarium-calmness as before. I rode my seat, holding on, and waited for the helicopter to slam into the ground. I stared distantly at the metal floor between my feet, refusing to look at either the dizzying approach of the earth outside or the faces of the doomed men around me. When death came, I wanted it to be a surprise. I had no desire to have the stricken faces of my friends burned into what little memory I had left.

By an odd quirk of the brain's function, I almost laughed aloud as I recalled an old Bill Cosby routine about how to survive an airplane crash. "Just before the airplane hits the ground," he had quipped, "jump up."

That gave me a wild idea. The Mekong Delta was a vast swampy prairie of sloughs and canals and lakes and rivers and flooded rice paddies and reed plains. What if, at the last moment, I leaped from the helicopter into the water? I might survive if the water was deep enough.

Any chance was better than no chance.

Instinctive survival drew my eyes toward the door, past which the dreadful wind howled. I saw that we were drifting slowly to the right now as we fell. Two streams below glinted in the midmorning sun. We were floating toward them.

I scrambled out onto the skid without hesitation. Wind howled and buffeted my helmet, but the absence of engine noise made the sky almost cathedral. Lieutenant Keppel and Doi seemed to have read my mind. They gingerly climbed out onto the skid next to me. Sergeant Wallace, Miller, and the door gunner soon occupied the other skid. We held on and looked through the empty cabin at each other.

Afterward I recalled the mechanics of autorotation and the procedures for evacuating a crashing helicopter. A falling chopper's dead blades would pick up speed as it dropped through the air, so that at the last moment, just before impact, the blades would have built up sufficient lift for the pilot to pull it out of its fatal dive into a more or less controlled crash. Passengers were supposed to jump, roll, and get the hell out of the way the instant before it hit.

While the others assumed I was preparing for the crash, the truth was that I had forgotten everything I should have known about emergency landings. The only thing I thought about was getting out of that loose elevator. I assumed the others were following my example.

The Huey sailed across the first river, still too high for us to jump. I watched the second river coming swiftly up and toward me. I tensed. The aircraft was coming down fast. The river was my last chance. Nothing but flooded rice paddies lay beyond it.

"Get ready to jump!" Lieutenant Keppel shouted. The only thing I heard was *"Jump!"*

Adrenaline, like a giant hand out of the sky, grabbed me and flung me off the skid. The last thing I saw was the look of total disbelief that flashed over the lieutenant's face as he saw me swan dive into space fifty feet above the water— five stories from the ground.

I twisted my body in a desperate effort to hit the narrow river.

Saw too late that I was going to miss it.

I sailed over the river, glimpsing green rice shoots sticking up through a sheen of water, and saw the helicopter reflected in the natural mirror.

Then I landed.

Two or three feet of water covered the rice plants, underneath which was another foot or so of soft mud. I struck on my nose, belly, and toes with enough forward velocity so that I motorboated fifty feet across the field, shooting up a prow wave and leaving a wake behind me.

When I finally stopped skidding, I scrambled to my feet and discovered to my surprise that my body was relatively intact. I had damn near drowned myself, but . . .

"I'm *alive!*" I shouted with uncontrolled relief and joy— just as the helicopter dropped ahead of me in a tremendous eruption of mud and water. Soldiers exploded from it, hitting the rice water and running. All had survived.

I was still jumping around like a madman. "I'm alive! I'm alive! *I made it!*"

Don't answer the door, Mom.

Sergeant Wallace and the other survivors joined me in a moment of unbridled exhilaration at our deliverance, pounding each other on the back and shouting. We were on a tremendous high. Ron Miller, still with his radio strapped to his back, pointed out that this was his second helicopter crash. "They ain't so bad, once you get used to 'em," he said, grinning warily.

"Beautiful dive," Sergeant Wallace dryly congratulated me. "You missed the river."

"Any landing you walk away from is a good one, right?" the door gunner babbled.

We were too busy congratulating each other to realize that while we had escaped one calamity we might have fallen into another, more desperate, situation. Even as the other three helicopters dropped low to circle protectively overhead, gunfire rattled from the tree line at the distant edge of the rice paddy. Geysers of water erupted around us.

Door gunners above began working out on the trees as we survivors dashed for the cover of the nearest paddy dike. We crouched behind it knee deep in brackish water. Miller's PRC-25 came alive among the buzzing Hueys, giving us some idea of our predicament:

"Charlie all over the goddamn place," shouted one pilot's voice over the air. "Running like rats."

"Dalton Two?" said another voice. "Dalton Six. See the little bastards? At your two o'clock. Victor Charlies. One, two, three . . . six of 'em."

"Dalton Six, we're on 'em. Goddamn, did you see that? Shot the dink's legs clear off."

"Like cockroaches. My God, Dalton Three has gone down in deep shit. The woods are full of Indians."

Lieutenant Keppel looked at me. Bullets seared the air explosively above our heads. "Doc," he said, "how's your aid bag? And how's this for our luck? We must have crashed right in the middle of a VC battalion base camp or something."

48

I hadn't noticed the hooch until now. It was huge, easily four times the size of a normal one, with a thatched roof and two doors. It occupied the edge of the woods away from the rice field. Gooks flushed from it as if from a hay barn set afire.

Because of the unexpected contact, Colonel Hackworth scrubbed First Platoon's original mission. The rest of the platoon swiftly offloaded and splashed online. We were to throw pressure against the gooks and hold them until Battle Company could be airlifted in to reinforce. Sergeant Richardson directed prep fire against the building's mud sides while the gunships stationed themselves aloft and chewed at the structure with their M60s. Dust and smoke spurted from the hooch as if from a rug being beaten.

In the background, a twin-bladed CH-47 Chinook helicopter lifted its downed smaller cousin out of the rice paddy and flew away with it toward Dong Tam.

The hooch was a battalion-size field hospital, like our BAS at Dong Tam. That meant it serviced a considerable force of VC—and probably NVA—operating in the vicinity. We had truly stumbled into the core of the wasps' nest. The Vietnamese hadn't had time to booby-trap the facility as they ordinarily would have. Someone had recently vacated the dental chair, no doubt disturbed by our unannounced crash landing. A bowl of rice sitting on a table in the operating room was still warm. Beds in the ward had been abandoned on the run. Patients had left behind some of their personal belongings.

Little Arles Brown kicked open a door as Sergeant Wallace's fire team stormed through the building. The small room beyond was filled with cases of drugs, medications, and other medical supplies. There were also books and stacks of medical literature on every topic from debriding a wound to delivering a baby.

I joined Arles as he bristled, his voice suddenly taut as a tripwire: *"Motherfuckers!"*

Arles was too wholesome to freely employ obscenities. Something must have really set him off. I took a look and felt my jaw stiffen to match his: *"Motherfuckers!"*

We stood shoulder to shoulder and filled the room with invective. Glaring back at us, taunting us in English stamped on the boxes, was the source of the supplies: "Donated by the University of California, Berkeley."

Bitter tears filled Brown's eyes. "How *could* they?" he demanded. "We're being killed over here, and our own people are sending stuff to help them."

I had no answer.

Arles tilted the muzzle of his M16 and sprayed the boxes, shattering bottles. He seemed to feel better after that, as if he had somehow struck back at Jane Fonda and the other war protesters and their chants that echoed even across the ocean and cut us to the heart: "Ho-ho-ho. Ho Chi Minh is going to win."

Signs warning of *tu dia*—danger—were posted along the well-worn paths leading into the jungle beyond the hooch. No doubt the area was heavily booby-trapped.

Higher-higher ordered Lieutenant Keppel to confiscate all the medications from the hospital and torch the building. Choppers throbbed back on-site like frantic bumblebees to airlift the platoon another klick south of the hospital in an effort to block the retreating enemy and force him into a fight. A thick plume of black smoke from the burning hospital smudged the blue sky. I hesitated an instant before scrambling into the belly of my assigned slick. Then I shrugged. What the hell. A man could get used to anything.

The choppers deposited us in a rice field without enough cover to conceal a mouse. The nearest wood line was 300 meters away across a flat of green shoots sticking speared heads above shallow water crossed with low, flattened dikes. The sun sucked up tendrils of steam from the field, distorting the figures of two VC running through the trees.

Dale Gass, the farm boy, was humping the M60 machine gun. He sprang out of his helicopter with the heavy weapon wedged against his hip, the carrying strap over his shoulder, and leaned on the trigger. Empty brass leaping from the eject port sparkled in the sunlight; tracers pale in the daylight arced low over the field. Bullets thudding into the thick verdure echoed in a drumlike rhythm. The VC vanished into the forest. Boonie rats spread out across the rice field as the slicks hopped back into the air, taking with them the sense of urgency created by their whining engines and pulsating blades.

The resulting silence was shattered a moment later by the muffled, earthy cough of an exploding mine. Leonard Gauerke's helmet went sailing. The concussion threw him back and deposited him in a screaming heap amid a cloud of smoke on the nearest dike.

No one had to shout "Medic!" I ran to Gauerke.

"Doc, get the fuck off that dike!" Sergeant Richardson yelled.

Gauerke's left leg had been chewed bloody. I ripped off what remained of his trouser leg, slapped on pressure bandages, and tied them down.

I hadn't quite finished with him when another explosion and another cry of pain and surprise jangled my already exposed nerve endings. The voices of Lieutenant Keppel and Sergeant Richardson slashed through the turmoil like rapiers: "Everybody! Stand where you are. Goddammit, *stand still!*"

What was going on? Helicopters crashing into the center of an enemy base camp, other choppers dropping us into the middle of a minefield of booby traps. It was as if First Platoon had lived a charmed life for too long, and now everything was happening at once.

I concentrated on finishing up on Gauerke. I heard moaning from the next dike.

Gauerke clenched his teeth. "Doc? Doc, it's Gass. He's hurt bad."

Not the farm boy. Not Dale.

I finished and glanced up. About twenty meters of rice paddy water separated me from the next dike where Gass lay crumpled like a pile of old clothes. Wisps of smoke curled from bloody holes ripped through his combat fatigues. His machine gun lay next to him. He sounded as if he wanted to scream but was chewing on his tongue to keep silent.

Boonie rats stood frozen, staring, as if they had been stuck in the mud and water and left there to grow. Like terrified mannequins in a museum display.

I was the medic. The Doc. My men needed me. I couldn't let them suffer while I watched, bobby traps or not. I took a deep breath, adjusted my glasses, and stepped off toward the suffering farm boy.

"Doc?" It was Sergeant Richardson's Okie drawl.

I kept going through silence watched and preserved by the platoon.

"Doc," Richardson called out, "I'm coming too. I'll meet you there."

"Nobody else move," the lieutenant ordered.

We both made it, guided and drawn by the farm boy's beseeching eyes. An initial medical assessment told me Dale's condition was much worse than Gauerke's. Shrapnel from the mine had shredded both lower legs. Blood and greenish bowel material oozed from deep lacerations in his abdominal cavity; his intestinal tract had been punctured. There was a ragged hole the size of my finger through his neck and esophagus. As if this wasn't enough, the center of his left hand had been blown out, leaving shards of bone and dangling tendons and nerves exposed. The fingers twitched spasmodically.

I crooned reassurances as I worked over him. I pretended this was some stranger, a soldier from another outfit. I didn't want to see the farm boy lying there suffering and perhaps dying. It *couldn't* be Dale. Not *my* Dale, who always took out photographs of his prize porkers to show to the cherries, not the farm boy with whom I had eaten and slept and shared Vietnam experiences so personal that only those of us who lived them would ever understand them. A Doc had to rise above his emotions. A Doc must never let his tears show.

Gass's voice escaped hoarse and blood-gushy from his mangled throat. "Jim . . . ?"

Sergeant Richardson grasped the farm boy's good hand firmly in both of his.

"Jim? Am I . . . am I going to die?"

The platoon sergeant's eyes darted to find mine. Richardson looked so anguished I felt almost as sorry for him as for Dale.

"No," I barked. *"No!"*

My personal war continued. Doc against death. Doc against his personal enemy. Sometimes the enemy won. But not this time.

"Hear that, Dale?" Sergeant Richardson said. "The Doc says no. You know the Doc never lies. You gotta hang in there. You've got the million-dollar wound. You're going home. Your dad's going to need your help back in Illinois raising all those hogs."

That seemed to revive him. "I'm going back to the farm?"

War hardened some people, but Gass had remained wide-eyed and innocent throughout, his face open and trusting like the farm boy he was.

"The farm is where you should have been all along," Richardson said. His eyes misted. He looked quickly away to hide his emotions.

"Doc?" Gass pleaded, faltering. "Doc . . . can I have a drink of water?"

"Not yet, Dale." I felt as if I'd denied a meal to a starving orphan. "You'll be in surgery within the hour. They'll have you patched up as good as new."

I silently prayed for it to be true. In the background Fullmer requested medevac for two WIAs, *urgent.*

The ordeal was still not over for unfortunate First Platoon, which had lost its charm and incurred the wrath of the gods. I thought my heart had exploded when the next mine went off. Sergeant Richardson shot erect, already looking. "Goddammit. I told nobody to move."

"Sarge, they were already on the dike and trying to get off," came an explanation.

"I don't give a damn where any of you are. *Stay!*"

This time it was Larry Fentress and Bob Howell, who was attached to us from the mortar platoon. Two for one. Fentress's buddy, Faulkenberg, looked coiled; the two were virtually inseparable.

"Stay right where you are," Sergeant Richardson warned Faulkenberg. "Let the Doc handle it."

It was the dikes that were heavily mined, so I stayed in the water. The bobby trap had riddled both soldiers with shrapnel and opened Fentress's left foot like a butterfly with its wings spread. He also had a shard of steel in one eye, swelling it closed. I wrapped both eyes to protect them, stopped the bleeding from his foot with a tourniquet, and gave him an injection of morphine. Howell's wounds appeared less serious. By the time I completed aid, blood stained my arms up to the elbows. The distant thumping whine of the arriving dust-off came welcome to my ears.

Get the WIAs out of here. Get us *all* out of this rice field.

Two rifle shots rang out from among the distant trees, shooting water geysers up. Boonie rats fell in the water wherever they stood, cursing our luck, bobbing with only their faces, helmets, and weapons exposed.

When would this shit stop?

"Dust-off's coming in anyhow," Fullmer called out, shouting between conversations over his radio. "Have the wounded ready."

Lieutenant Keppel popped green smoke to mark our position and guide the medevac into the almost nonexistent wind. I assigned soldiers to help me carry the wounded to the chopper once it touched down. It circled the field. Richardson nudged me and nodded toward the tree line.

Charlie had also popped green smoke in an effort to confuse the helicopter and lure it into a trap. That the bird wore a giant Red Cross on its belly meant nothing to the enemy. They had probably never even heard of the Geneva Accords.

Lieutenant Keppel popped red smoke. The VC released red smoke.

Then yellow smoke rose from the field mirrored by yellow smoke from the woods.

"The chopper's not fooled by it," Fullmer assured the lieutenant. He hunkered down in filthy water and shouted into his radio mike. "He has us spotted," he said. "He's coming in fast right on top of us. Be ready."

God bless the dust-off jockeys.

The chopper hovered, its pulsing blades whipping the

water into a mini-typhoon, while we carried the wounded to it and loaded them aboard. Someone lay in on the M60 to provide covering fire. Gass was only semiconscious. I gave him a farewell pat on the shoulder. The platoon wouldn't be seeing him again; he had a million-dollar wound. He was going home.

"I'll send you guys a case of beer just as soon as I reach the world," Fentress promised as the chopper lifted off. Faulkenberg looked forlorn, lost, gazing up toward the sky as his buddy was carried away. He and Fentress had been together since the beginning, since the initials of their last names had placed them next to each other in boot camp.

"Larry got it," Faulkenberg said morosely. "I figure I'm next."

Slim Holleman yelled at him: "That's sooner'n you expect, you don't get your white ass down. They is shootin' at us."

The chopper's engine had masked the sound of enemy fire. It was coming in fairly hot, but not so accurate at such long range. I water-crawled behind the dike and peeped over the top. I couldn't see anything. Off to my right. Sergeant Richardson had the farm boy's abandoned machine gun rockin' and rollin' in a long-distance duel with the VC. Charlie Reese lay belly down next to him with the other big gun. Rockin' and rollin' together. The barrels smoked, overheating, as the guns rhythmically pumped supersonic tracer bees in arcs across the rice field. Bullets plunged—*thump! thump! thump! thump!*—into the thick green verdure from which Charlie Cong tormented us.

When the guns went silent, the Mattie Mattel popping of the tinny M16s sounded weak and ineffectual in contrast.

"Ammo!" Reese pleaded. "We need ammo."

No one wanted to stir and further tempt fate and the ubiquitous mines. But what the hell. I still had my guardian angel. I leaped to my feet to my own background score from *The Sands of Iwo Jima* and scrambled around collecting belts of ammunition. Bullets screamed past my ears as I lugged the belts to Reese and Sergeant Richardson at a run. I hit the mud face down and slid up between the two silent machine guns. Richardson glanced at me in amazement, but said nothing.

"Safe at home plate!" Henderson bellowed in his best umpire's voice.

Sergeant Richardson slapped a fresh belt into his feed tray and got back on the trigger. Two VC who were foolish enough to expose themselves went down hard in the hail of lead he poured into the trees. The platoon cheered. "Fuck them motherfuckers *up!*" Mario Sotello roared. The platoon sergeant swept the gun muzzle back and forth. The barrel glowed a dull red; it hissed and smoked. He was burning it up.

I had never seen the sergeant like this before. He was usually so contained, so controlled. But now his bronzed face was sharp and grim and deadly, blue eyes like knife slits aiming down the barrel of the machine gun. He had "kill" in his eyes. Tears of rage and sorrow over the useless wounding of his men streaked the grime on his face.

He fired the machine gun in one long continuous burst that seemed to go on and on. He fired until no more answering shots came from the jungle. He fired until the platoon ran out of M60 ammunition. Even then he kept the trigger depressed on the silent gun while the barrel smoked and glowed.

Lieutenant Keppel knelt next to him and placed a gentle hand on his shoulder. Richardson blinked, as though emerging from a daze.

"Jim? Jim, it's okay," the lieutenant said. "They're all gone. The choppers are coming in for us. We're being extracted."

<u>49</u>

The helicopter crash in the rice field had launched a contact with the enemy that continued on through March. The Green Machine of the 4/39th ground away at Charlie, pursuing him day and night. Although Recondos began referring to the month as "bloody March," Hardcore esprit remained high and seemed to grow stronger each day. Recognition of the Hardcore Battalion's exploits in *Old Reliable*, the 9th Division's newspaper, and in *Stars and Stripes* did wonders for morale. The men were cocky and kicking the shit out of Charles—but Charles was kicking back, too.

"As I started giving back to the men many of the privileges I'd stripped away so savagely at the outset of my tour in order to bend them to my will," Colonel Hackworth noted later in his memoirs. "I couldn't help but get the feeling the 4th Battalion, 39th Infantry, was on the verge of something big."

A tremendous blow to morale and confidence occurred a few days after First Platoon's disastrous encounter with the minefield that had left four seriously wounded. Two platoons of Dagger Company were attacked in their own ambush position by a VC element that had probably been watching them all day. The company had fallen asleep at the wheel. Dagger's casualties were nearly twenty dead and wounded; the company commander was also killed.

Hackworth appointed a good guerrilla commander, Captain Ed Clark, to pick up the pieces of Dagger Company. In the early morning hours of March 23, Dagger's listening posts on an ambush position spotted enemy troops slipping into attack positions. Figuring the enemy knew all too well where his people were located, Captain Clark fooled Charlie by moving his unit back a couple of hundred meters. Minutes later two companies from the Main Force VC 261st Alpha Battalion launched an attack on Clark's old position with rocket launchers and light machine guns blazing.

When the VC realized their prey had slipped away, they moved slowly forward. Clark held his fire until the last moment. Then a VC tripped a claymore mine and the fight was on. Dagger extracted payback by gutting the enemy's attack formation with machine guns and individual weapons. By the light of popping flares, gunships helped break the attack and placed effective fire on Charlie and his probable escape routes. Artillery also joined in.

By dawn the enemy was in full retreat. Using tracker dogs to follow blood spoor and LOHs flown barely above grass level, Alert and Dagger Companies hot-trailed the escaping VC into their defensive perimeter. Thirteen air strikes again sent the enemy on the run. Dagger set up on the most likely escape route, where the company killed forty enemy soldiers during the night.

Hackworth's Hardcore killed 143 enemy soldiers, demolished 261st Alpha's base camp, and captured the defeated battalion's colors. The 4/39th suffered eight casualties in the action, none of them serious enough for immediate medical evacuation.

"It ain't over yet," L. J. Henderson predicted, chewing his cigar. "In fact, you ask me, it's just beginnin'."

As for Platoon Sergeant Richardson, he seemed to have lost something personal and deep inside himself after the day in the mined rice field. Quiet to begin with, he became even more subdued. On the day we received the bad news that Sergeant Svatek had been wounded, Richardson uttered not a single word. He walked alone to the wire at FSB Danger and stared out across the grass plains for a long time. He had acquired the fabled 1,000-yard stare in a tiny room.

Lieutenant Torpie, the leader of Second Platoon, to which Svatek had transferred, had dispatched Svatek and a squad to set up an ambush on a river trail. The radio antenna of Svatek's RTO, Nigel Poese, had hit a trip wire concealed in tree branches. The explosion had killed Poese and riddled Svatek with shrapnel. We heard at first that Svatek had died. Then we heard he was in serious condition but that he would live. He was shipped to a hospital in Japan, where he joined Dale Gass the farm boy in recovering.

Lieutenant Keppel urged Sergeant Richardson to take R&R. "You need to get away for a while, Jim. A little I&I—intercourse and intoxication—in Bangkok or somewhere."

Richardson stared at him with blank eyes. He looked around at the platoon. He felt responsible for us. "Not yet," he said.

Lieutenant Keppel argued that, given Dagger's decimation of the VC's 261st Alpha, Charlie wasn't up for much more fighting for a while. It would be a good time for Richardson to take off. The platoon sergeant finally acquiesced and took R&R leave. Sergeant Wallace and Sergeant Marty Miles more or less took his place.

50

March 25, 1100 hours

The platoon was scheduled for an eagle flight, a recon-in-force to check out a wood line near where Dagger Company had concluded its battle with the 261st Alpha the previous day. VC were supposed to be moving back into the area. After checking out the first target, choppers would lift First Platoon up near Moc Hoa on the Plain of Reeds. Everyone except Henderson, who was always predicting disaster, expected the day to be little more than a long walk in the sun.

Little Arles Brown stayed behind as the platoon saddled up and went out FSB Danger's back gate to the chopper pad; Henderson had dropped a machine gun on Arles's foot and broken it. RTO Harry Fullmer also stayed behind to take care of some personal affairs; Specialist Bob Eaton would function as Lieutenant Keppel's radio operator. A helicopter full of women from the TV series *High Chaparral* dropped in and landed just as we were loading up to depart—miniskirts and legs everywhere to entertain the troops. Arles grinned happily.

"You guys take care of Charlie," he quipped. "Ol' Arles will take care of the women."

Henderson, chewing on his cigar, rode next to me. Faulkenberg sat across from us with Slim Holleman. The choppers flew northwest for six miles and descended upon another wide field that reminded me of the minefield six days earlier, except that this one was totally flat and dry.

"We lost four of us in a place open like this," Henderson said. "You know, I'm startin' to really get tired of this shit. Hear what I'm sayin', Doc?"

March 25, 1235 hours

Unknown to anyone in First Platoon, hostile eyes peered from the jungle as the flight of slicks deposited us near a shallow stream with high banks that bisected the clearing. A searing midday sun sucked moisture out through our skin.

Lieutenant Keppel and Sergeant Miles lined out the outfit and got it ready to assault the wood line once the Cobras and hogs finished prepping it with rocket fire. Dug into the woodline, dug in deep, was the Dinh Tuong Provisional Headquarters of the North Vietnamese Army. Surviving elements of the 261st Alpha VC Battalion that had engaged Dagger Company, along with the 502nd Main Force VC Battalion and the 279th Vietcong Security Force also watched silently from deep cover. In the woods, in bunkers capable of withstanding the Cobra attack, lurked 200 to 400 heavily armed enemy soldiers.

First Platoon was a force of about twenty men.

Xin loi—sorry about that.

The field was about 400 meters across. Except for the bisecting stream and a narrow strip of head-high weeds that grew from a point on the little creek toward the wood line, the hard-packed clearing supported only short rice stubble on slightly rolling terrain. First Platoon began moving toward the wood line. Sergeant Wallace led his half of the platoon to the right of the weeds; I accompanied the lieutenant's squad to the left.

I hadn't felt well when I awoke that morning. Parasites or something—or simply too much humping the boonies with poor food and too little asleep. I felt half dead, dragging, zombied out. I kept online with my peripheral vision as we slogged toward the wood line. The sound of the buzzing Cobras and their bombs was deafening. I tuned it out. All I thought about was getting this day over with and returning to FSB Danger where I could crash.

Suddenly I became aware that I was walking alone on the barren field. I looked around. Lieutenant Keppel and the rest of the squad lay prone behind me. The lieutenant frantically motioned for me to get down. I read his lips—something about "head up your ass."

Beyond the weeds, Sergeant Bill Gregory was lobbing missiles from his M79 into the woods as fast as he could load and pull the trigger while Charlie Reese fired long bursts from his M60 machine gun.

I felt much better immediately. It always surprised me how long it took to go from standing to prone. I low-crawled rapidly back to the stream bed and fell over the bank into Mario Sotello's arms.

"Doc, it's Faulkenberg."

I remembered what Faulkenberg had said when his buddy, Fentress, got it: that he would be next. "Dead?" I asked.

"He's still moving. He needs a medic fast."

"I'm on my way. Where is he?"

"He's lying directly in front of an enemy bunker."

What could I say? "Don't mean nothing," I said.

I ran along the bottom of the stream, using it for cover, until I had to get out of it. I saw Faulkenberg's body lying like an empty bundle of clothing on the field almost at the edge of the distant wood line. Just beyond him, where the first trees grew, was an enemy bunker almost level with the ground and camouflaged with jungle growth. I glimpsed movement at the firing ports. A pale blue pall of gun smoke hovered over the bunker. The VC inside were stitching the field with .51 caliber machine-gun fire. Troops lay scattered about, flat on their bellies and afraid to move.

Guardian angel, you watching this?

I recalled what Doc Holley had told me that time when I walked point, about how most Medals of Honor were awarded posthumously. He had also said no one would think any less of me if I didn't try to reach the wounded under fire. But that was my man out there, hurt. A medic had no choice.

"Medic coming up!" I yelled as I threw myself over the lip of the stream bank and began low-crawling across the field like a fast lizard. A string of little geysers erupted off to my right.

Sergeant Marty Miles joined me. "Doc, you'll need help," he said. Marty was from Tenafly, New Jersey. "New Joisey," he called it. Like me, he had played football and was All-City his senior year. A lot of colleges were interested in him until they learned he weighed less than 150 pounds.

Sergeant Wallace's pinned-down squad and Lieutenant Keppel's men in the stream laid down covering fire on the bunker. Sergeant Miles and I crawled underneath the stream of singing lead. I thought it incredible that we reached Faulkenberg unhurt. He groaned in greeting.

"Glad to see you, Doc. Didn't I tell you I'd get it too?"

He was pale and looked to be going into shock. Blood covered his chest. He lay on his back. You could tell how serious a man was injured by how he lay. A man not critically wounded always protected his belly by keeping it next to the ground.

"Don't talk," I said. "We have to hurry."

Bullets flew over our heads and thumped into the nearby bunker. Working from as close to the ground as I could get, my mouth dry and my tongue sticking to the roof of my mouth from raw fear, I ripped Faulkenberg's jungle shirt off to reach his wound. The bullet had penetrated his right lung lobe. Lung material bubbled from the puncture—a sucking chest wound. I sealed the front wound with Vaseline-coated gauze and the plastic wrap from a field dressing and secured it with adhesive tape.

I turned him over onto his belly to seal the exit wound. He spat up something hard and dark-colored. "Jesus!" Miles exclaimed.

"Butterscotch candy," Faulkenberg said.

Miles took one side of the wounded GI, and I took the other side. Still low-crawling, we dragged him fifty yards to the streambed. It was a hell of a way to treat a patient, but at least I made house calls. Wallace and his men folded in behind us. Two machine guns played rat-a-tat on our asses.

Lieutenant Keppel was frantic on the horn with higher-higher, but I don't think he or any of us realized the extent of the contact we had made. He reported enemy of approximately squad size.

Exploding grenades prevented a dust-off from picking up Faulkenberg. A Loach observation helicopter, *Commanche One*, radioed Eaton, the RTO, that a branch of our little stream split off from the main artery to our left flank and angled across the clearing away from the hostile wood line.

"Battle Red 56," instructed the pilot, "follow the branch-off for about two hundred meters. I'll mark an LZ for the dust-off."

Four other grunts, running, helped me carry Faulkenberg along the stream to the landing zone. Within a few minutes, the wounded Recondo disappeared into the belly of a Huey bearing the big Red Cross. I figured he'd end up in Japan with his partner, Fentress. At the present rate of attrition, there would be enough First Platoon soldiers in the hospital in Japan to hold our first annual reunion.

51

March 25, 1320 hours

Battle Company's CO, Lieutenant Knapp, was off on R&R. The acting CO was Lieutenant William James Torpie, Second Platoon leader. He was tall and dark and lanky, always wearing a grin that made him appear cool and unflappable. Like almost everyone else in the company, he was in his early twenties. Boy soldiers. Many of the VC, however, were even younger.

The rest of Battle Company inserted out of range on the LZ used by the medevac. As the platoons offloaded the slicks, Lieutenant Torpie directed them up the streambed to seed in on First Platoon's flanks. Third Platoon, with its undisciplined Soul Patrol, was now led by a tough specialist fourth class by the name of Donald Lee Hooker, a former gang leader of the Chicago Black Stone Rangers. Hooker now had the Soul Patrol under control. The Third fed onto First Platoon's left flank. There was little exchange of fire with the wood line as Cobras worked it over and *Tamale 14*, an air force forward air controller in a small military version of a Cessna, flew overhead, preparing the air for the jet fast-movers.

I mingled with the newcomers, who included three medics—Company medic Elijah Frazier, Third Platoon medic Mike Hill and my friend Rick Hudson of the Second Platoon. I hadn't worked with Rick since the night the guy almost died on us from the insect bite. Hudson filled me in on Sergeant Svatek and we loitered, gossiping.

"You're too late for the action," I told him. "By the time the artillery, the gunships, and the jets get through with that wood line, there won't be a rat left walking or a snake left crawling."

"Better them than us."

Two men in Hudson's platoon had had premonitions of death. Machine gunner Dennis Richards had told a buddy that "something is going to happen tomorrow." He had been wounded twice before, but neither had been preceded by foreboding like the one he had experienced the previous night. "I'm not going to make it," he had said with sharp finality.

The other man, Platoon Sergeant Ron Sulcer, had been chatting up one of the *High Chaparral* girls on the FSB Danger helicopter pad just before lifting off to reinforce First Platoon at the clearing. She was a beautiful brunette from Temple, Texas, Sulcer's hometown. A cold hand had rested on the sergeant's shoulder, and a voice had said, "Today is the day." Sergeant Sulcer pivoted to take a look. There was no one behind him.

"Have your guys had premonitions like this?" Rick Hudson asked me, looking troubled.

"Most of the time it doesn't mean anything," I said.

"Have you ever had a premonition, Dan?"

I shook my head. "I have a guardian angel."

I adjusted my glasses. We watched the distant tree line in awed silence as F-4 Phantoms streaked in low, roaring, and dropped ordnance into the palms. Strings of giant flash explosions hurled palm trees fifty feet into the air. Black smoke rolled, coughing, smudging the sky. Battle Company GIs strolled leisurely around the open field, visiting, laughing, smoking cigarettes, eating, and watching the spectacular fireworks show as all the power available to the Green Machine in Vietnam concentrated on what we assumed were a few scraggly Vietnamese stupid enough to let themselves be tagged.

"Nothing left out there but shattered trees and bomb craters," observed Third Platoon's Doc Hill.

I hoped he was right.

Colonel Hackworth was now sending in Alert company, just in case. Soldiers were filling up the clearing. More spectators for the air show.

"What are we supposed to do if there *is* an NVA division out there?" a lieutenant asked.

"Give them a road map."

"Salute and say, 'No fuckin' slack, sir. Recondo!'"

Then the fireworks ended abruptly. Black smoke oozed out of the trees, punctuated by licking tongues of red flame. Nothing could have survived such a lambasting.

"It's time for the infantry to go to work," said Private Marshall Hayes. "Infantry—the queen of battle."

52

March 25, 1515 hours

Eugene O'Dell of the mortar platoon carried a heavy 90mm recoilless rifle. It weighed 35 pounds and was usually left in base camp. No one in Battle Company could remember the last time anyone had humped the big gun on a mission, but now O'Dell had it.

"What's the objective?" O'Dell asked Lieutenant Torpie.

"We're taking a walk in the sun," the company commander answered, meaning it would be a low-risk operation after the Phantoms finished their bombing runs. "A body count for the Dich Board."

Alert Company remained in reserve in the streambed while the Battlin' B strung out its platoons for the 300-meter slog into the smoke and rubble left by the air force jets. First Platoon took point in a long file, followed by Second Platoon with Third Platoon to Second's left flank.

First Platoon's own point element consisted of seven men—Tiger Scout Doi and Private Earl Marshall Hayes, the two of them twenty-five meters in advance of a five-man security team led by Sergeant Wallace and including Wallace's RTO Ron Miller, big Aztec-looking Mario Sotello, and Jim Fabrizio, the redheaded "Wop Number One" from Chicago.

"Where's your fifth man?" Lieutenant Keppel called out as the point piled out of the stream and slowly spread out walking toward the smoldering wood line.

Wallace looked around and pointed at Slim Holleman. "Get on up here, Slim."

"I ain't goin', man. I done did my share."

"We ain't complete without a soul bro'," Sergeant Wallace rapped. "Get up here."

Unhappy with the order and snarling under his breath, Holleman slouched toward the sergeant, dragging the butt of his M16 on the ground.

"Get with the program, Holleman," the lieutenant shouted, impatient. "Get your weapon up."

Holleman slowly, defiantly, hoisted his rifle. The point element spread across the baked, short-rice landscape. Sergeant Gregory, leading the first squad, fell in behind. Strung out to his rear were Charlie Reese, carrying the M60 machine gun, and Sugar Bear Bauer, bringing up the tail. The command post element—made up of Lieutenant Keppel, RTO Bob Eaton, Sergeant Marty Miles, and me—filled in the gap between first squad and trailing second squad. We spread out so broadly across the flats that Doi and Hayes up front were about to reach the tree line while Third Platoon, 40 yards to our left and behind First Platoon, was still crawling out of the stream and up the steep bank. Lieutenant Torpie and the rest of the company CP directed operations in the streambed.

And in the woods, VC and hardened NVA were crawling out of their tunnels and air raid shelters. They waited and held their fire. Vietcong called the tactic of fighting at close quarters to neutralize American support "hugging the belt."

Doi and Hayes entered the wooded area.

The crack of doom descended upon them. Hundreds of Chinese Communist AK-47s and light machine guns literally exploded in their faces. Joe Holleman and Jim Fabrizio actually saw bullets plunging through the two men, making them dance on their feet like marionettes. Chunks of flesh and globs of bright blood blew out of their backs, as if in slow motion. They were dead before their mutilated corpses hit the ground.

The same furious fusillade took out Wallace and Fabrizio. They fell together, while slightly behind them Sotello, Slim Holleman, and Ron Miller hit the dirt face down. Machine-gun bullets turned the PRC-25 on Miller's back into a pile of useless, mangled metal. Miller lay with dirt in his mouth while bullets spanged off the radio.

Wallace's M16 saved his life. A bullet that would have gone through his abdomen deflected off the weapon's selector switch, lacerating his hand between the index and middle finger. The weapon was useless. He cast it aside. It was the swarthy sergeant's fifth Purple Heart.

"I feel blood running down my leg," Fabrizio exclaimed.

The two men were less than ten feet apart and made eye contact without lifting their heads.

"How bad is it?" Wallace asked.

"It still feels okay, but I must have lost about a quart of blood."

"Put a field dressing on it."

"I'll probably pass out if I look at it."

Sergeant Wallace and Sotello crawled to Fabrizio beneath a stream of deadly gunfire.

"Which leg is it?" Sotello asked.

"God! Can't you see, Mario? It's my left leg."

In spite of the situation, Sotello snickered. "James, it's your canteen that's wounded, man. Not you."

The hot water had felt like blood. "Be goddamned," Fabrizio said, and managed a sheepish grin.

Boonie rats were spread out face down all over the field without enough cover to shield a snake. Hostile incoming was so intense we dared not raise our heads. Communication with the point element had been cut off; we thought everyone out front must be dead. Fifty yards back from Sergeant Wallace's men, Sergeant Gregory and Sugar Bear Bauer pumped M79 grenades at the tree line. I fired my M16.

"Stop shooting, Doc, before you hit your point guys," Marty Miles yelled.

The earth was as hard as concrete, dry and cracked. I was getting an up close and personal introduction to it. Rice shoots grew about six inches tall. I wished I was skinny enough to melt right down into the rice plants.

Lieutenant Keppel, behind me, shouted something to the effect that we had to get all the men in front of us—including those surviving on point—back to the stream ditch so we could call in artillery. The lieutenant sounded excited but in control. He was proving himself. I thought Sergeant Richardson would have been proud of our young officer.

"Sergeant Miles, see if you can get a machine gun off to our right flank and lay down a field of fire so Wallace can withdraw."

"Yes, sir."

Charlie Reese was the nearest machine gunner. Miles pointed out where he wanted him to go. Reese jumped to his feet. He stumbled and fell fifteen feet in front of me. I crawled to him and found he had a clean bullet hole through the muscles of his right thigh. No arterial or bone involvement. I patched him up with field dressings and told him to stay put.

"How are we going to get him to the rear?" Sergeant Miles asked.

"His wound's not that bad," I explained. "We'll leave him right where he is until nightfall and then low-crawl out."

"I'm not going anywhere," Reese said. He had a million-dollar wound, a ticket back to the land of the Big PX if—that big unspoken *if*—we could get him out of here alive.

No one on the field dared move. Sergeant Miles took Charlie Reese's M60 and loosed a burst of fire into the distant wood line. Situation: FUBAR—fucked up beyond all recognition. We were in one bad position. All we could do was wait until nightfall. If we could hold out that long.

Lieutenant Keppel crawled toward us, paused about ten meters away, and lifted himself up on his elbows.

"Doc, do you need a dust-off for Charlie—"

He exposed himself enough to catch a slug through the left chest wall. The force of the bullet flipped him onto his back and threw his legs bicycling into the air.

"*Mommy! Mommy!*" he shrieked, then lay still, looking up at the light blue of the sky and the low floor of deadly lead scything across the field. I figured the bullet had gone through his heart, that he was dead.

"Is he—" Charlie Reese asked in a hushed tone, staring.

We all stared, stunned by how quickly life flowed through and out. I almost felt myself aging.

Minutes passed. The lieutenant groaned. His legs moved, kicking feebly as he regained consciousness.

"Doc?" Sergeant Miles said.

"I see him."

I started crawling toward the lieutenant. An enemy machine gunner picked up the movement and hosed the area. I stopped. The machine gunner stopped. I crawled forward again. The machine gun came back on. I remembered someone in boot camp saying that he had been the only GI to survive an ambush in a Korean rice paddy by lying still and close to the ground. I lay now with my left cheek pressed into the dirt. Only my buttons prevented me from getting any closer to the ground. I counted bullets as they flew inches over my head. I stopped counting after eight. They made a cracking noise as they passed my right ear. The hair on the back of my head stirred as they went by. Rounds thudded into the hard earth a few inches behind my feet.

"Doc?" It was Lieutenant Keppel's weak, croaking voice. "Doc, go back. I'm going to die anyhow."

Tears suddenly filled my eyes. I remembered how, sometimes in base camp, the lieutenant talked about how war was the natural state of human affairs and peace the anomaly. Recondos sometimes referred to him as the "pacifist lieutenant." He had lasted longer with the First Platoon than any of our previous leaders; most of the guys had come to accept him on a par with Sergeant Richardson.

"Go back, Doc," he managed. "You'll get yourself killed."

"L.T., you forgot I have a guardian angel."

"How . . . how could I ever forget that?"

I finally reached the lieutenant an instant before the Second Platoon medic, Rick Hudson, slid down next to me. Although he'd been under cover in the streambed when the ambush was sprung, he hadn't stayed there. Recognizing that men were wounded on the field of battle, he had thrown himself into harm's way. Clutching his aid bag with one hand, firing his M16 with the other, no longer a conscientious objector, he had raced two hundred meters across that deadly field, darting and dodging, while every Vietnamese in the tree line tried to bring him down. Where, I wondered again, did the army find such valiant men?

The lieutenant protested that we were too late to save him. We had to try. Death, our old enemy, wouldn't win without a fight. Keppel was hyperventilating and sweating so profusely that adhesive tape wouldn't stick to his wet skin.

The entrance wound was small and sealed and bloodless between his clavicle and first rib. His left side was paralyzed, preventing his trying to crawl to cover on his own. The exit wound was a bloody hole the size of my fist torn out of his back two inches below the rib cage. It made a gurgling sound. The lieutenant himself took a field bandage, wadded it up and stuck it into the crater. Hudson and I sealed both wounds with Vaseline gauze and secured the dressings in place by wrapping a cravat around his chest. That wasn't accepted procedure at Fort Sam's medic school, but Fort Sam wasn't stuck out here on this bloody field, pinned down by hostile fire while good men suffered and died.

Trying to drag the weight of the tall officer over the length of two football fields under withering enemy fire to the safety of the streambed would have been willful suicide for all three of us. As Lieutenant Keppel drifted into unconsciousness, I whispered to Hudson, "We have no choice. We have to wait until dark before we can get him out."

"Can he last that long?" Hudson wondered. He lifted his eyes toward the bright sky without raising his head off the ground. Nightfall was hours away. "Can any of us out here on this damned field last that long?"

53

March 25, 1610 hours

The tropical sun beat down upon the field of death, seeming to press the dead and the wounded into the pale dry field of rice plants, returning earth to earth. Second Platoon, to First Platoon's rear, was also pinned down on the flats and getting hell shot out of it. Hostile fire poured out of the woods both to our front and to Second Platoon's right. Wounded men cried out for relief.

Lieutenant Ross Sterling, the redleg artillery officer assigned to Battle Company, faced a dilemma. He needed heavy support in order for Battle to survive, but he required pinpoint artillery accuracy to avoid collateral damage. We were out of range of the 105mm batteries at FSB Danger. Howitzers would have to be airlifted within range, which would take time. Sterling decided to call for ARVN artillery, which was always unreliable. Their first rounds hit so far off-target that Sterling called a cease-fire rather than add friendly fire to Battle's problems.

A U.S. Navy cruiser steaming through the South China Sea volunteered to pour in a few rounds from its five-inch guns, but its marking rounds also missed the target by 200 meters. For Battle Company's safety, the artillery officer terminated the fire mission. That left the air force fast-movers and army hogs—but the lead elements of First Platoon would have to pull back from the wood line, out of the kill zone, before air support could accomplish much. The VC knew what they were doing by fighting "close to the belt." GIs caught in the open couldn't move at all.

Eugene O'Dell, with his 90mm recoilless, found himself on the company's left flank when the battle began. He hoisted the heavy weapon onto his shoulder and jogged along the streambed until he reached a point past the pinned-down Second Platoon. Firing the gun with any accuracy required him to clamber out into the open and assume the classic kneeling position. Rounds for the gun, each weighing nine pounds, had been distributed among the members of Second Platoon. GIs had to spring up under fire and deliver the rounds to O'Dell as he began sighting in on the enemy positions. Lieutenant Sterling ran to him and helped him adjust.

While enemy fire chewed up the ground around them, O'Dell and Sterling methodically knocked out three VC bunkers before they expended their available high explosives. The last shell was an antipersonnel canister, or beehive, filled with thousands of razorlike fleshettes. O'Dell slammed the shell home, but left the breech unlocked. The beehive would be used only as part of the final protection fire if the company was about to be overrun.

Meanwhile battalion sniper Dan Conney positioned himself in a patch of weeds forward of the stream and scanned the wood line through the 5X scope mounted on his Winchester Model 70. VC had positioned their own snipers in trees. Conney picked out the VC sharpshooters one by one and knocked them out of the trees.

Simultaneously, Company medic Elijah Frazier treated the wounded in the rear as fast as they were brought to him—until a bullet smashed his arm, putting him out of action. Lieutenant Sterling was dressing the wound when he witnessed one of those freakish incidents sometimes produced by battle. A green tracer ricochet landed on Frazier's chest and spun like a top. Sterling flipped it off with his finger. He appropriated Frazier's aid bag and began treating WIAs.

Third Platoon, with former gang leader Donald Lee Hooker goading it on, maneuvered online parallel to the woods and initiated a charging assault to relieve pressure on the other two platoons. RPG-7 grenades erupted like geysers all through the platoon, filling the dangerous air with shrapnel, smoke, and dust. The advance soon faltered in the face of overwhelming resistance.

"Medic! Medic!"

Mike Hill crawled to the man.

"I think I sprained my ankle," the guy complained.

"You stupid ass," Doc Hill exploded. "Guys are dying

and you whine about a sprained ankle? What do you expect me to do about it?"

Suddenly, what felt like a heavy hammer banged Hill's own leg. He felt himself going into shock as he attempted to treat his own ragged injury. He popped a Darvon-65. Sergeant Craig from Second Platoon finished bandaging him.

As the young medic lay on the battlefield, drifting in and out of awareness, he began praying. "Lord," he prayed, "I can't think of a good reason why you should let me, but I'd sure like to live."

The company now had two medics remaining who were able to function—Rick Hudson and me, and we were pinned down halfway across the field.

At this point, out of ammunition for his 90mm recoilless, Eugene O'Dell began evacuating wounded to the rear. He carried three men to safety before his luck finally ran out. A green tracer knocked his left knee out from underneath him, sending him sprawling across the body of a fourth trooper he was attempting to hoist into his strong arms. The bullet shattered his knee, exited through his thigh, and grazed his rib cage. A second green tracer slammed into his back as two other soldiers started dragging him toward the streambed. The force of the shot blew off his glasses.

The enemy still wasn't through with O'Dell. Charlie had zeroed in on the little group. Bullets gnawed at the men. A third round struck the already critically wounded O'Dell in the right buttock and penetrated his intestinal tract. A fourth shot ricocheted off the ground and took him in the left buttock and destroyed more intestine.

The little group of GIs fell to the ground, unable to withstand the hail of gunfire. Frank Ellis dropped with his head resting on O'Dell's right shoulder. His helmet leaped twenty yards into the air as a large-caliber bullet ripped off the top half of his head, spilling brains and gore.

Paco Melchor crawled to the aid of the wounded men and was shot in the right forearm. Freddie Downs and Sergeant Craig then attempted to reach the pile of bleeding, moaning men. Craig glanced back over his shoulder and saw about twenty men running in the woods. They wore uniforms. He momentarily mistook them for American reinforcements, then realized they were NVA regulars.

He tossed O'Dell over his shoulder and took off running for the rear. Melchor ran with him, holding his torn arm close to his chest. Downs struggled with Ellis who, remarkably, was still breathing even though most of his skull was gone. The little group slid down the bank into the streambed and made its painful way toward a flat next to the creek where a medavac was coming in fast and low, its blades kicking up a whirlwind of dust.

Downs, still clutching the unconscious Ellis, turned his head away to keep the rotor dust from blinding him. To his horror, he watched, in slow motion, a pair of green tracers arc above the stream, growing larger and larger as they descended toward him. They looked the size of meteors by the time they plunged into his body, one penetrating his chest wall with a breath-stopping thump, the other striking his wrist and spinning him in his tracks. He dropped with Ellis on top of him.

He sprang up immediately and threw himself into the belly of the dust-off. Other GIs tossed Ellis's body in on top of him and Paco Melchor. Sergeant Craig found the litters in the chopper filled with injured, terror-stricken GIs. He placed O'Dell sitting up on the blood-smeared floor littered with gore-stained bandages. O'Dell was weak from his four wounds, but he bravely flashed Craig a thumbs-up as the bird lifted its skids off the ground. He tottered forward and for a breath-stopping moment appeared about to plunge out of the helicopter's open door. Then the chopper banked away, and O'Dell fell back inside the cabin.

At FSB Danger, Arles Brown, a cast on his foot, crowded into the ops center with other troops to listen to the desperate chatter of radio transmissions emanating from the dry rice field. His buddies were out there under fire, fighting for their lives. Agitated, unable to take the suspense of not knowing, feeling helpless and REMF-useless and more than a little guilty for not being out there, he finally tore off his cast, taped his foot tightly so it would fit into a combat boot, then jumped onto the next helicopter flight headed into the battle. One for all, all for one.

* * *

Colonel Hackworth had placed Dagger company on stand-down in Dong Tam after its victory over the enemy in the same vicinity in which Battle Company's fight was now heating up. Division had scheduled an awards ceremony for the warriors. Hackworth attended the ceremony, but before he left Fire Support Base Danger he had briefed Major Bumstead, his operations officer, on what he had in mind for the day. He felt uneasy about leaving. He wanted units to return to Dagger's battlefield of the previous day to police up VC who might come back to pick up their dead.

"Under no circumstance," he cautioned the major, "are you to become decisively engaged while I'm away."

It had been First Platoon's misfortune to stir up the hornets' nest. Headed back to FSB Danger in his command helicopter following the awards ceremony, Hackworth contacted the Hardcore Battalion as soon as he came within radio range. Major Bumstead sounded exhilarated as he reported that he had a great contact going and everything was fine.

Hackworth flew straight to the battlefield. Horrified, he discovered Alert Company digging in and Battle Company getting the shit shot out of it in a 400-meter dry rice paddy devoid of both cover and concealment. Men lay all over the field, some of them on their backs. The company was pinned down by at least four machine guns, snipers, and a continuous barrage of RPG rounds. GIs couldn't effectively return fire for fear of hitting their own men. Every time Lieutenant William Torpie, the young acting company commander, tried to get the men low-crawling to the safety of the streambed, they drew more fire. It wasn't that the men couldn't get out; it was that they were hampered by their simultaneous efforts to withdraw their seriously wounded with them.

Something had to be done—*fast*. Battle Company couldn't wait until nightfall. It was taking far too many casualties.

54

March 25, 1700 hours

The walk in the sun had become a trip through the meat grinder. Nearly two hours had passed since Luke the Gook initiated his devastating ambush. Two hours that seemed like two years to those of us pinned down on the open field. Time had gone into slow motion. Minutes seemed like hours. An hour was an eternity; an hour for some of us was the rest of our lives.

Charlie Reese's leg had swollen and stiffened on him. Lieutenant Keppel drifted in and out of consciousness. "Gotta get my people outta here," he raved. "Get my people . . ."

Rick Hudson and I had teamed up to care for the wounded in the vicinity, most of whom had bullet holes in legs and arms, which could be simply treated with pressure bandages. We crawled around on the hard earth until we wore holes in our trousers. I watched the westering sun, trying to estimate how much longer before dark. The sun was still bright and hot enough to bake us and suck out our bodily fluids, but it looked to be only about three inches off the horizon.

"Halfway home," Hudson murmured, also waiting for the blessed night.

I had never thought I would pray for darkness in Vietnam.

Odd the thoughts that passed through your mind at such times. They passed so rapidly through that as soon as you grabbed on to one it slipped through the clumsy fingers of your mind and another slipped in.

Don't answer the door, Mom.

Dianne saying, "I wish you had gotten me pregnant before you left. At least I'd have something to remember you by."

219

Dianne writing, "As far as I'm concerned, you're not my husband."

The girl at the bridge giving me the Saint Christopher medal. "*Bac-si,* put it around your neck. You protected now. VC no kill you now."

Trying to watch the Vietnam casualty movies in medic school, having to run outside to get fresh air. Now I found myself starring in one of the movies, only it was for real, even though it didn't always seem real.

Doc Whitmore had warned me when I replaced him as First Platoon's medic not to become personal friends with the troops, but he had also said he knew I wouldn't follow his advice. And I hadn't. Grunts who were no longer with the platoon were now lined up wearing their bloody bandages as they marched through my mind. I saw their faces: Richard Forte, Teddy Creech, Gene Abrahamson, Albert Fletcher, Eugene Harvill . . .

And in just the last week alone: Leonard Gauerke, Dale Gass, the farm boy, Larry Fentress, Bob Howell, Sergeant John Svatek, Charlie Reese, Lieutenant Roger Keppel, Larry Faulkenberg . . .

How many more were there out on the field whom I didn't know about yet? Probably Sergeant Wallace and the entire point element. Others . . . Others.

Shouting and screaming all around. I was in Dante's *Inferno.*

I was in combat—been there, done that, bought the T-shirt—but I still couldn't figure out what it was I had thought to prove when I volunteered for this. How to fill sandbags, dig ditches, treat VD and gunshot wounds? How to watch your friends die in the sun? It hadn't been this way for John Wayne.

What was it all about? Troops always said it meant nothing, but it *had* to mean something, which was what they really meant, except they didn't know what.

Evans, keep your head down and do your job.

Maybe that was the only thing it was all about.

Up ahead of me I saw L. J. Henderson and his assistant gunner, Eusebio Fernandez, pouring machine-gun lead non-stop into the woods. The black man with the chewed-up cigar stub in his mouth seemed frozen on the trigger while

Fernandez kept feeding belts to him. Sergeant Gregory popped M79 grenades and shouted for his squad to pull back. "People, goddammit! Keep down, but pull back." The point men were undoubtedly KIA; no use trying to retrieve their bodies and getting more people killed.

Every time somebody moved, he attracted fire.

RPG grenades and rockets walked through First Platoon, upheaving soil, smoke, and shrapnel and contributing to the hellish din and confusion. The grenades stepped toward me in giant 10-meter footfalls. The first one 40 meters away, then 30, then 20 . . .

I started crawling. Then I buried my head underneath my arms.

The grenades walked back in the direction from which they had come—30, then 40, 50 . . .

Back toward me again—40 . . . 30 . . . 20 . . .

Taunting, torturing . . . 30 . . . 40 . . . 50 . . .

I figured a tree must be blocking Charlie's field of fire, preventing his walking the grenades directly into and over me. I sometimes made light of my guardian angel, joked about it. But maybe I really did have a guardian angel looking over me.

55

March 25, 1720 hours

Cobras with their sharks' grins and Huey hogs buzzed the wood line like a swarm of enraged killer bees, working it over at close range with everything they had. As the most forward element, point under Sergeant Wallace was exposed and vulnerable. Doi the Tiger Scout and Marshall Hayes were already dead. Somehow Wallace and the others were unharmed. The sergeant organized a withdrawal behind covering fire provided by the helicopters. The rest of the company had already marked Wallace off as lost.

Sergeant Wallace brought up the rear with Fabrizio and Ron Miller, still carrying his busted radio, Mario Sotello and Slim Holleman crawling ahead of him.

"Man, don't none of us need to be *here*," Holleman panted. "Especially not no soul brother."

Wallace heard the bullet hit the black grunt's head, sounding like a melon thumped by a ball peen hammer. The bullet hit the bull's-eye on a pack of Lucky Strike cigarettes that Holleman carried in his helmet cover band. It pierced the helmet and went into his forehead and out with a gush of brain gore behind his right ear. He grunted once and relaxed unconscious on the ground.

Wallace had no more field dressings; he fished a clean pair of socks from his ruck and improvised a pressure bandage.

"Slim, don't you die on me, hear? Listen to me, asshole. Don't you dare die on me."

Above, in his C&C helicopter, Colonel Hackworth tried everything he could think of to give his Recondos some air and provide Lieutenant Torpie room to maneuver. It was a hell of a mess on the ground. Having run out of options to get the wounded out of the way so the fast-movers could swarm in with HE and napalm, he was about to add to the Hackworth legend.

He ordered the other gunships to keep fire going on the woods where the enemy machine guns were blazing, to keep Charlie's head down, while he directed his pilot to land within 30 feet of Sergeant Wallace's element. As the C&C bird swooped in and flared for landing, Wallace automatically sprang to his feet to guide the chopper in as he normally did. He caught himself and dropped flat again. Hackworth had landed almost in front of an NVA machine-gun emplacement. He and Major Bumstead were already standing on the skids. They dropped to earth while the helicopter was still six feet off the ground. Bullets punched holes through the aircraft.

"Lads, we're getting you the hell out!" the colonel shouted as he and his ops officer sprinted toward the prone troops.

His only saving grace was gunships swooping down one by one to hose enemy positions during the entire few minutes the C&C rested on the field of fire.

Wallace and the colonel snatched Holleman off the ground, ran back to the chopper, and tossed him into the cabin to an air force doctor. Hackworth figured Wallace was also wounded. Before the sergeant could object, the battalion commander had him tossed into the cabin.

Fabrizio was next. He was covered with Holleman's blood, but still untouched. He had intended to hug the ground until the chopper left, then crawl on back to his platoon and the streambed. Instead, he felt himself jerked off the ground by the two C&C officers and deposited inside the chopper with Holleman, Wallace, and the Air Force doctor. Mario Sotello and Ron Miller jumped up and ran to rejoin the platoon, using the chopper as cover.

There wasn't room in the chopper for Hackworth, so he leaped onto the skid and put on his crash helmet so he could tell the pilot to take off. The pilot was as low to the floor as he could get, using the console as cover. Hackworth's tongue had welded itself to the roof of his mouth from pure fear. He had to open his canteen and take a swig of water before he could speak. "Let's get this mother out of here!" he shouted into the mike.

The bird jerked, leaping into the air. Fabrizio grabbed the colonel around the waist to keep him from falling.

"Colonel," Fabrizio said, as the bird clawed for altitude, "you wouldn't happen to have a cigarette on you, would you?"

Hackworth laughed.

Although Fabrizio was unhurt and Wallace had suffered only the minor hand wound, Colonel Hackworth ordered them to stay behind at FSB Danger. They had administered mouth-to-mouth to Slim Holleman during the flight, crouching over his body on the floor of the helicopter, but the soldier was already brain-dead and would stop breathing shortly after his evacuation.

"You two men have done enough for one day," Hackworth told them before he returned to the fight.

With the point element withdrawn from the kill zone, the Hardcore Battalion commander used every weapon at his disposal to dislodge the enemy from the wood line—napalm, artillery, tear gas, white phosphorous, air strikes, the works. Now that the point element was no longer a factor in the equation, Hackworth couldn't understand why Lieutenant Torpie wasn't doing something to get his men off that field and consolidated at the streambed, but Torpie still kept radioing that he was pinned down.

Hackworth lost his temper and chewed Torpie's ass over the radio: "Lieutenant, you listen to me, sir. Get cracking and get my soldiers out of that paddy. Like *now*. Is that understood?"

"Lima Charley, sir. Loud and clear."

"Then do it, sir. Do it now."

The force of the Hardcore commander's word propelled the young lieutenant to his feet. He began running from man to man all over the field to get them to move back. He wouldn't last long. Battle Company had only two officers left who were not already dead or wounded.

56

March 25, 1740 hours

Lieutenant Torpie bravely organized a frontal assault on the wood line. He and the company command, consisting of RTO Tom Smith and Sergeant Ron Sulcer, worked their way forward from the streambed as the battle progressed. Muzzle flashes sparked from firing slits in the enemy bunkers. Smith and two Hueys were dueling it out with one of the emplacements when a bullet slapped the RTO's left arm, paralyzing it temporarily. Smith lay on the ground and patched himself up.

Farther back, Sergeant Lester from Second Platoon flopped down next to Sergeant Sugar Bear Bauer.

"What's the sitrep on the point element?" Lester asked.

Bauer told him he thought the men had been extracted by Hackworth's helicopter.

"Lieutenant Torpie wants the company to get online to assault the woods," Lester explained.

"That's fucking stupid," Ron Frampton fussed. "What's the point?"

"We can't just stay out here while they pick us off."

"Assholes," Frampton said.

Lieutenant Torpie breezed past, running. "Let's go! Let's go, people! Come on, people! Get up and move into the wood line. They're not even firing at us."

Frampton, Sugar Bear, and a number of others reluctantly scrambled to their feet and joined the charge, rushing toward the thick and smoking woods. Three enemy soldiers jumped up and fled, Torpie pursued them.

"Don't do it!" Sulcer warned him." "Let 'em go!"

The lieutenant's lean body suddenly jerked short. His weapon flew from his numbed fingers as a round punched through both lungs from left to right. Smoke hissed from the bullet holes as he crumpled.

"Battle 46 is hit and down!" Tom Smith radioed from where he nursed his own wound.

Sugar Bear had built up momentum. Running low, he zigzagged toward one of several low-built enemy bunkers constructed at the edge of the woods. Green tracers buzzed from the firing slit. The bunkers were so well built underneath layered roofs of logs and mud baked as hard as concrete that bombs dropped by the air force Phantoms simply bounced off.

Bauer ran past a LAWs rocket—a light antitank weapon—that someone had dropped on the ground. He darted back to retrieve it as a Huey gunship with weapons blazing made a low run at the bunker, causing the defenders inside to drop low and stop firing. Sugar Bear popped up, shouldered the rocket, extended it, sighted, and pressed the trigger. To his delight and relief, the contrail of thin smoke stretched from the weapon through the firing slit as the penetrating rocket entered the bunker. The confined explosion lifted the roof a full two inches and puffed smoke, dust, and fire out the weapons slit. The bunker went dead silent.

Off to Sugar Bear's left, Sergeant Sulcer contended with another bunker. Lieutenant Torpie's assault had run its course; Recondos once more took to their bellies, unable to break through the Viets' defensive line. Withering fire continued to pour from the woods.

Sulcer stayed behind to provide cover fire while the wounded RTO, Smith, and a grunt from Donald Lee Hooker's Soul Patrol dragged Torpie toward the rear. Fighting the bunker directly ahead of him, Sulcer sprang to his feet to maneuver to a more advantageous position. Two bullets snapped past his helmet. He pivoted to confront the enemy soldier.

Muzzle flash winked from the bunker's darkened firing ports. The report from the discharge clapped against his ears. Green bee flying. It cut into his abdomen, went completely through him. Sulcer fell on his back only thirty feet or so in front of the bunker. So near to the Vietnamese that he made out their features as they looked out the slit and laughed at his helplessness. He realized he was paralyzed and at the mercy of the NVA inside the bunker.

He managed to stuff a field bandage into the fist-size exit wound in his back. Then he lay there, his terror-stricken eyes riveted on his enemies as they taunted and played with him, like cats toying with an injured mouse. It was an old VC trick to use a wounded GI as bait, hoping other soldiers would attempt to rescue him and be lured into their trap.

Sulcer watched the VC as they pantomimed shooting him. They made pistols with their hands and pulled imaginary triggers, imitating the sound of gunshots. They took careful aim at the defenseless GI with their rifles. Sulcer's muscles tensed, waiting for the impact of the shot that never came. He heard derisive laughter instead. The VC seemed much amused by their sadistic game.

"Fuck you, assholes!" Sulcer roared defiantly. "Shoot me, goddammit. If you're going to shoot me, *shoot me!*"

The enemy hooted with laughter. Sulcer stared at them, making eye contact, not flinching. He thought he was dying anyhow.

Rick Hudson and I were busy treating WIAs when the company commander, Torpie, ordered his attack and grunts sprang up all over the field to follow him. Moments later, transmissions echoing from radio to radio reported Lieutenant Torpie down, hurt badly. He needed a medic. Hudson and I started working our way toward the wood line, crawling. We were both blood-crusted.

Torpie had already been passed on to Tom Bever, Dennis Richards, and Sugar Bear Bauer. Bever was six-four and long-muscled. He hoisted the bleeding company commander into his arms and started jogging with him toward the rear while Sugar Bear and Richards helped support him and Mario Sotello provided cover fire.

As the little group approached my location, running in a tight bent-over cluster, Richards's throat exploded blood in a pink mist that drenched the other GIs. Slow motion again took over. I actually witnessed the tracer enter the left side of the grunt's neck and exit, dragging with it a strip of skin that seemed to stretch out toward me and flap at the end like a cracked whip. Blood gushed thick from Richards's mouth, nose, and bullet holes. He clutched his throat with both hands as he fell, as though trying to hold his own blood in.

Bever stumbled. The soldiers went down in a pile. Sugar Bear shouted that he had been hit when he saw all the blood covering him.

Hudson crawled rapidly to Richards's aid while I took Lieutenant Torpie. Richards died within seconds. Hudson rolled toward me while Bever and Sugar Bear spread wide and opened fire with their M16s. Torpie lay still, his face relaxed and peaceful, eyes rolled back in his head. Both lungs had collapsed, but he was still breathing. I didn't know how he could. A medic could never give up, though, as long as a single breath remained in a maimed GI's body.

Torpie's wounds weren't as big as Lieutenant Keppel's—and Keppel was still alive. Hudson and I worked feverishly trying to seal the wounds to trap and preserve what breath Torpie retained. We spoke in crisp monosyllables, feeding each other the patient's pulse rate and respirations, both of which were dropping quickly. Darkness would set in within an hour, but the lieutenant couldn't wait that long. I didn't know if he would make it even if we dusted him off immediately. We worked a collapsible litter underneath him, just in case we got a chance to run with him.

Lieutenant Torpie revived suddenly. He rolled his head and looked directly into my eyes. His dark thin face seemed calm. "Can I borrow a dime?" he asked.

"What do you want a dime for?"

"I got to call my girlfriend and tell her I'm okay."

He gasped. His eyes remained open. I started artificial respiration, blowing into his lungs desperately.

Blood and froth came back up. I tasted it in my mouth. My stomach revolted, but I kept it up until I felt a hand on my back. Sotello or Sugar Bear or someone murmured gently, "Doc, he's dead."

"He's not dead!" I snapped.

"Doc, listen to me. You can't do anything else for him."

I felt so damned tired. I dropped my head onto my arms. Death, my old enemy, had won another round.

"Medic! Medic!"

"Doc? Doc, you're needed."

57

March 25, 1840 hours

The longest day of my life just kept going on and on and on. The sun seemed not to have moved at all. After Lieutenant Torpie and Dennis Richards died, I crawled back to check on Lieutenant Keppel and Charlie Reese and learned that they had been medevac'd. Pushed by his survival instinct and an adrenaline rush, Keppel had jumped up off the ground and *run* to the dust-off when it landed. He didn't have enough energy left to climb into the helicopter, though; other wounded pulled him inside. Sergeant Lester from the Second Platoon, wounded in the arm, cradled the lieutenant's head in his lap and comforted him during the flight to the surgical hospital in Dong Tam.

Rick Hudson and I crawled forward again under continuing enemy fire. Desperate cries of *"Medic! Medic!"* still rang out from the open field.

Bob Goldberg took a bullet through the hand. Dan Moreno felt a sharp blow to his left ankle as an AK-47 round smashed through it. He fell forward, and another bullet slammed into his left shoulder.

Sergeant Marty Miles motioned to me. "It's on the radio," he said. "The zoomies are going to make a very low, very close bomb drop. Get your head into the dirt, Doc. We're close enough to get shrapnel. Pass the word along."

There were grunts to my left. I crawled to them with the word. I heard the jet engines. The Phantom leader was so low to the ground I saw the pilot's head in the cockpit. The lowering sun glinted dully off the bombs released from his wings. To my surprise, the bombs tumbled through the air instead of falling straight down as in the old World War II movies. They tumbled across the sky above our heads—Oh, Jesus Christ, I thought, wasted by my own air force!—and, then, to my amazement and relief, slammed into the wood line, where they exploded in tremendous bursts of flame and smoke that made the ground underneath me shudder.

For the safety of the American troops still on the field, most of the jet fighter bombers flew parallel to the wood line. One pilot, however, spotted Sergeant Sulcer still lying wounded in front of the bunker where the VC were tormenting him and trying to bait other Americans into attempting foolish rescue missions. Sulcer had been lying there for over an hour. The pilot circled and came in perpendicular to the woods, flying in so low that Sulcer could have counted the rivets in the jet's belly.

The Phantom released a napalm canister as it approached. Sulcer knew he was a crispy critter, roasted by the air force instead of shot by the NVA in the bunker. What was the difference? American GI dead all same-same.

The jet jockey knew what he was doing. The napalm barrel had the momentum of its fast-moving carrier. It whistled through the air above the disabled soldier and bashed into the bunker. The rich odor of gasoline rode the whoosh of flame and black oily smoke fifty feet into the air. Tremendous heat instantly transformed the VC inside the bunker to blackened half-cooked corpses.

Hot winds from the explosion scorched Sergeant Sulcer's hair and eyebrows, but he waved with what strength he had left and croaked out a thin cheer of gratitude. He only regretted he could not have watched his tormentors being immolated. As far as he was concerned, they deserved to be burned alive.

The Phantom air strikes continued, run after run. Dirt filled my mouth, I was so close to the trembling earth. I passed out, maybe from bomb blast, from fear, or simply from being so overwhelmed that I fell asleep to mentally escape. When I regained consciousness minutes later, Sergeant Miles and Hudson were gone, and I couldn't place where I was. The nipa palm trees in front of me were now a wall of flames and smoke so intense it must have jacked up the ambient temperature on the field by three or four degrees. I pushed myself around in a three-sixty turn before I finally became oriented again.

I hoped this was a nightmare from which I was awakening. It wasn't. I gradually became aware of Sergeant Miles directing air force strikes over his radio. I pointed to a big tree in the corner of the field ahead, where the wood line became an L. "There's a sniper in that tree," I said. "He's the one who killed Dennis Richards."

"Let's give him the hot seat," Miles exclaimed and got back on the radio. The next air strike demolished the tree. Payback for Dennis.

The word finally came, relayed mouth to mouth from rear to front: withdraw. Best news I'd heard since the eagle flight started at 1100 hours, decades ago. Boonie rats scrambled to the rear. Two grunts from Third Platoon stopped me.

"Ron Sulcer is still up there," they said, pointing. "He needs a medic bad."

Everyone was to go to the rear, I guess, except the medics and the wounded. Hudson, who had been at my side since the beginning, immediately volunteered to accompany me. So did two grunts from Third Platoon. Sergeant Miles would remain on post to relay radio messages for us.

The grunts provided a quick sitrep. "Sulcer is lying directly in front of a bunker." They didn't realize friendly napalm had silenced it. "He looks paralyzed, but he's still alive. He yelled at us to stay back. Gooks are still in the woods."

Since we were abandoning the battlefield to the enemy in defeat, I stuffed what medical supplies I thought I would need into the cargo pockets of my pants and destroyed the remainder. I rolled Torpie's body off the collapsible litter and stripped his corpse and Richards's of ammo and anything else the enemy might be able to use. Then, dragging the collapsible litter, the four of us crawled once more toward the chattering guns of the enemy. As we reached Sergeant Sulcer, I noticed shadows suddenly stretching halfway across the field from the tree line. The sun was now red and low. It was a deep red, a fitting color to end this day. Darkness would settle within fifteen minutes. Night always came quickly to the tropics, like the charge of a big cat.

I patched Sulcer's entrance wound; Hudson took the exit.

"I-I kept thinking they were going to kill me," the suffering sergeant said.

I patted his shoulder. Such men, these young American soldiers. Such courage and self-sacrifice.

"Sergeant, we're here now. We'll get you out," I promised.

"I believe you, Doc."

Sergeant Marty Miles crawled forward. He shouted, "Doc, I've got a chopper coming in to lay smoke for you. Get ready."

We slipped the litter underneath Sulcer. "We'll try to give you a gentle ride," I told him.

"Do what you have to do, Doc. I'd give you my last C-rat can of peaches even if you dragged me out by one foot."

The four of us attached ourselves to the corners of the litter as the helicopter came in low and fast, laying a thick cloud of white smoke along the tree line between us and the enemy. We jumped up and ran with the patient. I felt the wind once I was on my feet. It was blowing the wrong direction. Smoke billowed past us, once more exposing us to the Viets. Bullets snapped past us.

"Get down!"

We dropped. Sulcer stifled a scream. Sweat speckled his face.

"Sorry, Ron."

"It don't mean nothing."

The army always had a Plan B. That went into effect now. The two Third Platoon grunts and Sergeant Miles provided security while Hudson and I dragged Sulcer on his stretcher, a foot or two at a time, toward the distant streambed. We crawled backwards ahead of the stretcher to the length of our arms, pulled the sergeant up to us, then repeated the procedure. Sulcer moaned from his pain, but fought valiantly to restrain anything that might be construed as a complaint.

Darkness fell. Green tracers flying overhead became luminous, like lightning bugs that came out at night. With Marty Miles still providing cover, Hudson and I and the two Soul Patrol boonie rats bunched our muscles, sprang up, and ran with our patient, concealed now by wonderful darkness.

The first soldier we encountered was Major Bumstead, hiding with his RTO in a strip of weeds that had separated First Platoon from the other platoons when the action began and Faulkenberg was hit. The colonel had dropped Bumstead onto site to take charge. We learned that Battle Company had only one officer remaining.

"Is there anyone else out there?" the major asked.

"I think we're the last," Marty Miles said. "Sir, would you mind calling us a dust-off?"

First Platoon—those who remained—came running to embrace us roughly and slap our backs. "Assholes," they said. "Fuckin' grunts," they said with that rough affection not altogether smothered by their words. The tall Aztec Mario Sotello; the broad, pleasant face of Sergeant Bauer, who really did look like a Sugar Bear; tiny Arles Brown, unable to stay out of the fight while his buds, his brothers, were in it, limping around peering through his thick glasses while he helped the wounded; Ron Miller, who had finally shed his busted radio; the tall homeboy L. J. Henderson with his flashing, welcoming grin and his cigar.

"Jesus, Doc," Sugar Bear exploded, "we heard you were dead. That was the report."

"It's news to me."

Henderson looked me over just to make sure. "Doc, don't you *dare* get dead on me, man. Hear what this nigger's sayin'?"

58

March 25, 2230 hours

The last wounded man medevac'd off the field was the company commander's RTO, Tom Smith, who'd been hit in the left arm early in the fight just before Lieutenant Torpie and Sergeant Sulcer went down in front of the wood line. Smith had stayed on the battlefield to help in the rear with the wounded until well after dark, when Doc Hudson noticed blood oozing from the radioman's arm.

"It's not that bad," Smith protested.

"You're on your way out," Hudson told him.

Smith got out of the dust-off at Dong Tam to find a truck and driver waiting for him.

"Where's the KIA?" the driver asked.

"I'm the only passenger, and I'm not dead," Smith explained.

Two green body bags containing corpses lay at the doorway of the 3rd Surg Hospital when Smith walked in. He was further evacuated to a hospital at Tan Son Nhut. As he walked through the door, he was greeted by a soldier sitting up in bed holding his spilled intestines in his hands and screaming, "I don't want to die. I don't want to die!"

On the field, the morale-shattered remnants of Battle Company dug in for the night. It was too late to extract us. Colonel Hackworth had thought to get something else going with the enemy, to seal off the area and sweep it in force. His C&C helicopter, however, took a full spray of machine-gun bullets through the belly, which hit the artillery officer in the gut and shattered Hackworth's leg. Colonel Hardcore found himself being carried into 3rd Surg, where the wounded troops cheered him robustly and shouted, "Hardcore Recondo, sir!"

On the battlefield, Captain Winston, an officer of Alert

233

Company, which had been sent in to take the pressure off Battle Company and salvage the fight, was busy having a full-blown nervous breakdown. He walked around telling every soldier he met, from private on up, that, of all the units in Vietnam, *his* company was the only one selected to be resupplied with yellow smoke grenades. Alert Company troops kept receiving a strange radio transmission to pop yellow smoke; they ignored it and dug in.

Battle Company had lost virtually its entire chain of command and 30 percent of its strength. Sergeant Marty Miles, now acting company commander, was in charge. He spread the survivors in a defensive line along the streambed and planted claymores out front to fend off one or two half-hearted enemy probes.

The company had expended all its machine-gun ammo, and half the men were without ammunition for their M16s. Almost all the M79 grenades had been used. Machine guns had been fired so hard their barrels had overheated and warped. VC rocketed one of our resupply helicopters as it tried to negotiate a too-small landing zone in the darkness. The bird hit a tree and crashed to the ground, trapping one of the door gunners inside the wreck and burning him alive. His screams grated against the nerves of every GI on the field. The chopper burned brightly, exploding ammunition for the rest of the night.

"We're down to throwin' rocks at 'em," L. J. Henderson lamented. "Hear what I'm sayin'?"

Major Bumstead went operationally paralytic with the fall of night. Consequently, there was no security patrol and no sweep of the area. Leaderless, Alert and Battle Companies merely squatted in our holes until morning, when the NVA and VC units probed a few times, then ran away. The U.S. arsenal was extensive enough to blow the wood line completely off the map come dawn.

The battle, said Colonel Hackworth later, was "a stinging defeat and a waste of good men's lives." Seven men were known dead; five of their bodies still lay on the battlefield. About twenty had been seriously wounded. First Platoon was down to less than a dozen men still on the battlefield and able to fight.

Medic Mike Hill of Third Platoon hobbled into 3rd Surg

using his M16 as a crutch. Other medics cut off his trousers and boots. A doctor wearing a golf shirt took one look. "This man needs a shower first," he snapped.

After treatment, Hill dozed off in one of the wards. At 2230 hours, Dong Tam came under attack from 120mm mortars, the largest in the enemy's arsenal. Wounded boonie rats from the battle at the dry rice field were dragged to bunkers while rockets rained down on 9th Division's base camp. About 500 tons of ordnance and fuel exploded when mortar rounds hit the army's fuel supply depot. Four men were killed there and sixty others wounded.

Colonel Arnold, commander of the 9th Medical Battalion and the only American in Vietnam I had grown to hate because of his chickenshit rules and regulations, took a shard of shrapnel through his right radial artery. He would have bled to death if he hadn't been in the middle of a medical unit. He wouldn't be around anymore to transplant palms and pass out Article 15s.

I had to hand him one thing, though. If it hadn't been for his chickenshit, I might have spent the war as a REMF in Dong Tam. Someday, when my unborn son asks, "What did you do in the war, Daddy?" I wouldn't have to tell him I'd driven garbage trucks, treated VD cases, and vaccinated whores.

The night on the rice field had grown cold. Sergeant Miles and I found a bed of hay and crawled into it for warmth. I lay for the rest of the night listening to negative situation reports on the radio. I was bloodstained, filthy, and totally exhausted, but I couldn't sleep. I had asked myself simple but vital questions before coming to Vietnam: Could a green twenty-one-year-old with ten weeks of medical training do a job? Could I really save lives?

"The day will come when you will be called upon," the medic school instructors had preached. "The troops will depend upon you. Their *lives* will be in *your* hands."

I *had* been called upon. I had done what I could. Maybe it was not always enough. Some of the men I treated had died: Richard Forte, Lieutenant William Torpie, Dennis Richards. But others had lived: Lieutenant Roger Keppel, Ron Sulcer, Larry Faulkenberg, Larry Fentress, Eugene Harvill, Charlie Reese, Dale Gass, and others. Sometimes the war was a Twilight Zone. At other times, amid the horror, I saw a certain nobility in acts of individual courage and sacrifice. Many of those who were wounded and killed on the battlefield had been attempting to help their comrades.

"It don't mean nothing," the grunts said. But I felt that my being in Vietnam *did* mean something. My work had had some value. The war was crazy, it was insane, but the medics were there to alleviate some of the suffering. Surely that meant something.

L. J. Henderson slipped into the hay next to me.

"Doc, how's your guardian angel?"

"Must be still watching, L.J."

"Doc . . . ?" The burning resupply helicopter illuminated his dark face. He took out his cold cigar and squeezed my shoulder. "Thanks for bein' with us, Doc," he said. "You are one good combat medic. Hear what I'm sayin'?"

I heard him.

AFTERWORD

The Vietnam War ended for me, Doc Daniel E. Evans Jr., four months after the battle in the rice field, on July 30, 1969, when I DEROS'd back to the United States. For me, First Platoon was never the same after that battle. I continued to do my job, treating the wounded, but I did not bother to learn the names of the men who replaced First Platoon's dead and wounded. I didn't want to lose any more friends in Vietnam.

For my service as a combat medic with the U.S. Army 9th Infantry Division, I was awarded the Combat Medical Badge; the Distinguished Service Cross, the nation's second highest award for heroism; the Bronze Star with *V* for "Valor," with three oak-leaf clusters; the Army Commendation Medal with *V* for "Valor," with two oak-leaf clusters; a Purple Heart; the Vietnam Service Medal; the Vietnam Campaign Medal; and the National Defense Service Medal.

I refused to read newspapers or watch television reports about the Vietnam War once I returned home. I had difficulty sleeping each night until after I relived in my mind the bloody battle of March 25, 1969. Why did I live? Why didn't I do more? Did I let anyone down?

I am now a doctor of veterinary medicine practicing in Ohio. I have been married to my present wife, Sandy, for over twenty years. We have a son, Ryan, and a daughter, Kelly.

Many of the wounded from Vietnam endured months of surgeries and rehabilitation. Some of the wounded were maimed and remain in pain for the rest of their lives. A few of the more seriously injured wished they had died. For many Vietnam veterans, the war has never ended, nor will it end during their lifetime.

The families of those killed in Vietnam were also casualties of war. Sons are supposed to bury their parents, not the other way around.

The exploits of the man with the 90mm recoilless rifle reached legendary proportions during the months following the March 25 battle. Eugene O'Dell was wounded four times. His heart stopped beating twice during surgery. He recovered from his wounds by Christmas. He was recommended for the Congressional Medal of Honor, but it was downgraded to the Distinguished Service Cross. His citation only mentioned that he was wounded once. Marty Miles and Colonel (then Lieutenant Colonel) David H. Hackworth were also awarded the Distinguished Service Cross for their heroic deeds on March 25.

Sergeant Ron Sulcer awoke on the morning of March 26 in the 3rd Surgical Hospital at Dong Tam. In the bed next to him lay a VC who had also undergone surgery the night before. The VC stared directly at Sulcer, giving him flashbacks of how he had been tormented by the enemy soldiers in the bunker after he was wounded. He frantically screamed for a nurse and demanded she remove the gook.

Now married with three children, Sulcer works for Disabled American Veterans, assisting disabled veterans and active duty servicemen.

Lieutenant Roger Keppel and Larry Faulkenberg underwent surgery at the military hospital at Can Tho. They awoke to find themselves attached to the same chest suction pump. Faulkenberg eventually caught up to his friend Larry Fentress in Japan. Fentress and Faulkenberg live within twenty miles of each other. Faulkenberg is a heavy equipment operator by night and a farmer by day. Fentress is totally disabled. Lieutenant Roger Keppel recovered completely and is now an environmental biologist with a large electrical utility company.

*   *   *

AFTERWORD

From the *Marion* [Ohio] *Star,* March 29, 1969:

Dennis R. Richards
Killed in Viet Fight

Spec. 4 Dennis R. Richards, 21-year-old son of Mr. and Mrs. Robert Richards . . . was killed in Vietnam Tuesday, the third Marion youth to fall in six days.

His parents received word Friday that Dennis was mortally wounded in combat with his unit, B Company, 4th Battalion, 39th Infantry, 9th Infantry Division, near Dong Tam.

A 1965 graduate of Harding High School, he attended Ohio State University's Marion campus for two years prior to entering the army. He went into the service Dec. 8, 1967, and left for Vietnam Oct. 10, 1968.

An athlete in school, he was a starting lineman on the Harding football team during 1964.

He was a member of Emanuel Lutheran Church and employed by the Hollyday Rug Co. while attending college.

Also surviving is a sister, Nancy Jane, a student at Bowling Green State University, and his grandmother, Mrs. Amos G. Uncapher. . . .

Spec. 4 Richards is the 13th Marion County serviceman to lose his life in Vietnam.

Richards had written a last letter to his parents and sister on March 24, 1969, the day before the fight in the rice field where he lost his life.

March 24

Dear Mom, Dad & Tuny,

Things have really been happening big this past couple of days. Last night one of the companies in our battalion (4/39) ran into a NVA base camp and killed over a hundred. They called the rest of us out to help and right now the total body count is well over 200 enemy dead. We captured three machines guns, around twenty AK rifles, and some rocket launchers. The colonel has some reporters over there now so you will probably read about it in the paper.

If you see anything about 4th Battalion 39th Infantry or the 1st Recondo Brigade, that's us. The colonel is really excited. It will probably mean a promotion for him. Ha! It's just another day closer to home for me. Today I have exactly 200 days left. I think I'll celebrate tomorrow. I see where Mickey Mantle finally retired. He was always one of my favorite ballplayers. I think it's time he got out, though. He was starting to slow down.

Is Ike Jordan's boy over here? Most of the airborne units are farther north and the 101st airborne is right on the DMZ with the Marines. That's where Mickey Wier is stationed. I'm sure glad I'm not up there. I'd rather fight a few local VC and some NVA than those boys up North. The only nice thing about up north is that they don't have booby traps like we do. Those booby traps can spoil your whole day.

Well, that's about all for now. I just wanted to let you know about all our adventures. Keep an eye out in the paper for the 9th Div. Maybe you could cut the articles out and put them in my scrapbook. I feel just fine and tomorrow I finally break 200 days.

Lots of love and take care.

Love ya always,
Den

At 6:30 A.M. the day after Dennis Richards died, his mother was looking out the window of her house when two army officers pulled up in an official sedan. One of the officers didn't want to get out of the car. The other one shoved him out. They rang the doorbell with a prepared speech. Richards's parents came to the door, already dreading the news. The officers said Dennis had been shot through the neck from a distance of five feet and recommended the casket be kept closed.

"Would you like a military funeral?" the officer asked.

"No," replied Mr. Richards bitterly. "The army has done enough for us already."

Earl Marshall Hayes, who was killed on point with Doi the Tiger Scout, was still married, although his wife was legally separated from him after he went to Vietnam. The army couldn't find Marshall's wife. His five-year-old daughter, Marsha Marie, was living with Marshall's parents. The military finally sent the child a telegram on April 1, 1969:

April 1, 1969
Washington, D.C.

Miss Marsha M. Hayes,
Care of Mr. and Mrs. Leo F. Hayes
210 Oxford St.
Spindale, N.C.

The secretary of the army has asked me to express his deep regret that your father, Private First Class Earl M. Hayes, was killed in action in Vietnam on 25 March 1969 while on a combat operation when engaged a hostile force and was hit by napalm from a friendly air strike directed at hostile force. Please accept deepest sympathy. This confirms personal notification made by a representative of the secretary of the army.

Kenneth G. Wickham, Major General U.S.A. F33 Adjutant General, Dept. of the Army, Washington, D.C.

Until May 1993 when I contacted the Hayes family and corrected the error, Marshall's parents thought their son had somehow made a personal mistake and had been killed by friendly fire. Those who prepared his body for transport must have assumed he died from napalm, since it had covered his body during the air strikes after his death.

Charles Reese died of a massive heart attack in his early forties. According to Social Security records, Leonard

AFTERWORD

Gauerke died in 1971. Stephen Seid, Robert Eaton, Harry K. Fullmer, and Eugene Harvill were not found.

Sergeant John Svatek spent many years recovering from his wounds. He now works for HUD in Washington, D.C. He visits "the Wall" every year on March 20, the anniversary of Nigel Poese's death.

Sergeant Don Wallace blamed himself for the death of Richard Forte and the wounding of the others during the ambush on Widow Maker Alley. For twenty-four years, Teddy Creech thought Sugar Bear Bauer had died in that March ambush. On Thanksgiving Day 1993, Creech learned that Bauer was alive and telephoned him. Creech remembered that no one in the squad had given the order to ride the Jeep back to Vinh Kim; the order had come from higher-higher via the radio.

Teddy Creech owns a 327-acre farm in Kentucky. He raises livestock and tobacco and still hunts. Tim "Sugar Bear" Bauer is employed by the U.S. Postal Service. He was so impressed with medics in Vietnam that he became a member of his hometown emergency response team. Don Wallace, the human magnet, collected six Purple Hearts in Vietnam. Wallace is a single parent working as a supervisor of a fabrication center in Silicon Valley.

The driver of the Jeep on December 23, 1968, James M. Fitzpatrick, was awarded the Distinguished Service Cross. Numerous attempts to locate him were unsuccessful. Will Stevens, Albert Fletcher, and Gene Abrahamson were wounded seriously enough to be evacuated from Vietnam. All three men made full recoveries. Abrahamson's arm was not amputated as we were told in Vietnam.

Lieutenant Robert Knapp, Ed Hogue, and Arles Brown remained in the military. All three are now retired and starting second careers. Robert Knapp is an executive officer of Butler International Construction Company. Ed Hogue works as a computer programmer for a property and casualty software writing company. Arles Brown is attending college and plans to become a sociologist.

* * *

Glenn Smith was the only member of the platoon who was not wounded. William Joye received a medical discharge from the army in 1980. He presently works for HUD as a program analyst. Sgt. Jim Richardson, L. J. Henderson, Mario Sotello, Dale Gass, Ron Miller, Frank Ellis, Eusebio Fernandez, James Fabrizio, and William Gregory all survived their tours in Vietnam. Dale Gass continues to raise registered pigs. Fernandez became an attorney and practices law in Florida. Bill Gregory returned to his job at Pfizer Pharmaceuticals and is in research and development. Jim Richardson is a business owner and rancher in Oklahoma. Ron Miller installs windows in skyscrapers. Henderson works for an electrical power company in Texas. Sotello works for a bread company, also in Texas. Fabrizio is a truck driver, and Ellis works for a large shopping mall in California.

Medic Rick Hudson won a Silver Star for his actions on March 25, 1969. He lives in Oregon, where he owns a marine engine repair business. Medic Mike Hill operates a construction business. Dr. Byron Holley became an ophthalmologist following his tour in Vietnam. He published a book, *Vietnam 1968–1969: A Battalion Surgeon's Journal.*

In contacting former soldiers with whom I served in Vietnam, I received two letters that eloquently summed up the Vietnam experience for the combat line grunts. The first was from Jim Whitmore, the medic Evans relieved at First Platoon:

> When I got back from Vietnam, the first two to three years I couldn't talk about my experiences. First, because I didn't think there was any way anyone could relate to what I went through over there. It wasn't worth the effort. Second, if I did try to tell anyone about my experiences, I'd get halfway through the story and find myself almost flashing back to that experience and then spacing out and unable to finish the story. Thankfully, I had a very close circle of friends who were very understanding and gave me the space and time I needed to come

out of my shell. Without those friends at my side, I seriously doubt I would be as well adjusted to life as I am today. I feel very fortunate.

The Vietnam experience was so intense, so nerve-racking, and so probing, it dissected your brain and really made you aware of who you were as a person. It exposed all of your strengths and your weaknesses. All of us who were there can relate to the hundreds of experiences that tested our minds, our courage, and our bravery. The camaraderie that developed as a result of these experiences we shared is deep and will last a lifetime. For all of the good and bad (mostly bad) I experienced in Vietnam, I'll never know any other feelings equal to the ones I felt when I was able to save someone's life. It all seemed worth it, if only for a little while. I've always wondered what happened to all those guys I bandaged up and put on choppers. Were they okay? Did they make it? How are they doing now? How have their wounds affected their life since Vietnam? Sure hope they're okay.

Whitmore is now vice president of a medical catheter manufacturing company in the Southwest.

The second letter was from a platoon member who preferred not to be identified. He concluded his reminiscences on Vietnam with this sentence: "I love my wife and children dearly, but when I die, it will be Vietnam that I will see, hear, taste, smell, and feel last."

To say I was gung-ho to go into the military would be an understatement. I went to Vietnam believing that I was indestructible. No matter what I did, I was going to come home at the end of my tour. With this attitude, war was an adventure, a new experience, the passage from boyhood to manhood. Looking back, I can see that these traits are probably a sign of immaturity and naïveté, with a touch of stupidity.

My tour of duty as a combat medic was by far the most rewarding part of my life. I never had nightmares about Vietnam, but for many years I couldn't go to sleep until I relived every second of March 25, 1969. I was convinced that because I didn't die that day, I didn't do enough, and the only logical explanation for that would come under the category of cowardice.

I got out of the army at 11:00 A.M. on January 3, 1970. Twenty-one hours later I was sitting in a genetics class on the campus of Youngstown State University trying very hard not to look as if I'd just gotten out of the military. Vietnam veterans were looked down on, spat on, and called derogatory names that would have made a drill instructor blush. GI educational benefits enabled me to pursue a second career in veterinary medicine that is just as satisfying as being a medic.

Finding and talking with the men in my platoon and company has also been a very rewarding experience. It was great to hear that those I'd treated had recovered from their wounds. Most of us got together for our first reunion in Reno, Nevada, in 1993. Slides and pictures brought back fond memories, and we shared stories of the good old days in Vietnam. Sharing these stories has been a great honor for me. All of these men are heroes to me.

The word "Vietnam" is a tragic icon that represents one of America's greatest failures. "Success has many fathers, failure is an orphan," is a saying I first heard in veterinary school. Vietnam is no orphan. Many men, both military and political, who formulated our Vietnam policy and direction must be blamed for the consequences of that war.

Many people now think that we shouldn't have been in Vietnam. Hindsight is great but as a nation we can't dwell on the fact that we shouldn't have been in Vietnam. We were there. We made mistakes, wasted billions of dollars, and lost more than 58,000 men and women. We owe it to those who died to find out why our country followed the path it did and to make sure we never follow that route again.

GLOSSARY OF
MILITARY TERMS

Ambush position the position in which an ambush is being established

AO area of operations

APC armored personnel carrier

Article 15 nonjudicial punishment for disciplining soldiers

Artillery either the weapons or used as in "call in artillery" or "artillery falling"

"Arty" GI term for artillery

BAS battalion aid station

CID Criminal Investigation Division

Concertina coiled razor wire

Conex large metal shipment container

Dich Board a casualties tally board

Drive-on rag also called "catch me-fuck me" rag; cloth cravat soldiers wrapped around head or neck to catch sweat

Grunt term for combat infantry soldier, of whatever rank

HE high explosive ordnance

"Jody" draft dodger, or male of military age who avoided Vietnam

LAWs rocket light antitank weapon, shoulder-fired rocket

LBE load-bearing equipment, like a web harness for carrying combat supplies on person

LCM landing craft (mechanized)

Light Colonel a lieutenant colonel

LOH or Loach small surveillance helicopter

MEDCAP Medical Civic Action Program

GLOSSARY

MOS   Military Occupational Specialty

P-38   small can opener issued for opening C-rations

RPG   rocket-propelled grenade

Six-Actual   military radio jargon for the commander of a unit

Slick   unarmed helicopter

SNAFU   Situation Normal, All Fucked Up

Strak   term meaning strike, sharp, outstanding